CONSCIENCE AND POLITICS

JOHN RAE

CONSCIENCE AND POLITICS

THE BRITISH GOVERNMENT AND THE CONSCIENTIOUS OBJECTOR TO MILITARY SERVICE 1916–1919

London
OXFORD UNIVERSITY PRESS
NEW YORK TORONTO
1970

Oxford University Press, Ely House, London W.1

GLASGOW NEW YORK TORONTO MELBOURNE WELLINGTON
CAPE TOWN SALISBURY IBADAN NAIROBI DAR ES SALAAM LUSAKA ADDIS ABABA
BOMBAY CALCUTTA MADRAS KARACHI LAHORE DACCA
KUALA LUMPUR SINGAPORE HONG KONG TOKYO

SBN 19 215176 2

Printed in Great Britain by Hazell Watson & Viney Ltd
Aylesbury, Bucks

TO MY WIFE, DAPHNE

whose encouragement made
it possible

PREFACE

This book describes the relations between the British Government and the conscientious objectors to military service in the First World War. The treatment of the conscientious objectors in the First World War has been the subject of two books: John Graham's *Conscription and Conscience* published in 1922 and David Boulton's *Objection Overruled* published in 1967. Both these accounts were written from a point of view sympathetic to the conscientious objectors and hostile to what may collectively be known as the 'authorities'; neither account made use of all the official records and private papers of political leaders that are now open to inspection. John Graham was writing soon after events in which he had himself been involved; wounds were still open, departmental records still closed. David Boulton evidently did not obtain access to many official documents, including Cabinet Papers.

The material for the present book was collected during three years research in the Department of War Studies at King's College, London. The book itself is not designed as a corrective to the accounts already published nor is it an attempt to vindicate the policies of the government of the day. My aim has been to produce the first historical study of these events that is based upon all the public and private documents that are now available.[1]

I am indebted to so many people for their help and kindness that these brief acknowledgements must seem inadequate, but my gratitude is no less sincere for being concise. As the dedication of this book indicates, my greatest debt is to my wife; she persisted in encouraging me to undertake this research in the face of my protests that I had no time, and continued to give encouragement through the disappointments and set-backs. I owe much, too, to Michael Howard, who, as Professor of War Studies at King's

[1] See Note on Sources, p. 259.

College, London, supervised my research; without his sharp criticism and unfailing kindness, I should have made little progress. I am most grateful to my father for helping to pay my fees at King's College; to Dr. R. L. James and Mr. Charles Lillingston, the Headmaster and Senior History Master of Harrow School, who helped me to continue my research while trying to fulfil my obligations as an assistant master; and to Edward Milligan, the Librarian of the Society of Friends, whose friendship and co-operation have made my visits to the Library such a pleasure.

I would also like to record my appreciation of the help I received from the following: Lady Allen of Hurtwood; Mr. J. K. Bates of the Scottish Record Office; the Deputy Keeper of Western MSS., Bodleian Library, Oxford; Constance Braithwaite; Vera Brittain; Lord Brockway; the late Randolph S. Churchill; Rachel, Lady Clay; the County Record Office, Bedford; the late Rt. Hon. Arthur Creech Jones; the Director of Army Legal Services, Ministry of Defence; Lord Denning, the Master of the Rolls; the Departmental Record Officers of the Board of Trade, the Home Office, the Ministry of Health, and the Ministry of Labour; Mr. W. L. Emmerson; the Fellowship of Reconciliation; Mr. David Garnett; Mr. Martin Gilbert; the Greater London Record Office; Earl Haig; Mr. Denis Hayes; Mr. James Henderson; the House of Lords Record Office; the Imperial War Museum; Mr. D. W. King, Librarian of the old War Office Library; the Librarians and staff of the Battersea Central Library, the British Museum Newspaper Library, the British Library of Political and Economic Science, the London Library, the National Library of Scotland, and the Library of the Trades Union Congress; Sir Basil Liddell Hart; the London Mennonite Centre; Mr. Norman Monk-Jones; the National Council for Civil Liberties; Mrs. Hubert Peet; Mr. Reginald Pond; the Keeper of Public Records and the staff of the Public Record Office; the Hon. Sir Steven Runciman; Earl Russell; the Marquess of Salisbury; Mr. George Sutherland; the late Mr. James Strachey; Mr. Stephen Thorne; the Town Clerks of Camberwell, Harrow, and St. Marylebone; Mrs. Julian Vinogradoff; the War Resisters International; Dr. Bryan Wilson.

I wish to express my gratitude to Her Majesty the Queen for her gracious permission to publish material from the Royal Archives. I would like also to thank Mr. Robert Mackworth-Young, the Librarian at Windsor Castle, for his help.

I thank the following for their kind permission to quote from material which is in their possession or of which they own the copyright:

Lady Allen of Hurtwood (Clifford Allen Papers)
Beaverbrook Foundations (Lloyd George Papers)
Mrs. Mary Bennett (H. A. L. Fisher Papers)
Mr. Mark Bonham Carter (H. H. Asquith Papers)
Rachel, Lady Clay (Margaret Hobhouse Letters)
Mrs. Arthur Creech Jones (Arthur Creech Jones letter to Dr. Salter)
Lord Davies (David Davies letter to Gilbert Murray)
E. M. Forster (letter to the author)
Librarian, Friends' House (T. E. Harvey Papers; Friends Ambulance Unit material in Arnold Rowntree Papers; Yearly Meeting Proceedings)
Greater London Council (County of London Appeal Tribunal Minutes)
Harrow Town Clerk (Minutes of the Harrow-on-the-Hill U.D.C. 1916)
Ministry of Health (Tribunal Records in PRO MH.47)
Isobel Henderson (Gilbert Murray Papers)
Controller of H.M. Stationery Office (material from records that are Crown Copyright)
Home Office (The Home Office and Conscientious Objectors: A Report prepared for the Committee of Imperial Defence 1919)
Independent Labour Party (I.L.P. City of London Branch Minutes)
Ministry of Labour (Pelham Committee Papers; the Recruiting Code)
Lord Lothian (Lothian Papers)
New College, Oxford (Milner Papers)
Passfield Trustees (Beatrice Webb Papers)
Mr. Peter Rowntree (Seebohm Rowntree letter to Lloyd George)
Lord Samuel (Herbert Samuel Papers)
Lord Scarsdale (Curzon Papers)
Scottish Home and Health Department (Records of the Lothian and Peebles Appeal Tribunal and other tribunal material from departmental records of the First World War)
Southwark Town Clerk (Camberwell Local Tribunal Minutes)
Mrs. Alix Strachey (James Strachey letter to the author)

Westminster City Council (St. Marylebone Local Tribunal Minutes).

In conclusion I wish to say a special word of thanks to the Carlyle Trustees for enabling me to enjoy membership of the London Library at a reduced subscription; to Mr. Richard Brain of Oxford University Press for his encouragement and guidance; and to Mrs. Jean Frampton who has typed the manuscript and corrected my spelling mistakes with great efficiency. The errors of grammar and history that remain are entirely my own responsibility.

Taunton School,
Somerset
January 1970

CONTENTS

Preface vii

List of Illustrations xii

Abbreviations xiii

Holders of Government Offices principally concerned with conscientious objectors from the formation of the Coalition Government in June 1915 to January 1919 xv

CHAPTER ONE: The Drift into Conscription 1

CHAPTER TWO: The Drafting of the Military Service Bill 22

CHAPTER THREE: The Military Service Bill in Parliament 33

CHAPTER FOUR: The Change to Conscription 52

CHAPTER FIVE: The Conscientious Objectors 68

CHAPTER SIX: The Tribunals at Work 94

CHAPTER SEVEN: Obstinate Mules and Rampant Griffins 134

CHAPTER EIGHT: The Home Office Scheme 162

CHAPTER NINE: Conscientious Objectors who accepted the Tribunal's Decision 191

CHAPTER TEN: The Absolutists 201

CHAPTER ELEVEN: Aftermath 234

APPENDIXES 246

NOTE ON SOURCES 259

SOURCES 260

INDEX 271

LIST OF ILLUSTRATIONS

Fenner Brockway *facing page* 64

Wyndham Childs 64

Lord Derby 65

Walter Long 65

From the front page of the *Daily Sketch*, 15 April 1916 80

Lord Curzon and Lord Milner 81

Stephen Hobhouse 81

ABBREVIATIONS

The following abbreviations are used in the footnotes:

ACI	Army Council Instruction
AO	Army Order
CAB	Cabinet Papers in Public Record Office
HO	Home Office Papers in Public Record Office
MH	Ministry of Health Papers in Public Record Office
RA	Royal Archives
SHHD	Scottish Home and Health Department
SR&O	Statutory Rules and Orders
WO	War Office Papers in Public Record Office

Hansard references are given as follows:

5 HC 99, col. 1151, 20 November 1917

which refers to the House of Commons Debates, fifth series, volume 99, column 1151.

HOLDERS OF GOVERNMENT OFFICES PRINCIPALLY CONCERNED WITH CONSCIENTIOUS OBJECTORS FROM THE FORMATION OF THE COALITION GOVERNMENT IN JUNE 1915 TO JANUARY 1919

Local Government Board

President:	Walter Long	June 1915–Dec. 1916
	Lord Rhondda	Dec. 1916–June 1917
	W. Hayes Fisher	June 1917–Nov. 1918
	Sir Aukland Geddes	Nov. 1918–Jan. 1919
	C. Addison	Jan. 1919
Pmt. Under Sec.	W. Hayes Fisher	June 1915–June 1917
	Stephen Walsh	June 1917–Jan. 1919
	Waldorf Astor	Jan. 1919

War Office

Sec. of State	Lord Kitchener	June 1915–June 1916
	H. H. Asquith	June–July 1916
	D. Lloyd George	July–Dec. 1916
	Lord Derby	Dec. 1916–April 1918
	Lord Milner	Apr. 1918–Jan. 1919
	W. S. Churchill	Jan. 1919
Pmt. Under Sec.	H. J. Tennant	June 1915–July 1916
	Lord Derby	July–Dec. 1916
	J. I. Macpherson	Dec. 1916–Jan. 1919
	Viscount Peel	Jan. 1919

Home Office

Sec. of State	Sir John Simon	June 1915–Jan. 1916
	Herbert Samuel	Jan.–Dec. 1916
	Sir George Cave	Dec. 1916–Jan. 1919
	Edward Shortt	Jan. 1919
Pmt. Under Sec.	William Brace	June 1915–Jan. 1919
	Sir H. Greenwood	Jan. 1919

CHAPTER ONE

THE DRIFT INTO CONSCRIPTION

From January 1916, eighteen months after the outbreak of the First World War, until August 1919, nine months after the war's conclusion, conscientious objectors to military service constituted a minor but intractable problem for the British Government. That they did so was chiefly the result of official inexperience not only of conscientious objection but also of the whole field of compulsory military service. The introduction of conscription in 1916 caused widespread confusion. In the case of the conscientious objectors this confusion aggravated the difficulties inherent in dealing with men whose claim to be excused from active service was neither popular nor susceptible of proof. Yet confusion was not inevitable. The penalties imposed by inexperience could have been mitigated by an attempt to anticipate the problems of compulsory service, and the specific difficulty of providing for conscience eased by discussions with those who understood the grounds on which objections would be based. The absence of any preparations on these lines was the direct consequence of the policy pursued by the Liberal Prime Minister, H. H. Asquith. By refusing to face conscription until he was satisfied that there was overwhelming popular support for its adoption, Asquith denied to the civil and military authorities the opportunity to plan ahead.

Asquith's policy was inspired by his belief that there existed a formidable sum of active and dormant hostility to the principle of compulsory military service; and that it was necessary therefore to demonstrate that the resources of the voluntary system had been exhausted before asking Parliament for compulsory powers. This approach ensured that the main recruiting efforts of 1915 were devoted to schemes for encouraging men to volunteer; with the exception of the National Register taken in August, no government measure before the end of the year could be regarded as preparatory to the introduction of conscription. The Military Service Bill of January 1916 was not the product of careful planning; it was a hastily constructed alternative to which Asquith withdrew when the voluntary system became untenable. The effect of Asquith's policy on the character of the Bill and particularly on the law relating to conscientious objectors was profound; in the final stages of the Prime Minister's retreat from the principle of voluntary recruiting were sown the seeds of those administrative difficulties whose complexity successive governments were unable to disentangle.

For the British people 1915 was a year of adjustment. As the hopes of a swift victory over Germany receded, the generals, the public, and the politicians had to come to terms with the demands of a long war whose character they had not foreseen. The process of adjustment was sometimes haphazard, always difficult. It involved the abandonment not only of familiar military tactics but also of cherished beliefs in the extent of individual freedom and the limits of government control.

In the previous year the fluent and dramatic German advance had been contained north of Paris. Within a few months a campaign characterized by movement had become a deadlock of trenches. Reluctantly, the German General Staff recognized that 1915 would witness the start of a conflict of attrition sustained by the flow of shells and men. The controllers of British policy were less certain: the Generals believed that a breakthrough in France was still possible; leading members of Asquith's Cabinet, including Lord Kitchener, the Secretary of State for War, believed that it was not and that the main military effort should be made elsewhere. The campaigns of 1915 brought little comfort to either party. In France the one positive attempt to break through the German lines at Loos petered out in mid-October with the loss of sixty thousand casualties. Greater finality marked the failure of those who advocated a strike against Germany's ally Turkey. The Dardanelles affair discredited for the remainder of the war the belief that it was strategically possible to outflank the rigid network of trenches in France and Belgium. When the allied soldiers were evacuated from the beaches of Gallipoli in December, there appeared to be no strategic alternative to a war to the death in the fields of northern France.

Victory in such a war would depend upon the efficient mobilization and control of the nation's resources; once this truth was accepted, a system of voluntary recruiting would be an anachronism. It was a change in the requirements for a military victory rather than pressure from the conscriptionists or the failure of voluntary recruiting that made compulsory service inevitable. This does not mean that the elaborate and devious manoeuvres with which Asquith succeeded in postponing the introduction of conscription were irrelevant or unjustified: the Prime Minister's tactics not only affected the character of the Bill; they helped to ensure that the Bill would be passed with a convincing majority.

Asquith had succeeded Campbell-Bannerman as Prime Minister and leader of the Liberal Party in 1908. Two years later he had led his party to victory at the polls but his overall majority in the Commons had depended on Irish and Labour votes. By August 1914, Conservative by-election victories had made this dependence more obvious: there were now 260 Liberals in the Commons and 288 Conservatives; Asquith's premiership was made possible by support from the 84 Irish and 38 Labour M.P.s. For the first nine months of the war Asquith's Liberal Cabinet remained in office. At the start it had lost the advocates of neutrality, the Gladstonian, Lord Morley, and the trade union leader, John Burns; the rest of the Cabinet and the parliamentary party accepted Asquith's decision to go to war and, having committed themselves, they also accepted the need to win. No doubt many of them believed that victory could be achieved without violating Liberal principles: men of military age would be invited to volunteer, free trade would fill the market for munitions, the nation as a whole would be encouraged to exercise economy. Government initiative, direction, and control would be kept to a minimum. Success in the field could be left to the service departments. Voluntary recruiting and *laissez-faire* economics would provide the means: the Admiralty and the War Office would achieve the end.

Asquith shared his party's view of war as the business of the professionals. He saw no reason to consider the formation of a coalition or national government, but to disarm Conservative criticism he lost no time in appointing Lord Kitchener to the Cabinet a few days after war had been declared. As with a number of Asquith's political strokes, the appointment appeared inspired at the time and unfortunate in retrospect. Kitchener's military success in the Sudan and South Africa had made him a popular hero, but as a member of the Cabinet he was inarticulate and ill at ease.[1] He was not accustomed to working with colleagues and it was soon apparent that his talents did not lend themselves to the politico-military role he had been assigned. At first, Asquith was not unduly concerned. His own leadership, patrician and remote from military affairs, needed Kitchener's colossal prestige both to embarrass critics of the Government's conduct of the war and to lend credibility to an unbellicose administration. For several months Kitchener's presence was sufficient to inspire volunteers and to guarantee a wide measure of support for the Government's *laissez-faire* policy.

The limitations of this policy were to some extent disguised by the overwhelming response to the call for volunteers. Between August 1914 and June 1916, when universal compulsory service came into force, 2,675,149 men volunteered for the army[2] and the great majority of these came forward in the first nine months. The flood of recruits embarrassed the War Office who had neither the personnel nor the equipment to undertake their training. It did not embarrass the Government. Throughout 1915 Asquith was able to defend the voluntary system on the grounds that it produced the men. Strangely, the advocates of compulsion allowed him to keep the debate on recruiting on this numerical plane. The case for conscription had nothing to do with numbers: a conscription act would check rather than stimulate the flow of men and would increase the claims for exemption.[3] But it would bring indiscriminate recruiting under control and be a first step towards the rational use of manpower without which victory in a long war would prove elusive.

By making the recruiting figures the criterion by which to judge the success or failure of the voluntary system, Asquith left himself vulnerable to the first significant fall in the monthly total. This occurred in July 1915. Adroit political tactics enabled him to

[1] Viscount Samuel, *Memoirs*, London, 1945, p. 117. Samuel was a Cabinet colleague from January to June 1916.

[2] General Annual Reports of the British Army for the period from 1 October 1913 to 30 September 1919 (Cmd. 1193), 1921, p. 9.

[3] Between 1 March 1916 and 31 March 1917, 371,500 men were compulsorily enlisted: up to 30 April 1917, however, 779,936 men had been exempted from service by the tribunals. For these figures see Cmd. 1193, 1921, p. 60, and *Statistics of the Military Effort of the British Empire during the Great War 1914–1920*, London, 1922 (hereafter *Military Statistics 1914–1920*), p. 367.

postpone the surrender of voluntaryism until the end of the year, but it was not easy. From May he was no longer dealing with a Cabinet constituted only of Liberal colleagues. Faced with the 'scandal' of a shortage of shells and a political crisis threatened by the resignation of the First Sea Lord, Admiral Fisher, Asquith agreed on 17 May to the formation of a coalition. The new Cabinet contained eleven Liberals, nine Conservatives, the leader of the Labour Party, Arthur Henderson, and Lord Kitchener, the guest of honour who had become an embarrassment but who could not be asked to leave. There was a rough balance in the distribution of offices between the two major parties but this was numerical rather than real. Asquith remained Prime Minister; Bonar Law, the Conservative leader, had to be content with the Colonial Office. Liberals held the key positions: Sir Edward Grey was Foreign Secretary, Sir John Simon Home Secretary, and Reginald McKenna Chancellor of the Exchequer. But while the leading offices were still held by Liberals, the Cabinet now contained a nucleus of politicians whose desire to prosecute the war was not inhibited by a devotion to the principle of *laissez-faire*. On the issue of compulsory military service this nucleus was most likely to press for a decision.

The intensity of feeling aroused by the prospect of conscription reflected the power of historical tradition. The English had for so long been able to conduct their military affairs without recourse to compulsory recruiting that they had come to regard this method of raising troops as inconsistent with their traditional liberties and alien to their national character. The fact that continental powers with long land frontiers and territorial ambitions had found it necessary to impose some form of conscription only reinforced the Englishman's determination to preserve a freedom that set him apart from other people. The truth was however that he owed his freedom from conscription to the accidents of history and geography rather than to any exclusively English virtue.

Before the restoration of Charles II in 1660, Englishmen had been liable to three forms of military compulsion: the general and feudal levies that provided troops to meet the threat of invasion, and the practice of impressment.[1] The levies had some basis in law: the King's Press, so damnably misused by Falstaff, had not.

[1] There is an admirable summary of the history of the forces in the *Manual of Military Law*, War Office, London, 1914, Ch. IX.

The power to impress had been assumed by the Crown during the anarchy of the Wars of the Roses and carefully nurtured by the Tudors as a royal prerogative. In this, as in other matters, the Stuarts found Parliament less acquiescent. In 1640, the Long Parliament declared impressment illegal, though it was the unconstitutional exercise of the royal power and not the principle of compulsion that they were rejecting. When it came to the Civil War both sides practised impressment without hesitation and it was left to the radicals to protest. All this was changed by the reorganization of the military system after 1660: impressment was outlawed for good and the feudal levy abolished; an obligation to serve in the militia remained but the element of compulsion was diluted by the system of ballots and parish quotas and the numerous exceptions allowed under the Militia Acts. In place of the old compulsions, the first steps were taken to create a regular military force. The handful of regiments that Charles II was permitted to maintain became the core of a standing army based on voluntary enlistment.

The final rejection of impressment for the army and the establishment of a standing volunteer force fixed the nation's attitude to recruiting for two hundred and fifty years. Between 1660 and 1914 war was the concern of the professional soldier. The long struggle against France in the eighteenth century and the remote campaigns of Victorian imperialism were fought by volunteers. The success of these volunteer armies and the width of the English Channel allowed the nation to entertain the belief that freedom from conscription was one of its ancient liberties. By the beginning of the twentieth century there appeared to have been no slackening of pride and confidence in the voluntary system; in the summer of 1902, shortly after the end of the Boer War, Lord Salisbury, the Conservative Prime Minister, rejoiced that the enemy had been defeated by soldiers attracted to the army 'not by coercion but by the emoluments and the honours of a great and splendid vocation'.[1] But while the Prime Minister and the public flattered themselves that voluntary recruiting had once again proved its worth, the seeds of a conscription lobby had already been sown. In February of the same year a National Service League had been founded whose aim was to promote the ideals of compulsory military service.[2]

[1] Quoted in Denis Hayes, *Conscription Conflict*, London, 1949, p. 28.
[2] For the early days of the League see Hayes, op. cit., pp. 36–50.

For some years the National Service League made no impact on public opinion; though the League talked of the threat of invasion, the mass of Englishmen refused to believe that a military situation could develop in which it would be necessary to accept a curtailment of individual liberty. Nevertheless the League did make some useful progress during the last years of peace: its branches in Australia and New Zealand were instrumental in persuading the political leaders of these countries to adopt compulsory peacetime training; and in Britain the absence of popular interest was offset by the increasing support of influential public men. In July 1909 a Bill to impose compulsory territorial training on all men between the ages of eighteen and thirty was narrowly defeated in the House of Lords.[1] The chief advocates for the Bill were members of the League: the President, Lord Roberts of Kandahar, and Lord Curzon, the former Viceroy of India. The fate of this Bill illustrates the conscriptionists' problem: they could not command a majority in the Lords, while in the Commons their support was negligible; they wielded influence but not political power. Neither of the great parties was prepared to be associated with the concept of compulsory military service, the Liberals as a matter of principle, the Conservatives as a matter of politics. Nor did the outbreak of war have any immediate effect on this position; the high tide of volunteers left no foothold to the conscriptionists. But in May 1915 the formation of the Coalition Cabinet brought the conscriptionists into positions of political power at the very moment when the tide of volunteers began to ebb.

The new Cabinet did not divide on strictly party lines. Two of the Liberal members—David Lloyd George and Winston Churchill—had no doctrinaire objection to conscription; of the other Liberals, some apparently possessed a fundamental dislike of all state direction, but when it came to the point only one—Sir John Simon—resigned rather than be associated with a conscription Bill. The Conservatives in the Cabinet, with the single exception of Lord Lansdowne, favoured the introduction of conscription. Some, like Lord Curzon, wanted a change to compulsory service without delay; others, like Walter Long, though no less convinced of the need, were prepared to await a sign from Kitchener. Kitchener,

[1] By 123 votes to 103; for the debate see 5 HL 2, col. 255–470, 12 and 13 July 1909.

however, appeared to regard conscription as a purely political question on which it would be wrong for him to give a lead.[1]

Outside the Cabinet, the demands for conscription were vociferous and unequivocal but they were not an expression of popular sentiment. Although the confusion and injustices of voluntary recruiting had reconciled many Liberals to the need for some form of manpower control, the campaign for conscription remained a private crusade. In 1915 the leading crusaders were Lord Milner and Lord Northcliffe.

Milner, like Curzon, had returned to England in 1905 after a period of proconsular eminence. As High Commissioner of South Africa and Governor of Cape Colony he had won devoted admirers and alienated Liberal sympathies.[2] Outside politics and with no popular following, Milner was nevertheless a force; in a narrow but influential circle that included a Cabinet Minister, Lord Selborne, and a rising young officer-M.P., Leo Amery, he was still revered as a great administrator, divorced from the enfeebling manoeuvres of political intrigue and endowed with those very qualities of leadership and intellectual vigour that Asquith was failing to display. The most ardent Milnerites, contemptuous of 'Squiff' and his patrician Liberal colleagues, cast their hero in the role of Prime Minister.[3] In July 1915 Milner became Chairman of the General Council of the National Service League; from this position he launched his campaign against the Government's failure to bring in a measure of compulsory recruiting.

Milner's views were given wide circulation by Lord Northcliffe's newspapers; *The Times* and the *Daily Mail* joined him in condemning a policy of drift. Neither Milner nor Northcliffe showed much respect for Parliament; they preferred to see the debate on conscription conducted in the morning papers rather than in the House. They demanded firm leadership and implied that anyone who failed to place the defeat of Germany above party and above principle was not fit to hold office. Their activities were bitterly resented by

[1] Kitchener's motives may not have been this simple. Asquith may have nobbled him by insinuating that the demand for conscription was an oblique attack on Kitchener's own position. See Philip Magnus, *Kitchener*, London, 1958, pp. 352–4.

[2] In 1906 Milner had been censured by Parliament for permitting the illegal flogging of Chinese coolies in the Transvaal.

[3] See A. M. Gollin, *Proconsul in Politics: a study of Lord Milner in opposition and in power*, London, 1964, p. 276.

those who wished to give voluntary recruiting a fair chance, but for Curzon and the other conscriptionists in the Cabinet, Milner and Northcliffe provided a degree of pressure that could not safely be applied within the Cabinet itself.

Asquith did not allow these activities to deflect him from his policy; he remained convinced that the country was not yet ready to accept conscription and that any attempt to force the issue would endanger national unity at a critical period of the war. It is a policy that has won him little credit: the very success with which he was able to neutralize the opposition to conscription has encouraged the view that he overestimated the opposition in the first place.[1] This view is not sustained by the evidence. In the summer of 1915, there were four identifiable groups hostile to the introduction of compulsory military service: the members of the Liberal Party in Parliament and in the country who had not yet abandoned faith in voluntaryism; organized labour; the left wing of the Labour movement exemplified by the young men of the Independent Labour Party; and the religious groups whose pacifist or eschatological beliefs precluded service in the armed forces.

It is not possible to calculate the exact strength of the Liberal opposition. In the Cabinet there were in addition to Simon three Liberals who actively opposed conscription until the end of 1915—Grey, McKenna, and Walter Runciman.[2] In the Commons it is possible that as much as three-quarters of the Liberal membership would not have supported Asquith if he had attempted to introduce conscription in the midsummer of 1915. Six months later, when the failure of the voluntary system had been made to appear final and complete, 34 Liberals voted against the Military Service Bill and about 110 abstained, altogether more than half of the total membership of 260.[3] To this active and passive opposition within his own party, the Prime Minister had to add the Labour and Irish members who would at best abstain. There is little doubt that Asquith was correct in thinking that a conscription Bill introduced in say June or July 1915 would have exposed to allies and enemies alike a crippling division of opinion in the Cabinet and the Commons.

Outside Parliament the most formidable opponents of conscrip-

[1] See, e.g., Roy Jenkins, *Asquith*, London, 1964, p. 394.

[2] President of the Board of Trade.

[3] See the analysis of voting figures on p. 37, below.

tion were the trade unions.[1] Their opposition was not symptomatic of hostility to the war itself; the unions had cooperated in the recruiting campaign and their members had volunteered in their thousands, though they risked not only life but the security of their families. Nor had the opposition of organized labour anything to do with abstract theories of *laissez-faire*. It sprang from a deep-rooted fear that conscription would be used to deprive the working man and his organizations of the legal rights that had been won in years of industrial conflict. The Fabian Socialist, Beatrice Webb, tried to explain this fear in a letter to Lady Betty Balfour, whose brother-in-law was a leading Conservative member of the Cabinet.[2]

> The feeling against conscription among thoughtful working men is intense. They feel that it is indescribably mean of the governing class to use the war to carry out a social revolution in their own favour. I think in this accusation they are wrong. I don't believe that even Milner and Curzon have any deliberate intention of cheating the people of their freedom on the plea of patriotism. I believe the conscriptionist lacks imagination. He fails to see that in asking the working man to give up his personal freedom to take work or leave it, he is asking him to give up all that makes daily life endurable.[3]

The Trades Union Congress meeting in September denounced 'the sinister efforts of a section of the reactionary press . . . to foist on this country conscription which always proves a burden to the workers and will divide the nation when absolute unanimity is essential'.[4] The Congress represented three million workers and its opposition to conscription could hardly be ignored; but the unions, like the Liberal Party, were committed to support of the war and could, therefore, be manoeuvred into a position where it would no longer be consistent for them to oppose compulsory service.

This was not true of the militant left-wingers of the Labour movement or the religious objectors to military service: the effec-

[1] For the trade union attitude see especially Malcolm Ian Thomis, 'The Labour Movement in Great Britain and Compulsory Military Service, 1914–1916', unpublished M.A. thesis, University of London, 1959.

[2] Arthur Balfour, First Lord of the Admiralty, Conservative Party leader 1902–1911.

[3] Beatrice Webb to Betty Balfour, 28 October 1915, Passfield Papers, II.4.g.f.45.

[4] Annual Register, 1915, p. 154.

tive prosecution of the war was not one of their commitments. These political and religious sources of conscientious objection are discussed in a later chapter, but it is useful to consider here their role in 1915.

The I.L.P. had condemned the war from the start. On 6 August 1914 the party leader, Keir Hardie, had called on members to resist the nationalist hysteria that was sweeping the country and in the same issue of the party's journal, the *Labour Leader*, the young editor, Fenner Brockway, had written:

> Workers of Great Britain, you have no quarrel with the workers of Europe. They have no quarrel with you. The quarrel is between the RULING classes of Europe. Don't make this quarrel yours. . . .[1]

The workers of Europe had shown little inclination to put socialism before patriotism; Hardie's dream of international solidarity had been shattered by the zeal with which the working men had gone to war. When Hardie died in October 1915 and his parliamentary constituency was captured by a Labour candidate who repudiated pacifism, I.L.P. policy appeared to have suffered a final defeat. But the younger members of the party were not prepared to remain inactive. If they had failed to prevent the seduction of the proletariat by the militarist propaganda of the ruling classes, they could still strike a blow against militarism in their own country. Conscription gave them their opportunity.

Organized opposition to conscription had been proposed as early as November 1914; through the columns of the *Labour Leader* Fenner Brockway had invited men of military age to join in a No Conscription Fellowship (N.C.F.).[2] The response had been immediate but not overwhelming. It was always in the N.C.F.'s interests to magnify the extent of its influence; when it claimed in April 1916 to have a membership of fifteen thousand, this was almost certainly a tactical exaggeration.[3] In the spring of 1915, the N.C.F. set up its headquarters off Fleet Street and published a Statement of Principles. The latter declared that the members of the Fellowship were men who would 'refuse from conscientious

[1] Quoted in Fenner Brockway, *Inside the Left*, London, 1942, pp. 45–6.

[2] Brockway, op. cit., p. 66. There is a set of N.C.F. Letters and Reports in the Clifford Allen Papers; the author also has a set in his possession.

[3] N.C.F. Letter to the Prime Minister, 15 April 1916. The exaggeration is evident when the N.C.F. figure is compared with an analysis of conscientious objectors. See Chapter 5 below.

motives to bear arms' and who would resist every effort to impose compulsion; if conscription came, they would 'obey their conscientious convictions rather than the commands of Governments'.[1] This fusion of idealism with the promise of active resistance attracted young men with a variety of religious and political views, though the young members of the I.L.P. provided the initiative and the leadership. Fenner Brockway became Secretary; Clifford Allen, a member of the party's City of London Branch, was appointed Chairman. In 1915, both men were twenty-six.

During the first six months of 1915, the N.C.F. leaders were busy establishing a network of autonomous local groups and shadow officials that would be proof against police action.[2] From the headquarters a flow of instructions and propaganda guided members without as yet provoking the authorities. Under a banner proclaiming a common belief in the sanctity of human life, the N.C.F. made an alliance with two organizations of Christian pacifists: the Young Men's Service Committee of the Society of Friends and the Fellowship of Reconciliation. The former represented those Quakers of military age who adhered to the Society's traditional rejection of military service; the latter united Christian pacifists from many denominations.[3] The alliance helped to co-ordinate resistance to conscription, though for some members of the N.C.F. 'the sanctity of human life' was a flag of convenience rather than a banner of faith.

Of the nature and extent of religious objections to conscription neither Asquith nor his colleagues would have had much accurate knowledge. The position of the Society of Friends, already familiar though frequently misinterpreted, was confirmed in the Society's declaration to both Houses of Parliament in September 1915.[4] But beyond the tenets of the Quakers there lay a complex pattern of pacifist and apocalyptic beliefs on which little information was available. In February 1915 one of the larger non-combatant sects, the Christadelphians, petitioned Parliament to grant them 'legal exemption from military service' if conscription became law.[5]

[1] N.C.F. Statement of Principles, 1915.

[2] N.C.F. Report, July 1915.

[3] The history of the Fellowship of Reconciliation is told in Vera Brittain, *The Rebel Passion: a short history of some pioneer peace-makers*, London, 1964.

[4] Minutes of the Meeting for Sufferings, 3rd of the 9th Month, 1915.

[5] F. G. Jannaway, *Without the Camp: being the story of why and how the Christadelphians were exempted from military service*, London, 1917, pp. 32–5.

Other sects waited in obscurity. This was, however, one area of opposition that Asquith could safely ignore. The religious objectors represented a problem that would have to be faced after the decision to introduce conscription and not before.

In addition to those religious and political groups that rejected conscription on principle, there were organizations that opposed the continuation of the war and therefore any move that could be regarded as an escalation of the British war effort. Thus the Union of Democratic Control (U.D.C.) founded in September 1914 to obtain—as a first step to peace—democratic control of foreign policy, opposed any extension of 'Prussianism' in Britain whether it took the form of censorship under the Defence of the Realm Act or compulsion for military service.[1] The U.D.C. wielded some influence in political and intellectual circles; other anti-war organizations such as the Stop the War Committee did not.[2] All were in 1915 the subject of reports by the Criminal Investigation Department of Scotland Yard, but no action was taken to curtail their activities.[3] The prosecution of the members of these organizations would have aroused still further Liberal and Labour fears that in the interests of victory individual freedom was to be suppressed and the nation brought under military discipline.

Until the autumn of 1915, the debate on conscription was conducted in ignorance of the exact number of men available for service. A Parliamentary Recruiting Committee had attempted to establish reliable statistics by means of a postal canvass of eight million families, but less than half of the forms had been returned.[4] The need for accurate information was underlined by the War Office, who objected to the procedure for protecting men in essential work from the attention of the recruiting officers; from July 1915 all badges carrying this protection were issued by the Ministry of Munitions, but even before this date the War Office reckoned that the system of badging had gone too far.[5] In these circumstances it was difficult for Asquith to resist proposals that a national regis-

[1] For the U.D.C. see especially H. Hanak, 'The Union of Democratic Control during the First World War', *Bulletin of the Institute of Historical Research*, November 1963.

[2] The Stop the War Committee was organized by J. Scott Duckers; see his account, *Handed Over*, London, 1917.

[3] HO45/10782/278537.

[4] Arthur Henderson's statement, 5 HC 73, col. 146, 5 June 1915.

[5] Humbert Wolfe, *Labour Supply and Regulation*, Oxford, 1923, p. 37.

ter should be compiled of the total manpower resources of the country. A Bill for this purpose was introduced by Walter Long, the President of the Local Government Board, and while it roused the suspicions of those who saw it as a prelude to conscription, the opposition in the division lobby was negligible.

The new Act[1] empowered the Local Government Board to compile a detailed register of all persons between fifteen and sixty-five. The Register was taken on 15 August. When the forms were returned to the Local Government Board offices, the details of each man of military age, that is between eighteen and forty, were transferred to a pink form; a black star marked the forms of men in essential work. The Register showed that 2,179,231 single men of military age were not in the forces.[2] But while the National Register confirmed that the men were available to maintain the seventy divisions that Kitchener regarded as the minimum British contribution to the war, the Cabinet were no closer to unanimity on the methods by which these men should be obtained. The differences on this issue remained so sharp that rational discussion was all but impossible.[3] Outside the Cabinet Room the controversy blazed the more fiercely. Liberal journals such as the *Daily News* and the *Nation* tried to prevent the country being bullied into conscription by Milner and the Northcliffe Press. But once the results of the National Register were known, the conscriptionists held the initiative and had no intention of relaxing their grip. In September, two members of the National Service League, Curzon and Amery, drew up a 'Sketch of possible scheme of compulsory military service',[4] on which a conscription Bill could be based. It was also rumoured that Conservative members of the coalition had threatened to resign unless such a Bill were introduced. It now appeared probable that Asquith would be forced to adopt compulsion before he was satisfied that the opposition to it had been sufficiently reduced. In this situation, the unity of the Cabinet and of the country remained Asquith's overriding concern. His attempts to preserve this unity contributed to the acute growing pains of compulsory service in the following year, but it is unjust to dismiss his tactics as mere prevarication. He was convinced of

[1] 5 & 6 GEO 5, Ch. 60, 15 July 1915.

[2] The figure given by Lord Derby in CAB37/139/26.

[3] One point on which nearly all accounts of this period agree; see e.g. Lord Beaverbrook, *Politicians and War 1914–1916*, London, 1959, pp. 246–8.

[4] A sixteen-page typescript dated September 1915, in Curzon Papers, 10.

their necessity and it can be argued that events proved him right: when conscription was introduced it had the support of the overwhelming majority of both Houses of Parliament.

The tactics that so exasperated Asquith's opponents were marked by familiar flashes of political opportunism. As a first step Asquith persuaded Kitchener to accept one further effort of voluntary recruiting.[1] This effort, launched in October, became known as the Derby Scheme.[2] The choice of the 17th Earl of Derby as civilian Director-General of Recruiting was a characteristically Asquithian stroke. The fact that Derby was an enthusiast for conscription (he had been an Honorary Vice-President of the National Service League since 1904) left Asquith's critics momentarily off balance. But Derby was more than a conscriptionist. With his ancient title and vast Lancastrian estates, his bluff manner and lack of intellectual pretensions, he enjoyed the friendship of the King and the confidence of the people. He was a popular figure; if men did not volunteer now, Asquith could say with justification that the voluntary system had been given every chance and found wanting.

Derby made it clear that he regarded the scheme as the final effort of voluntary recruiting. While the Liberals may have hoped that the number of men coming forward would make conscription unnecessary, Derby and his fellow conscriptionists believed that sufficient would hold back to make it imperative. The precise point at which the Scheme would be judged to have failed was never published and probably never decided. Asquith spoke of the 'prescribed minimum' of volunteers without which compulsion would have to be used. On 16 October, in a secret note to Kitchener, he summarized what he wished to be understood as the Cabinet's position:

> Compulsion, to be effective, must be adopted with substantial general assent. If the prescribed minimum is not forthcoming, the Cabinet believe that the objection to compulsion, which now so widely exists, would be largely modified if not entirely removed, and hopes that such general assent would be secured.[3]

The following week, the Derby Scheme was launched. Asquith's note suggests that he anticipated failure, but he won either way.

[1] Magnus, op. cit., p. 353, and Beaverbrook, op. cit., pp. 246–8.

[2] For the Derby Scheme see Report on Recruiting by the Earl of Derby, K.G., Director-General of Recruiting (Cd.8149), 1916.

[3] Kitchener Papers 73/WS/30.

If the prescribed minimum was forthcoming conscription could be postponed; if it was not, the opposition to conscription would be undermined. No doubt on this last point he would have liked there to be a greater degree of certainty, but the progress of the Scheme might yet provide a further opportunity to secure the 'substantial general assent' he wanted.

The Scheme was initiated by a personal canvass of all available men between the ages of eighteen and forty. These men were invited to attest their willingness to serve when needed. Those who responded were placed in groups according to age and marital status, it being understood that the groups of young single men would be called upon first. This procedure for calling volunteers to the colours only when they were required was referred to as the Group System. Men who were compulsorily called to the colours under the Military Service Acts were placed not in groups but in classes, hence the Class System. For the first half of 1916 the Group and Class Systems operated side by side as the men deemed to have been enlisted by law were being called up at the same time as men who had attested under the Derby Scheme the previous autumn.

The burden of organizing the Scheme fell on the War Office and the Local Government Board. The War Office Recruiting Officers received and documented the men who were willing to attest and, in cooperation with the civic authorities, organized a door-to-door canvass of every man shown by the National Register to be eligible for service. The Local Government Board was responsible for the appointment of tribunals to which the men who had attested could apply for the postponement of their call-up on the grounds of personal hardship or essential work. Postponement of call-up was not exemption from service though it was sometimes referred to as such. On 26 October Walter Long, as President of the Local Government Board, instructed every Local Registration Authority to appoint a small tribunal of not more than five members who should be men 'of impartial and balanced judgement' and who should not be drawn exclusively from the Authority itself.[1] There was of course no question of appointing members with special knowledge of the problem of conscientious objection;

[1] Local Government Board (L.G.B.) to Local Registration Authorities, 26 October 1915. L.G.B. letters and circulars 1915–1919 are held in PRO MH 10/79–84. Most carry the initial letter 'R'.

under the Derby Scheme this problem did not arise, though a man who had voluntarily attested could express a preference for non-combatant work in the army.[1]

The local tribunals, and the Central Tribunal appointed to consider appeals against local decisions, were given statutory authority when conscription became law. Their experience under the Derby Scheme was not a good preparation for this statutory role. Under the Military Service Acts, the tribunals became independent judicial bodies responsible for giving impartial decisions on applications for exemption; under the Derby Scheme the same groups of men had been told that it was their duty to assist the military authorities in securing men for the army.[2] In 1915 the tribunal was just another manifestation of the local recruiting effort. Local councillors provided a majority of the members and were often those who had been active in the promotion of recruiting; not infrequently the chairman of the local recruiting committee[3] became the chairman of the local tribunal.

Even where the tribunal members did not wish to be regarded as part of the machinery for obtaining men, the local representatives of the War Office left them little choice. The Recruiting Officer[4] not only received and documented the men who were willing to attest, but also disposed of a number of the applications for postponement of call-up. If he was prepared to give his assent to postponement (in the form of relegation to a later group), this was granted without the formality of a tribunal hearing. If he contested an application he sent a Military Representative to the tribunal hearing to express his objections. The War Office safeguarded its interests still further by appointing in each district an Advisory Committee of men with knowledge of local industry, whose task was to scrutinize the applications and to instruct the Military Representative as a solicitor instructs counsel. The tribunal members, fresh from their recruiting activities and conscious of their patriotic duty, were reluctant to reject the combined

[1] Lord Derby, *Group and Class Systems: Notes on their Administration under the Military Service Act*, War Office, London, February 1916, p. 15.

[2] L.G.B. to Local Registration Authorities, 26 October 1915.

[3] Also called Parliamentary Recruiting Committees; appointed in most cases in September 1915; see N. B. Dearle, *Dictionary of Official War-Time Organisations*, London, 1928, p. 202.

[4] Usually a retired regular officer or senior N.C.O.; later, men no longer fit for active service.

opinion of the Recruiting Officer and his Advisory Committee and not infrequently allowed the tribunal hearing to be conducted by the Military Representative. Thus an application for postponement was unlikely to succeed unless it had the backing of the local military authorities, a situation it would be difficult to justify if service became compulsory.

The opening weeks of the Derby Scheme were a notable success: thousands of men who had been proof against previous recruiting campaigns attested their willingness to serve. The arrangements for postponing call-up, the personal canvass, the impact of propaganda, the chance to enjoy the prestige of the volunteer without the prospect of immediate enlistment, all contributed to this new surge of sacrifice.[1] Enthusiasm was not however the universal response. Some men made a modest living by attesting several times, receiving 2*s.* 9*d.* from each recruiting office; more profitably, the blind and crippled sold their War Office cards marked 'Not Accepted' for £15 on the black market.[2]

The Scheme also spurred the N.C.F. into more provocative activity. But the implications of this 'final effort of voluntary recruiting' forced the N.C.F. leaders to pursue an ambiguous policy: they set out to discourage men from attesting and by doing so helped to guarantee the failure of their main objective—the prevention of compulsory military service. This confusion of aims did nothing to diminish their zeal or dull their ingenuity. At recruiting rallies, while the civic and military dignitaries called for volunteers, the N.C.F. moved discreetly through the audience distributing membership forms. It is hardly surprising that the authorities regarded such behaviour as unpatriotic, even subversive. The Director of Public Prosecutions had already sent a Memorandum to the Attorney General summarizing the anti-war literature published by the N.C.F. and the U.D.C.;[3] and as the Derby Scheme progressed, police chiefs kept the Home Office fully informed of N.C.F. activity in their areas. Sir John Simon was in a difficult position. He was under some pressure to prosecute the

[1] As additional inducements, War Pensions were extended to the dependants of all soldiers (not just the wives and children of married men), and the War Office gave notice that the right to opt for any arm except the infantry would shortly cease.

[2] Report of the Select Committee on Military Service, 1917, MH 47/144; General Geddes's evidence.

[3] HO 45/10786/297549/10.

N.C.F., yet both as a Liberal and as an opponent of conscription he must have regarded such pressure with distaste. When reports of N.C.F. activity reached him, he wrote on the file, 'I think it is politic to avoid proceedings if possible.'[1]

Free from official interference the N.C.F. went ahead with plans for a National Convention to be held in London at the end of November. When the Convention met under Clifford Allen's chairmanship, the N.C.F. members and the 'fraternal delegates' from such miscellaneous progressive organizations as the Australian Freedom League and the East London Federation of Suffragettes, resolved to resist the machinery of conscription 'whatever the penalties may be'.[2]

Meanwhile the Derby Scheme had run into an unexpected difficulty. It was reported that the married men were reluctant to come forward unless there were some guarantee that all the available single men would be called up first. Asquith saw his opportunity. In the Commons he gave a solemn pledge that the married men who attested would not be held to their obligation to serve until all the unmarried men had been dealt with, if necessary by compulsion.[3] It was an adroit move. If, as now seemed likely, the conscription of single men had to be introduced in the new year, he would be able to present the move not only as a military necessity but also as the honourable redemption of his pledge to the married men. The reluctance of the married men to attest provided Asquith with the additional lever he needed to undermine Liberal opposition to a conscription Bill.

The Derby Scheme was scheduled to end on 12 December. During the last days long queues formed at the recruiting offices and it took several hours to reach the door. It was rumoured that compulsion was imminent and the men of military age wished to avoid the stigma of being conscripts. The last-minute rush led some observers to argue that compulsion would not be necessary after all. Amid these currents of rumour and optimism, the nation awaited Lord Derby's calculations.

While the nation might have believed that the fate of the voluntary system hung on the results of the Derby Scheme, those closer to the centre of power recognized that this fate had already

[1] HO 45/10782/278537/30.
[2] N.C.F. Letter to members, 9 December 1915.
[3] 5 HC 75, col. 520, 2 November 1915.

been sealed. A month earlier, Asquith had given his approval to the drafting of a Bill based on the compulsory service scheme prepared by Curzon and Amery;[1] the printed draft bears Curzon's uncompromising title 'Universal Military Service'.[2] But much more decisive as assassins of the voluntary system were the military developments of the first week of December. On 6 December the second Inter-Allied Military Conference at Chantilly recommended that, in 1916, the Austro-German armies should be subjected to attack with maximum forces in the principal theatres of conflict, and that until these attacks could be mounted, the enemy should be worn down by the vigorous action of those powers such as Great Britain which still possessed reserves of manpower.[3] The following day—7 December—the Cabinet at last acknowledged that the Gallipoli campaign had failed and agreed to evacuate the allied forces. The withdrawal from Gallipoli confirmed acceptance of a policy of using every available man to break the enemy's resistance in France. In the face of these far-reaching strategic decisions the voluntary system, the very antithesis of maximum effort, never had a chance.

Lord Derby reported to the Cabinet on 15 December.[4] His figures concentrated on the position of the single men and showed that although 1,150,000 of these men had attested, 651,160 who were not starred for essential work were unaccounted for. Derby later corrected these figures in the face of Sir John Simon's criticism and of the findings of a committee appointed to examine the results of the Scheme. He told the Cabinet on 1 January 1916 that, on the advice of the Chief Statistical Officer of the Registrar General, the total number of single men available should be reduced to 316,464; he had omitted to make allowance for men who were unfit or in reserved occupations.[5]

Asquith did not wait for these adjustments. On 15 December he appointed a Cabinet Committee as a first step towards the redemption of his pledge to the married men. The Committee, under Walter Long's chairmanship, was instructed to 'consider in con-

[1] Asquith's approval conveyed through Austen Chamberlain; Asquith to Chamberlain, 7 November 1915, a copy in Curzon Papers 10.

[2] Draft Bill 297–5, Asquith Papers 82, f. 90.

[3] *History of the Great War: Military Operations, France and Belgium 1916*, London, 1932, pp. 4–10.

[4] CAB 37/139/26.

[5] CAB 37/140/1.

sultation with the draftsman what form any amendment in the law in the direction of compulsion should take'.[1] The rather cautious wording of the terms of reference did not disguise the real nature of the Committee's task, which was to draft a Bill for the compulsory enlistment of single men. Three days after the Committee's appointment the first soldiers were evacuated from the Suvla and Anzac beaches of the Gallipoli peninsula. Imaginative strategy and *laissez-faire* recruiting had alike been discredited.

[1] CAB 37/139/27.

CHAPTER TWO

THE DRAFTING OF THE MILITARY SERVICE BILL

It is a commonplace for an Act of Parliament to be criticized as ambiguous. From time to time a Bill is left deliberately obscure, but the imperfections of the law more often have their origins in the circumstances of drafting than in the conscious policy of ministers. The draft of the Military Service Bill owed its imperfections both to the short time available for its production and to Asquith's determination to present conscription not as a radical departure from the British tradition but as an extension of the Derby Scheme. These limiting factors would have hampered the work of the most effective Cabinet Committee, but Asquith had entrusted the drafting to a Committee whose composition might have been designed to frustrate progress. Walter Long's colleagues included both Lord Curzon, the most consistent advocate of compulsory service, and Sir John Simon, the one member of the Cabinet who opposed compulsion as a matter of principle.[1] Simon's role in the Committee is not recorded, but as he denied that the Bill was either right or necessary it is unlikely that he did much to facilitate its drafting.

A set procedure for drafting parliamentary Bills was well established by 1915.[2] When the Cabinet had approved of the general proposals, it delegated to a Cabinet Committee the responsibility for giving detailed instructions to the draftsman. In the case of the Military Service Bill, the Cabinet Committee, in consultation with the departmental staff of the War Office and the Local Government Board, decided the substance of the Bill; the

[1] The other members of the Committee were F. E. Smith, the Conservative Attorney General, and Lord Crewe, the Liberal Lord President of the Council.

[2] See especially Sir William Graham-Harrison, 'An Examination of the Main Criticisms of the Statute Book', and Sir Granville Ram, 'The Improvement of the Statute Book', both in the *Journal of the Society of the Public Teachers of Law*, 1935 and 1951 respectively.

draftsman, who was Sir Arthur Thring, the First Parliamentary Counsel, expressed the substance in language and form that would produce the intended legal effect. It was then the normal procedure for the first draft to be amended by conferences of the Parliamentary Counsel and the departmental staff, questions of policy being referred to the Cabinet Committee or to a meeting of the whole Cabinet. Thus a Bill might be passed backwards and forwards several times between draftsman, civil servants, and politicians before the final draft was approved by the Cabinet and presented to the House.

It has long been the complaint of the Parliamentary Counsel's Office that politicians and senior civil servants underestimate the time required to complete this process; in the experience of a distinguished First Parliamentary Counsel 'a Bill of moderate length will take several months to draft'.[1] Walter Long's Committee was appointed on 15 December; the final draft of the Military Service Bill was printed on 4 January and introduced to the Commons the following day, just three weeks after the Committee's appointment. The speed with which the Bill had to be drafted was dictated by Asquith's approach. He had publicly tied the fate of the voluntary system to the results of the Derby Scheme. Once the Scheme had ended it was essential to avoid a long period of delay during which the conscriptionists could push for universal compulsion and the opponents of conscription organize their diverse objections in a united front. Asquith did not reveal the results of the Derby Scheme before Parliament dispersed for the Christmas recess; when the members reassembled in the New Year he intended to present them with both the figures and the consequences.

The difficulties of producing an effective final draft were further aggravated by Asquith's narrow conception of the Bill's purpose; the Prime Minister's political tactics forced the Cabinet Committee to accept particular solutions to some of the fundamental problems of conscription. The first of these problems concerned the overall responsibility for the organization of the call-up. This responsibility had to be placed on the War Office. There was no civilian department—such as a Ministry of Labour[2]—that was

[1] Ram, loc. cit.

[2] A Ministry of Labour was created in December 1916; a Ministry of National Service in 1917.

capable of undertaking this task. The Local Government Board could continue to be responsible for the tribunals but it had had no experience of recruiting. The War Office itself had made no preparation for conscription but it did possess, in its local recruiting offices and military representatives, the rudiments of a recruiting organization; it was, therefore, the only department that could take on the responsibility at short notice.

The military authorities did not welcome their new role.[1] They recognized that their organization, though expanded at the beginning of the war and given some order by the Derby Scheme, was still based upon peacetime recruiting and quite inadequate to cope with conscription. And, contrary to the belief of many conscientious objectors, the military did not wish to be responsible for taking men from civilian life; they wanted the call-up to be under civilian control and for the War Office to be responsible only for receiving the men destined for the army, a role to which it was accustomed and in which its motives were not open to misinterpretation. The experience of the Second World War was to show that a civilian recruiting procedure had many advantages, not the least of which was that it facilitated the task of dealing with conscientious objectors. But in 1915 there was no possibility of a civilian procedure being established: not only was there no time; the Bill had to be conceived in Asquith's terms and not as a radical change.

The second fundamental issue—to whom the Bill should apply—was also answered exclusively in terms of the redemption of Asquith's pledge to the married men. The Bill[2] provided that all men who had been unmarried on 2 November 1915 (the date of Asquith's pledge) and between the ages of eighteen and forty-one on 15 August 1915, the precise age-group canvassed under the Derby Scheme, should be deemed to have been enlisted for the period of the war. Every attempt was made to place these men in the same position as those who had attested. The Derby tribunals were given statutory authority and the Cabinet Committee added this prefatory note to the draft Bill:

The cases in which exemption can be obtained will correspond, as far

[1] For the military view see Report of the Select Committee on Military Service, 1917, evidence of Lord Derby and General Geddes.

[2] Draft Bill 297–7. Unless otherwise stated the draft Bills quoted are those in Asquith Papers 82.

as possible, to those in which exemption can be obtained under the Derby Scheme.[1]

It followed that there would be no legal provisions for men who objected to military service on the grounds of conscience. The first draft allowed only three grounds for exemption:

> on the ground that it is expedient in the national interest that he should, instead of being employed in military service, be engaged in other work, or on the ground that arrangements must be made for persons dependent on him, or on the grounds of health. . . .[2]

Ironically, Asquith's concept of the Bill prevented the inclusion of arrangements that would have made the Bill more acceptable to its Liberal opponents. The Cabinet Committee was certainly not unaware that conscientious objectors existed: quite apart from the petition of the Christadelphians and the agitation of the N.C.F., Sir John Simon had reminded his colleagues that among those they proposed to conscript were a number of 'Quakers, conscientious objectors and cranks'.[3] But the provisions for such men could not violate the principle of no change from the Derby Scheme. Under the Scheme an attested man had been allowed to express a preference for non-combatant duties; the Cabinet Committee presumably intended that this War Office arrangement should now be used to meet the conscientious objections of enlisted men. The views of those conscientious objectors who would refuse to perform any duties under military control were either not known or not accepted.

With these limitations the draft Bill was put before the Cabinet. The broad outlines were accepted on 28 December when the Cabinet formally agreed to conscript the single men who had not responded to the Derby Scheme.[4] A full draft of the Bill was printed on 30 December and discussed by the Cabinet on 1 January.[5] For Asquith these were the hardest days. The unity of the Cabinet for which he had fought and manoeuvred with great political skill was now in danger. At the Cabinet meeting on 28 December, McKenna and Runciman dissented from the decision to introduce conscription and said that they would have to consider

[1] CAB 37/139/67.
[2] Draft Bill 297–7, 2 (I).
[3] CAB 37/139/53.
[4] CAB 37/139/58.
[5] CAB 37/139/70. The draft discussed at this meeting was 297–7.

their positions.[1] The following day, Sir Edward Grey told Asquith that if McKenna and Runciman resigned he would follow.[2] The chances of Sir John Simon staying at his post were even more remote.

If these four leading ministers and Liberal colleagues resigned, the image of Cabinet unity would be destroyed and Asquith's own political pre-eminence, already weakened by the formation of the coalition, would be undermined perhaps decisively. With Sir John Simon, Asquith probably decided to cut his losses; the Home Secretary would not compromise on this matter of principle. Instead Asquith concentrated on Grey, persuading him not only to remain loyal but also to use his influence to conciliate McKenna and Runciman. All three men agreed to attend the Cabinet meeting on New Year's Day. At the meeting 'the difference of opinion manifested was very acute'[3] but there were no resignations. Sir John Simon, whose resignation had been announced that morning, found that he had gone alone.

By limiting the resignations to the one that was both anticipated and unavoidable, Asquith had succeeded in preserving at least the façade of unity; but Simon's departure had transferred the danger from the Cabinet to the House of Commons. If the former Home Secretary could rally to his cause the many Liberals who at heart deplored conscription, he would provoke the bitter parliamentary conflict that Asquith feared. Asquith regarded it as imperative that the debates and the division lobbies should reflect a convincing majority in favour of the Bill. If they did not, the opposition to conscription in the country—particularly that of organized labour—would be encouraged to maintain its stand, even to the point of making the law unworkable. The failure to make conscription effective might in turn provide Britain's ally, Russia, already crippled by the German summer offensive, with an excuse to conclude a separate peace. These considerations confirmed the need to prevent a Liberal revolt against the Bill. Simon himself and the hard-core opponents of conscription, such as the Quaker and I.L.P. members of the Commons, could not be wooed by a concession to Liberal opinion in the Bill, but such a concession might

[1] CAB 37/139/58.

[2] J. A. Spender and Cyril Asquith, *Life of Herbert Henry Asquith*, II, London, 1932, p. 204.

[3] CAB 37/139/70.

discourage other Liberals from aligning themselves with Simon.

Two days after Simon's resignation a new draft of the Military Service Bill was printed. It contained an additional ground on which exemption could be claimed:

> 'on the ground of a conscientious objection to bearing arms.'[1]

There is no best evidence that this amendment was specifically intended as a means of making conscription more palatable to those Liberal members whose support was in question, but the circumstantial evidence is strong. Though Asquith was later at pains to present the decision to recognize conscience as part of an established British tradition, his policy would appear to have been inspired by political necessity rather than historical precedents. Many years after, Simon wrote, 'I have long since realized that my opposition was a mistake,'[2] but by his action he had obliged the Cabinet to make a concession to Liberal opinion that has long been regarded as a fine example of the nation's tolerance.

The earliest date on which the decision to insert a conscience clause could have been taken was Saturday 1 January; this left just three days in which to draft effective legal provisions for conscientious objectors. There was no time for exhaustive research; the character of the provisions would be dictated by the need to find a quick solution and one that would not require alteration of the existing administrative machinery. There were no useful models in English law. In the Commons, Asquith could assure the conscriptionists, without much risk of contradiction, that there were precedents in the Militia Acts;[3] the statute book was littered with such Acts, some temporary and some permanent, and the task of analysing the precise position of the many classes of excepted persons would have been arduous indeed. The Militia Acts in question excepted the Quakers and Unitas Fratrum not as conscientious objectors but as two of the numerous categories of citizen, including peers, licensed teachers, and poor men with more than one child born in wedlock, whom the government thought it unnecessary to disturb.[4] Thus while the Acts were some help to

[1] Draft Bill 297–8, 3 January 1916, 2 (I)(d).

[2] Viscount Simon, *Retrospect*, London, 1952, p. 107.

[3] See Asquith's speech, 5 HC 77, col. 949–62, 5 January 1916.

[4] 43 GEO 3, Cap. 96, 27 July 1803, sec. XII and Cap. 120, 11 August 1803, sec. II. The Unitas Fratrum was a branch of the Hussites commonly called the Moravians.

Asquith in presenting the provisions for conscience to the House of Commons, they were no help to the draftsman or the Cabinet Committee. It is possible that the Committee consulted those sections of the Vaccination Acts that dealt with conscientious objection; Walter Long, the Committee's Chairman, would have appreciated the relevance of the experience gained under these Acts of testing conscientious objection by means of a tribunal hearing.[1] But the Vaccination Acts did not provide a formula that could be used for military service. Fortunately, a ready-made formula did exist in the Australian Defence Act of 1910; and it was primarily in terms of the provisions of this Act that the problems posed by Asquith's last-minute change of policy were solved. Bonar Law later told the Commons, 'the Government have practically introduced as far as they could the very method which was adopted in the Australian Act for dealing with this subject'.[2]

One of the results of the activities of the National Service League before the war had been the adoption by the Australian Government of compulsory peacetime training. Under the Defence Act, young men between the ages of twelve and twenty-six were obliged to attend a prescribed number of drills and an annual camp. From this peacetime training there was no legal exemption on the grounds of conscience, though some attempt was made to find a non-combatant role for those whose religious faith did not allow them to bear arms. The Act did, however, make provision for the exemption of conscientious objectors in the event of conscription being imposed in time of war, and it was these provisions that were used in the British Bill. Paradoxically, the Australians who had accepted peacetime training refused to accept conscription when war was declared, so that the provisions for conscientious objectors had never been tested. This fact does not appear to have deterred those responsible for drafting the British law.

The Australian Act[3] provided that 'persons who satisfy the prescribed authority that their conscientious beliefs do not allow them to bear arms' would be exempt from combatant duties. The prescribed authority was defined as a court 'authorised by regulations', and it was expressly stated that the exemption this court could grant did not 'extend to duties of a non-combatant nature'.

[1] See p. 43, below. [2] 5 HC 78, col. 428, 19 January 1916.

[3] Australian Defence Act 1910 (Act No. 37 of 1910); section 7 deals with conscientious objectors.

When these provisions were grafted onto the British Bill they underwent small but significant changes.[1] Where the Australian Act spoke of 'conscientious beliefs' the British draft used the phrase 'conscientious objection'. The Australian wording could be understood to mean that the Government was prepared to recognize only those cases in which refusal to bear arms was inspired or dictated by the beliefs of a religious body.[2] There would appear to have been two reasons why the British Cabinet avoided this wording: the phrase 'conscientious objection' was already familiar in British law as a result of the Vaccination Act of 1898; and this phrase also reflected Asquith's wish that the wording of the law should comprehend 'people belonging to various religious denominations *or* to various schools of thought'.[3]

The change from the Australian wording would not have been welcomed by the conscriptionists in the Cabinet or by the representatives of the War Office; the latter in particular regarded this broadening of the definition of conscientious objection with suspicion. The official military view—which remained unchanged throughout the war—was that exemption should be restricted to bona fide religious objectors. This view was held by Lord Kitchener and by the two senior officers responsible for the discipline of the army—the Adjutant-General, Sir Nevil Macready, and the Director of Personal Services, Brigadier-General Wyndham Childs. These men were primarily concerned to prevent exemption from service on the grounds of political objection; the N.C.F., with its left-wing associations and unashamed opposition to the war, was anathema to the military. To Kitchener, the N.C.F. was a 'growing and menacing body'; when he received a deputation on conscientious objectors shortly before his death in May 1916, 'he emphatically pointed out that he was dealing solely with the conscientious objector with religious views and impressed upon the deputation that he recognized no political right to object'.[4] But if Kitchener protested to Asquith in January there is no record. The military protest was made by Macready and Childs. At separate

[1] Incorporated in draft Bill 297–8.

[2] The Australian Defence Act of 1939 (Act No. 38 of 1939), 3, used the same phrase but added: 'In this section "conscientious beliefs" includes all conscientious beliefs, whether the ground thereof is or is not of a religious character. . . .'

[3] 5 HC 77, col. 957, 5 January 1916.

[4] Kitchener Papers 74/WS/73.

interviews these officers urged the Prime Minister to restrict the right of conscientious objection to men who applied on religious grounds.[1] Asquith gave a polite but firm refusal: he could not limit the right of conscientious objection in this way without simultaneously limiting the political usefulness of this section of the Bill. Middle-class Liberalism embraced pacifist opinions that were not exclusively religious in origin; the various schools of thought to which Asquith referred included the internationalism of the U.D.C. members and the intellectual rejection of the war characteristic of the group of writers and artists who frequented the Morrells' homes in Bloomsbury and Garsington and among whom were men Asquith knew personally.[2] It was to protect these intellectual rather than political objections that Asquith insisted on an unrestricted definition of conscientious objection. The military did not understand Asquith's reasoning: his answer, Childs recorded, was 'over my head'.[3] But while the military had been rebuffed on this occasion, Macready and Childs remained implacable opponents of any concession to the members of the N.C.F., an attitude that was to assume considerable importance when these two officers became responsible for all conscientious objectors under military jurisdiction.

The British Bill followed the Australian in recognizing a conscientious objection to 'bearing arms', but on Asquith's copy of the draft the words 'bearing arms' have been crossed out and 'undertaking combatant service' written in the margin.[4] This alteration was incorporated in a draft dated 4 January;[5] clearly 'bearing arms' was not an adequate description of the duties that might be required of a combatant soldier in 1916. When the extent of the conscientious objection recognized in law was to 'undertaking combatant service', it would have been consistent to prescribe a statutory exemption from combatant service only. The provisions of the Australian Act reflected this consistency of approach: if a man established a conscientious objection to bearing arms he could be exempt from this duty but not from duty of a non-combatant nature. But on this important point the drafting of the British

[1] See Major-General Sir Wyndham Childs, *Episodes and Reflections*, London, 1930, p. 148; and WO 32/2055/6923.

[2] For the conscientious objections of these men see Chapter 5 below.

[3] Childs, op. cit., p. 148.

[4] Draft Bill 297–8, 2 (I)(d).

[5] Draft Bill 297–9, 2 (I)(d).

Bill introduced an element of ambiguity. The sub-section on certificates of exemption had originally read:

Any certificate of exemption may be absolute, conditional, or temporary, as the Military Service Tribunal think best suited to the case.[1]

When a new phrase was added to provide for the exemption of conscientious objectors, the sub-section read:

Any certificate of exemption may be absolute, conditional, or temporary, as the Military Service Tribunal think best suited to the case, and in the case of an application on conscientious grounds may take the form of an exemption from combatant duties only.[2]

This wording was open to two interpretations: it could be understood to mean that the exemption from combatant duties only was the sole exemption available to applicants on conscientious grounds, or that this exemption was an additional alternative before the tribunal when dealing with conscientious objectors. It is not clear which interpretation the Cabinet accepted at the time of drafting. The former was acceptable to the Conservatives and to the military and was consistent with the recognized objection to 'undertaking combatant service'. The latter was more generous in that it allowed an absolute exemption for conscientious objectors but by the same token was inconsistent with the limited objection recognized in the Bill. Subsequently, the Cabinet made it clear that it accepted the more generous interpretation but the inconsistency (and therefore the ambiguity) was allowed to remain. As a result the tribunals' powers in conscientious cases were for many months a source of controversy and misunderstanding.[3]

Under the Australian provisions the applications for exemption were to be decided by 'courts authorised by regulations'. If the provisions had been implemented, it is probable that the Australian Government would have followed the New Zealand and South African practice of authorizing the magistrates' courts to decide these cases.[4] But in Britain there was no practicable alternative to making use of the existing tribunal system. It was for Parliament to debate the merits and limitations of the tribunals; what mattered

[1] Draft Bill 297–7, 2 (I).

[2] Draft Bill 297–8, 2 (I).

[3] See Chapter 6 below.

[4] New Zealand Defence Amendment Act, 1912 (Act No. 20 of 1912), 65 (2), and South African Defence Act, 1912 (Act No. 13 of 1912), 82 (3).

to the draftsman and the Cabinet Committee was that the insertion of a conscience clause should disturb as little as possible the concept of the Bill as an extension of the Derby Scheme. The tribunals appointed locally, and the Central Tribunal appointed by the Government under the Scheme, were now to be given statutory authority. Intermediate Appeal Tribunals would be appointed for each county area. From the Local Tribunal there would be an absolute right of appeal, but from the intermediate Appeal Tribunal this right could only be exercised with the permission of the Tribunal. The overall responsibility for the constitution and procedure of the tribunals was vested in the Local Government Board.[1]

The final draft of the Bill was printed on 4 January and was to be introduced to the Commons the following day by the Prime Minister himself. Even for such an accomplished and experienced parliamentarian, the task was one of peculiar difficulty. To achieve a convincing majority he would have simultaneously to persuade the Conservatives that the Bill was an effective instrument of conscription and to satisfy the Liberals that it was no more than a postscript to the Derby Scheme. The proposal to exempt conscientious objectors did not fit easily into this pattern: while it might pacify some Liberal opponents of the Bill, it would provoke the conscriptionists; and it could not be presented as an adaptation of the arrangements of the Derby Scheme. Asquith's notes for the speech reflect these considerations:[2] if the exemption of conscientious objectors could not be presented as a continuation of the Scheme, it would have to be justified on the grounds of precedent and tradition; and if it cast doubt on the Government's determination to prosecute the war, he would have to emphasize that the objector was willing—indeed anxious—to serve the country in a non-combatant capacity. It did not matter that the motives of the Cabinet and the views of the conscientious objectors would be misrepresented, any more than it would matter that the first conscription Bill in British history was being disguised as the redemption of the Prime Minister's pledge. Asquith was prepared to sacrifice accuracy to his immediate goal of a parliamentary majority.

[1] Draft Bill 297–9, Second Schedule. The tribunals were first called Military Service Tribunals but this was amended so that in the Act they were called Local, Appeal, and Central Tribunals.

[2] The notes are in Asquith Papers 29.

CHAPTER THREE

THE MILITARY SERVICE BILL IN PARLIAMENT

On the afternoon of Wednesday, 5 January 1916, the benches and gallery of the House of Commons were filled to capacity. It was a scene unique in British parliamentary history: of the 630 M.P.s, 165 were serving in His Majesty's Forces and many of these men had chosen to wear uniform for this occasion.[1] Though the majority of gallant members held recruiting or administrative posts, a few had returned from France to attend the debate. 'Not since the Cromwellian purges', *The Times* reported, 'have so many uniformed soldiers been seen on the floor of the chamber.'[2] When Asquith rose to speak he faced benches occupied entirely by men in khaki; other soldiers thronged the gallery from where Lord Derby looked down on the proceedings. With his lordship above and the uniformed ranks below, it was as though the conscriptionists were taking no chances.

Asquith's introduction of the Military Service Bill was consistent with his policy throughout previous weeks: he was not announcing a revolution in British life, just the redemption of his promise to the married men. In a tense and expectant House his speech was both a deliberate anti-climax and an attempt to limit the discussion to the one narrow issue of the need to honour his pledge.

The Bill that I am about to ask leave to introduce is one, I think, which can be sincerely supported by those who, either on principle, or, as in my own case, on grounds of expediency, are opposed to what is commonly described as conscription. The Bill is confined to a specific purpose—the redemption of a promise publicly given by me in this House in the early days of Lord Derby's campaign.[3]

[1] They are listed in 5 HC 77, col. 1117–23.

[2] *The Times*, 6 January 1916.

[3] This and subsequent quotations from Asquith's speech are taken from 5 HC 77, col. 949–62, 5 January 1916.

If there were members who wanted to make this an historic occasion, Asquith did his best to disabuse them. His flat rehearsal of the events that had led to the Cabinet's decision, his elaborate and confusing statistics for the Derby Scheme, and his laborious analysis of the circumstances in which his pledge had been given provided no cause for enthusiasm or dissent. In the same low key, he explained the details of the Bill. The main provisions for the call-up of single men passed without comment. The grounds on which such men could be released from service were, however, more likely to provoke interruption: both the conscriptionists and the military feared that Asquith had persuaded his Cabinet colleagues to accept a string of exemptions that would make the Bill—in the words of one Conservative member—'a rotten mutilated piece of compulsion'.[1] Already conscriptionist suspicions had been aroused by the news that the Bill would not apply to Ireland because that country had not been canvassed under the Derby Scheme. Asquith now turned to the grounds for exemption: that it was in the national interest for the man to be engaged in civilian employment; that his enlistment would leave those dependent on him without suitable means of subsistence; that he was infirm or in ill-health. 'The fourth ground for exemption', Asquith concluded, 'is a conscientious objection to undertaking combatant service.'

These words were a signal for a rowdy demonstration. Anger, dismay, derision, and the excitement that until now had been denied an opportunity for expression, provided the impetus for a long interruption. The *Daily Mail* reported, 'the biggest outburst of incredulous and contemptuous cries came at the news that COs were to be released from combatant service. The laughter was long and loud.'[2] Asquith let the interruption run its course. Then he continued with his prepared defence of this part of the Bill. First there was the argument of precedent and tradition:

I am rather sorry to hear those expressions of dissent, and even of derision from some quarters. Some Hon. Members are, perhaps, unacquainted with the history of legislation in regard to these matters. In the days of the great French War, when Mr. Pitt and his successors were in power, and when they enforced the compulsory Militia Bill,

[1] Captain Craig, the Member for South Antrim, 5 HC 78, col. 460, 19 January 1916.

[2] *Daily Mail*, 6 January 1916.

they expressly exempted the only people who in those days had conscientious objections to Government service—the people called Quakers. In these modern times our South African and Australian fellow subjects, who have both in various forms adopted compulsory military service, have both included in their Acts these very exceptions—and with the best results.

As a justification of the Cabinet's decision to recognize conscientious objection this was largely bluff. Not only were the Militia Acts doubtful precedents; with the Australian Act, Asquith was claiming 'the best results' for a section of the law that had never been implemented. Yet the bluff, though clumsy, caught the conscriptionists at their most vulnerable points. They had themselves cited the Militia Acts as evidence that there was nothing inherently alien about conscription, and it had been their propaganda that had won support for the compulsory measures in Australia and South Africa. To these echoes of their own case, Asquith had added a patriotic overtone: the exemption of conscientious objectors had been granted by Mr. Pitt in a situation no less critical and with no noticeable weakening of the nation's resolve.

This blend of history and deception, of bogus precedent and heroic tradition, checked Asquith's more vociferous critics but was not sufficient to reconcile all the conscriptionists in the House. To achieve a general acceptance of the conscience clause, Asquith felt it necessary to allay any fears that the clause would be used by selfish or unpatriotic men to escape their duty. He gave—or appeared to give—an assurance that men would not be excused service altogether on the plea of conscience and he drew a picture of the conscientious objectors as brave men who were prepared to risk their lives alongside the fighting soldiers; they did not want to take life but 'were quite willing to perform many other military duties', indeed a number were already fulfilling useful roles 'with the greatest bravery and courage, exposing themselves to the very same risks as those who go into the trenches to man the guns and use the rifles'.

Once again there was an element of bluff. Though Asquith did not know the exact position that different groups of conscientious objectors would adopt if conscription became law, he can hardly have believed that his portrait of the eager non-combatant was typical. Men with pacifist views had volunteered to join the Red Cross and the Friends Ambulance Unit but it did not follow that conscientious objectors to conscription would feel the same enthusiasm for this type of military service.[1] Asquith's assurances were therefore misleading, as was his explanation of how the law would be applied. He told the House: 'It is suggested in the case of such men that the exemption which they should get—and which I am certain is all they would claim—should take the form of an exemption from military combatant duties only.'

Asquith's misleading statements were perhaps necessary to calm the conscriptionists and to ensure that they did not abstain in protest against the 'mutilation of the Bill'; but these statements figured prominently in the reports of his speech so that, from the start, the ambiguous sub-section on exemptions was given a particular and, as it transpired, a wrong interpretation in the public mind. The *Daily Mail* explained that conscientious objectors 'are apparently released only from service in the actual firing line', and the *Westminster Gazette* stated categorically 'this does not exempt them from other military duties'.[2] Ministerial statements and departmental circulars never completely succeeded in correcting this misinterpretation of the Cabinet's wishes.

When Asquith sat down, the perfunctory applause was a mark of his achievement. He had set out to deflate the occasion, to reduce it to a level at which intensity of feeling would be out of place, and he had succeeded. The outburst provoked by the concession to conscience—a point of detail—only served to underline how completely he had frustrated the passions that had previously been aroused by the principle embodied in the Bill. The sense of anticlimax he had created made it difficult for the opponents of conscription to raise great issues, just as his narrow conception of the Bill had left them little room to manoeuvre. When Sir John Simon tried to establish that the debate was concerned with a fundamental change in the nation's life rather than with the redemption of a Prime Minister's promise, he was unable to convince the House; and in the light of Asquith's insistence that no question of principle was involved, Simon's defence of voluntaryism appeared irrelevant. Simon failed to damage Asquith's case because he was unwilling to fight on the very restricted field that Asquith had

[1] There were many shades of opinion among those who volunteered for the Red Cross and the F.A.U., but there was a common desire to serve; such a desire was not common to all conscientious objectors, particularly not to those who rejected the war.

[2] See the editions of these newspapers for 6 January 1916.

chosen; and where Simon had failed other opponents of conscription were unlikely to succeed. Their only hope was to force into the open the issues raised by this extension of the power of the state over the life of the individual, but few members showed any interest in the theoretical implications of conscription. Asquith had indicated how conscription could be adopted without controversy and the majority of those who heard him were inclined to follow his lead. The shifts and postponements of the previous months had engendered an impatience with further delay; even among those Liberal members to whom conscription was distasteful there had been a growing desire to see all effective measures taken to ensure victory.[1] Charles Hobhouse, who had been a member of the former Liberal Cabinet and had voted against the National Registration Bill, now told the House, 'I for one, whatever my belief as to the evils of a permanent enforcement of conscription, shall support this measure as one necessary to the successful carrying on of the war. . . .'[2]

The vote on the first reading was taken on 6 January. The mood of the debate left no doubt that Asquith's tactics had ensured a majority, and the Bill's sponsors were encouraged to bid for total success. Winding up for the Government, Arthur Balfour spoke of a 'fundamental unity of feeling' and invited the Bill's opponents not to force a division. The invitation was declined. Members of the I.L.P. and the Society of Friends could not acquiesce in the imposition of conscription, however desirable unanimity might be as a stimulant to allied morale. The voting figures showed that 403 members had voted for the Bill and 105 against; about 150 members, almost all of whom were Liberals, had abstained. Simon's defeat had been even more conclusive than these figures suggest. Of the hostile votes, 60 had been cast by Irish Nationalists who subsequently decided to abstain from voting on what was a purely British measure. The effective opposition consisted of 34 Liberals and 11 Labour, of whom about thirty-five maintained their opposition throughout the Bill's progress.

[1] Some Liberals had from the outbreak of war taken the line that 'being in, we must win'. For the different Liberal attitudes see especially G. R. Crosby, *Disarmament and Peace in British Politics, 1914–1919*, Cambridge, Mass., 1957, pp. 12–34.

[2] 5 HC 77, col. 985, 5 January 1916. Hobhouse had been Postmaster General in Asquith's 1914 Cabinet; he was no relation to the famous conscientious objector Stephen Hobhouse.

Asquith's victory was greeted with prolonged cheering. *The Times*, a newspaper that had found little to praise in the Prime Minister's policy, described the applause as a 'tumultuously triumphant demonstration' in his favour.[1] It was Asquith's last great parliamentary success. His political skill had reduced the hostile vote to negligible proportions. Though his tactics had saddled the country with a hotchpotch system of voluntary and compulsory recruiting, a less Asquithian approach might well have divided the nation; his delays and evasions, his refusal to extend the scope of the Bill beyond the redemption of his pledge, and the timing of his concession to conscience all contributed to the difficulties of administering the law but they made conscription possible by minimizing the opposition in the House of Commons. And as Asquith had hoped, a convincing majority in the House helped to disarm the formidable opposition of the trade unions.

The immediate union reaction was not encouraging. On 6 January a special Congress of Labour voted overwhelmingly against conscription.[2] As a result the three Labour members of the Government[3] announced that they would resign from the Coalition in order to be free to oppose the Military Service Bill. Asquith at once asked for a meeting with the Labour leaders. Before this meeting took place, Arthur Henderson, his resignation cocked but not fired, circulated a memorandum to his Cabinet colleagues urging that, in view of the hostility of the unions, the second reading of the Bill should be postponed while a last effort was made to obtain the necessary men by voluntary enlistment.[4] Secure in the knowledge of their parliamentary majority, the Cabinet rejected Henderson's plea. Asquith however still had one or two conciliatory gestures up his sleeve. He assured the Labour leaders that their fears of industrial conscription were unfounded, and on the strength of this assurance Henderson and his two Labour colleagues withdrew their resignations; their future cooperation would however depend on the attitude of the Labour Party Conference at

[1] *The Times*, 7 January 1916.

[2] G. D. H. Cole, *A History of the Labour Party from 1914*, London, 1948, pp. 26–7.

[3] Arthur Henderson was President of the Board of Education; outside the Cabinet, William Brace was Under Secretary at the Home Office and G. H. Roberts a Government Whip.

[4] CAB 37/140/17.

the end of the month. Asquith also announced that the Group System of the Derby Scheme, which had closed on 12 December, would be reopened and that he hoped sufficient single men would come forward to make the Bill a dead letter. His somewhat disingenuous optimism did nothing to delay the Bill's progress. Once the Bill had won a convincing majority on the first reading, its final passage into law was never in doubt. This certainty forced the Labour leaders to choose between their fears of conscription and their support of the war. At the Party Conference in Bristol on 26 January they reaffirmed the former but chose the latter. The Conference voted against the Military Service Bill but rejected proposals to agitate for repeal if the Bill should become law.[1] As the Bill had already passed through every stage in Parliament and was to receive the Royal Assent the following day, these votes marked Labour's grudging acceptance of Asquith's triumph.

The decision of the Labour Conference confirmed that the struggle to prevent conscription had been lost on 6 January. A certain futility marked the N.C.F.'s instructions to its members on 9 January: 'The Government proposal need never become operative.... Bombard the Prime Minister, Mr. Lloyd George and Sir John Simon at the House of Commons with suitable letters and get your friends to do the same.'[2] After the first reading there were only two courses open to the opponents of conscription: to accept the decision of Parliament and work for the equitable treatment of those who came under the new law, or to continue in opposition even though this might involve taking (or encouraging others to take) illegal action. The N.C.F. chose the latter course; the opponents of conscription in the Commons chose the former, and it was with their attempts to secure adequate safeguards for the men who would be compulsorily enlisted that the committee stage of the Bill was primarily concerned.

The committee stage was taken two weeks after the first reading. The two leading Conservatives, Bonar Law and Walter Long, shared the task of steering the Bill through the Commons, a logical and shrewd choice on Asquith's part. In practice, the lion's share fell to Walter Long; as President of the Local Government Board, he had to cope with the amendments to the law relating to

[1] *Annual Report of the Labour Party Conference, 1916*, pp. 95 and 124.
[2] N.C.F. Letter to members, 9 January 1916.

the tribunals and the grounds for exemption. In May, he performed a similar function for the second Military Service Bill that was to introduce universal conscription. Thus from the appointment of the Cabinet Committee in December 1915 until the second Military Service Act became law in June 1916, Long exercised a significant influence on the character of the provisions for conscientious objectors and on the administrative context in which these provisions would be implemented.

In 1916, Walter Long was in his early sixties and approaching the end of his political career.[1] His background and interests were not those usually associated with an understanding of the pacifist position. He was what a later generation would have called an establishment figure almost to the point of caricature. An Old Harrovian Tory squire, he was as devoted to the pursuit of the fox as he was convinced of the value of conscription. For centuries members of the family had stood for Parliament and shouldered the high sheriffdom of their county; with few exceptions, the tradition was one of steady but undramatic public service. Walter Long's paternal grandfather had sat in the Commons for thirty-three years without making a speech; his maternal grandfather had sat for twenty-eight years during which he had spoken for three minutes in support of a bill to prohibit pigeon-shooting.[2] Walter Long himself was both more articulate and more ambitious. He had won a seat in the Cabinet and had been a candidate (though a reluctant one) for the leadership of the Conservative Party in 1911. But that his career had not been entirely inconsistent with the family tradition is suggested by the frequency with which Prime Ministers asked him to serve at the Local Government Board, a department of state requiring thoroughness rather than political flair.[3] In office he was diligent and scrupulous but unimaginative. His virtues enabled him to bring to the problem of the conscientious objector a desire above all to be fair; his limitations prevented him from grasping the subtlety and complexity of the issues involved.

Long's task was facilitated by the mood of the Commons. After

[1] For Long's career see Charles Petrie, *Walter Long and His Times*, London, 1936, and Walter Long, *Memories*, London, 1923.

[2] Petrie, op. cit., p. 18.

[3] Long was Parliamentary Secretary to the L.G.B. 1886–1892; President of the L.G.B. 1900–1905 and May 1915–December 1916.

the committee stage, Herbert Samuel, Simon's successor at the Home Office, reported to the king: 'The atmosphere in the House has been far more favourable than was anticipated beforehand.'[1] The contrast between the hostile reception given to Asquith's reference to the exemption of conscientious objectors and the restrained discussion of this section of the Bill in committee is not difficult to explain. The overwhelming victory on the first reading had relaxed the tensions of the long struggle over compulsion. There was no longer any cause for khaki demonstrations; like the members of a secret clan, the conscriptionists doffed their uniforms and resumed the sober round of parliamentary business. While some might have wished to fight the conscience clause in committee, the majority were more concerned to see the Bill on the statute book without delay. A few perhaps had already grasped the lesson that was to be driven home as the war continued: once it had been decided to make conscientious objection part of the machinery of the Military Service Act, Liberal principles and conscriptionist aims to a large extent coincided; neither individual freedom nor compulsory service would benefit from the widespread arrest and imprisonment of conscientious objectors.

Much of the credit for the reasonable tone of the debates belonged to the Government spokesmen; Walter Long in particular drew tributes from the opponents of the Bill for his generous and tactful handling of the amendments.[2] The veteran Irish member, John Dillon, told the Commons: 'I only want to say, as an old member of the House, and one who has passed through many stormy scenes, that I have never seen a Bill which might easily have led to passionate and heated debate, conducted with greater skill and in a more conciliatory manner than this Bill has been conducted through the House.'[3] Long's achievement was to establish by his own example an impartial and common-sense approach to the discussions on conscientious objection; it was characteristic of his attitude that when it was suggested that no one with strong anti-conscriptionist views should be appointed to the tribunals, he replied that in that case he would be compelled to bar anybody who

[1] Home Secretary's Report to the King on the Proceedings in Parliament, Samuel Papers, 20 January 1916.

[2] See the tributes of Philip Snowden of the I.L.P., 5 HC 78, col. 750, 20 January 1916, and of Sir John Simon, 5 HC 78, col. 1013, 24 January 1916.

[3] 5 HC 78, col. 760, 20 January 1916.

held views in favour of universal compulsory service.[1] But the smooth working of the provisions for conscientious objectors required something more than an impartial approach: it was vital that the Government spokesmen should clarify the official view of what exemptions were available to applicants on conscientious grounds.

The amendments to that part of the Bill that concerned conscientious objectors fall into two categories: those that attempted to change the Cabinet's definition of conscientious objection and the proposed method of deciding applications; and those that sought to relate the exemptions available more closely to the position that the conscientious objectors were expected to adopt. Though it was only the latter that resulted in modifications to the draft Bill, the former are not without interest as evidence of the Cabinet's desire to strike a balance between the Conservative and Liberal approach to the problem of conscientious objection.

The Conservative view of how a conscientious objector should be defined in law was put by Mr Joynson-Hicks, the Member for Brentford. He proposed that the ground for exemption should be 'that the applicant was, on the fifteenth day of August nineteen hundred and fifteen, a member of the Society of Friends or of any other recognised religious body one of whose fundamental tenets is an objection to all war'.[2] This amendment also reflected the wishes of the military authorities and may have been inspired by them. But the Liberal view was that the right of conscientious objection could not be restricted to the members of specific religious groups and this view prevailed in the Cabinet. It was explained in the House by Bonar Law: 'If there is any right whatever for exemption on account of conscience, it does not apply to any particular denomination, and is a question of man's heart and conscience.'[3] Coming from the Conservative leader, this statement effectively checked any further attempt to restrict the conscientious objection recognized in the Bill. That Bonar Law and the other prominent Conservatives accepted Asquith's definition of conscientious objection is an interesting comment on the Prime Minister's continuing authority within the Cabinet.

[1] 5 HC 78, col. 741, 20 January 1916.
[2] Joynson-Hicks's speech, 5 HC 78, col. 422–7, 19 January 1916.
[3] 5 HC 78, col. 428, 19 January 1916.

The Liberal challenge to the Cabinet's proposals for dealing with conscience was made on the subject of the tribunals. Compulsory vaccination, introduced at the end of the nineteenth century, had shown that there existed a fundamental difference between the two major parties on the competence of a tribunal or court to decide matters of conscience. The Conservatives, who had allowed a right of conscientious objection in the Vaccination Act of 1898,[1] had insisted that the applicant for exemption should satisfy two Justices that he believed vaccination to be harmful to the health of his child. Despite Liberal protests that the Justices were deciding cases in an arbitrary fashion, the Conservatives had refused to amend the law. The Conservative answer had been given by Walter Long, whose department had been responsible for the working of the Act: 'The magistrates', Long insisted, 'are perfectly capable of interpreting an Act of Parliament, and to satisfy [sic] themselves whether those who apply for exemption have or have not a conscientious objection to vaccination.'[2]

The Liberals had denied the competence of any body to judge a man's conscience. During the debates on the Vaccination Bill, the party's case had been put by Asquith: 'I do not understand by what process of examination or inquiry you can get beyond a man's statement, "I do conscientiously object to vaccination." I cannot conceive of any inquiry in any court which would enable you to get behind that statement, unless it were to inquire into the grounds of belief.'[3] Asquith had advocated allowing the conscientious objector to make a statutory declaration under oath, a proposal that had aroused all the Conservative fears of opening the flood-gates to spurious claimants. To the Conservatives any move to make it easy for a man to opt out of his obligation under the law was an invitation to anarchy;[4] to the Liberals it was a guarantee of individual liberty. When the Liberals had come to power in 1905, they had amended the law in the way that Asquith had suggested.[5] Within a year, the number of certificates of conscientious objection

[1] 61 and 62 VICT Ch. 49, 12 August 1898. Section 2 (I) deals with conscientious objection.

[2] 4 HC 108, col. 769, 27 May 1902.

[3] 4 HC 62, col. 452, 20 July 1898.

[4] See for example Lord Rockwood's statement, 4 HL 64, col. 446, 8 August 1898: 'If people are allowed to set the law at defiance at their own sweet will, where are we to stop?'

[5] Vaccination Act, 1907 (7 EDW 7 Ch. 31, 28 August 1907), I.

issued had been doubled and Conservative fears had appeared to have been justified.[1]

It was partly as a result of this experience that in the case of military service the Conservative view prevailed. When the Liberal, R. L. Outhwaite, proposed that a declaration on oath should be accepted as sufficient evidence of a man's conscientious objection,[2] he used those arguments that Asquith had employed in 1898, but Long was unimpressed. Not only was Long's faith in the good judgement of local bodies as profound as ever (he was even considering establishing local tribunals to hear cases against food profiteers),[3] but common sense indicated that a declaration on oath would be unacceptable as a test of conscientious objection both to Parliament and to the public. Nor did Long's experience under the Vaccination Acts incline him to be sympathetic to a proposal that special tribunals should be appointed to hear applications on conscientious grounds.[4] He knew the Liberal arguments about the tyranny of locally elected men but he did not accept them. Instead he assured the House that it was the Government's intention 'to secure . . . the presence on these tribunals of men who by their training and experience will give full and fair consideration even to the more extreme cases'; if the Government failed to do this, it would have to deal with cases of 'the utmost difficulty and complexity'.[5] It is a facile comment that in the light of subsequent events Long's words appear ironic; at the time his wide experience of local government and his narrow conception of the nature of conscientious objection made him confident that the tribunals would be able to perform their role 'with single-mindedness,

[1] The number of Certificates of Conscientious Objection under the Vaccination Acts 1905–1910 were:

1905	44,369
1906	53,828
1907	76,709
1908	160,350
1909	197,342
1910	230,947

The law allowing a statutory declaration on oath came into force on 1 January 1908. For these figures see 40th Annual Report of the L.G.B. 1910–1911 (Cmd. 5978, 1912), Pt. II, p. xxix.

[2] 5 HC 78, col. 462–5, 19 January 1916.

[3] Long, op. cit., pp. 228–9; typically, he thought that these local tribunals should consist of 'responsible persons'.

[4] The proposal made by T. E. Harvey, 5 HC 78, col. 566, 19 January 1916.

[5] Long's speech on the tribunals, 5 HC 78, col. 738–45, 19 January 1916.

honesty and integrity'.[1] When the war had ended and 'the utmost difficulty and complexity' had been experienced, Long's faith in the tribunal system was less pronounced. He wrote (not quite truthfully), 'I always felt that it was not fair for Parliament to throw this responsibility on local committees. . . .'[2]

While Walter Long was not prepared to accept amendments to the role of the tribunals, he did attempt to clarify official policy on exemptions. That he was only partially successful was the result of various factors: his own inability to foresee the tribunals' difficulties of interpretation (a corollary of his exaggerated faith in their competence); the work of the draftsman and the Cabinet Committee which had imposed on Parliament a fundamental inconsistency in the law; and a certain ambivalence in the Cabinet's attitude. It has been shown that the draft Bill contained this sub-section on certificates of exemption:

> Any certificate of exemption may be absolute, conditional, or temporary . . . and in the case of an application on conscientious grounds may take the form of an exemption from combatant duties only.[3]

Those M.P.s who were anxious to safeguard the position of the conscientious objector wanted to know whether under this sub-section a successful applicant on conscientious grounds could be given a conditional or unconditional exemption from all military service. Their contacts with the religious and political groups that would be the sources of conscientious objection[4] left them in no doubt that the majority of objectors would refuse to undertake any work under military control. It was to protect these objectors that two Quaker M.P.s, Arnold Rowntree and T. E. Harvey, tabled an amendment that specified for conscientious objectors an exemption from all military service conditional upon the applicant being engaged in work of national importance.[5] Such an exemption had not been precluded by the original wording of the draft, but if the Government accepted this amendment it would be giving clear recognition to the need to provide for men who objected to non-combatant as well as to combatant military service. In a moment of realism and generosity the Cabinet decided to accept the amend-

[1] Ibid. [2] Long, op. cit., p. 225.

[3] Draft Bill 297–8, 2 (I).

[4] The Quaker M.P.s, T. E. Harvey and Arnold Rowntree, were in touch with members of the Society of Friends of military age; Philip Snowden knew the I.L.P. leaders of the N.C.F. and spoke at the N.C.F. Convention in April 1916.

[5] 5 HC 78, col. 430, 19 January 1916.

ment; it did not wish the first weeks of conscription to be marred by a clash with the more extreme objectors. Herbert Samuel explained to the king:

The Government realises that it is highly undesirable, when the Bill passes into law, to have to prosecute such objectors and to send them to prison or to tacitly accept their resistance, to take no proceedings against them, and to allow the law, so far as they are concerned, to remain a dead letter.[1]

The interpretation of this amendment was left to the tribunals; at this stage Long did not see the necessity of defining work of national importance or of establishing machinery for making this work available. What was worse, neither Long nor his colleagues seem to have grasped that so long as the recognized conscientious objection was to 'undertaking combatant service', tribunals would be tempted to argue that the maximum exemption they were empowered to grant was from combatant service only. Tribunals that did not know whether a particular occupation was of national importance or that were uncertain of their power to grant an exemption from all military service, refused to make use of the conditional exemption, with the result that men who would have been willing to do civilian work of national importance were forced into the army as unwilling non-combatants.

A similar but more intractable problem arose in relation to the tribunals' power to grant an *absolute* exemption to applicants on conscientious grounds. Once again the difficulty stemmed from the structure of the sub-section on certificates of exemption and from the limited nature of the conscientious objection recognized in law; and whereas the Cabinet was clear that a conditional exemption should be available to conscientious objectors, its attitude to the granting of absolute exemption was less unequivocal. After the Government had accepted the amendment proposed by Harvey and Rowntree, Herbert Samuel explained the official position as follows:

We say these men must do something—if not military service, then non-combatant service, and if not non-combatant service, then something else that will be useful to the nation in its economic, commercial and other activities.[2]

[1] Home Secretary's Daily Reports to the King on the Proceedings in Parliament, 19 January 1916.

[2] 5 HC 78, col. 452, 19 January 1916.

This statement appeared to exclude the possibility of granting an absolute exemption, yet a week later another member of the Cabinet, Lord Lansdowne, twice stated categorically that the tribunals would have power to grant such an exemption to conscientious objectors; he went so far as to say,

> In our view it is much better that the tribunals should be in a position to give what I may call, without disrespect, the out-and-out conscientious objector an absolute dispensation.[1]

The contradiction underlined the ambivalence in the Cabinet's approach: the Cabinet members wanted absolute exemption to be available, but only for exceptional cases; as a general rule, conscientious objectors should be required to perform some military or civilian alternative service. The two members of the Government directly concerned with the execution of the Cabinet's policy were the President and Parliamentary Secretary of the Local Government Board, Walter Long and W. Hayes Fisher. On 3 February, Long gave this interpretation of official policy to the tribunals:

> There may be exceptional cases in which the genuine convictions and circumstances of the man are such that neither exemption from combatant service nor a conditional exemption will adequately meet the case. Absolute exemption can be granted in these cases if the Tribunal are fully satisfied of the facts.[2]

In the following year, Hayes Fisher, now President of the Board, told Lloyd George's War Cabinet that in his view Parliament had intended that, although absolute exemption was not excluded, the conscientious objector applications would 'normally be dealt with by non-combatant service in the Army or by a requirement that in return for exemption from military service the objector shall undertake work of national importance'.[3]

The policy of Asquith's Cabinet was also implicit in the exact wording that was allowed to become law. Walter Long had inserted the single word 'also' to indicate that while certain exemptions were specified for conscientious objectors, these were in addition

[1] 5 HL 20, cols. 1068 and 1075, 26 January 1916.
[2] R.36, L.G.B. to Local Registration Authorities, 3 February 1916.
[3] CAB 23/4/246 (I). GT.1974.

to the general power to grant absolute exemption to all classes of applicant. In its final form, the much amended sub-section read:

Any certificate of exemption may be absolute, conditional, or temporary, as the authority by whom it was granted think best suited to the case, and *also* in the case of an application on conscientious grounds, may take the form of an exemption from combatant service only, or may be conditional on the applicant being engaged in some work which in the opinion of the tribunal dealing with the case is of national importance.[1]

Unfortunately this wording did not have the desired effect. While a few absolute exemptions were granted, their distribution was arbitrary. Whatever government spokesmen and departmental circulars might say about the out-and-out objector and the exceptional cases the tribunals interpreted their powers from the wording of the Act alone. The sub-section still suggested a distinction between the exemptions for conscientious objectors and those available to applicants on other grounds, and the limited nature of the objection recognized in law encouraged tribunals to make this distinction; in particular, the ambiguity of the law enabled tribunal members to rationalize their natural reluctance to release conscientious objectors from all obligation to serve. When conscientious objectors, who neither accepted the tribunal's interpretation of the law nor understood the ambivalence of the Cabinet's approach, demanded absolute exemption as their right, they were almost always refused. Like the men who had been denied a conditional exemption, they found themselves in the army with a certificate of exemption from combatant duties or with no certificate at all; and once they had come under military law, they presented an administrative problem that neither Asquith's Cabinet nor that of his successor was able to solve.

The provisions of the Military Service (No. 2) Bill received their final reading on 24 January and three days later became law.[2] This, the principal Act, remained the basis for the legal treatment of conscientious objectors for the remainder of the war. Subsequent legislation added new groups of conscientious objectors by con-

[1] Military Service (No. 2) Act, 1916, 2 (3).
[2] As 5 and 6 GEO 5, Ch. 104.

scripting married and older men,[1] but there was no alteration to the fundamental principles upon which official policy was based. The Conservative members of Asquith's Cabinet had no doubt that the provisions for conscientious objectors were generous, perhaps too generous. Bonar Law had told the House that the Government had done everything possible to meet the case,[2] and Walter Long, after he had witnessed the law in action for a year, wrote that he was convinced that if the matter had to be discussed again neither Parliament nor the country would accept such a degree of latitude for the conscientious objector.[3]

The generosity of the Cabinet's provisions for conscientious objectors can be assessed by a comparison with the provisions of those Acts that imposed conscription in other countries during the war. In allowing exemption from non-combatant service the British Act was more generous than the pre-war Colonial Defence Acts that had served as a model to the British draftsmen; but it is more significant that the provisions of the British Act were also more generous than those of the wartime conscription Acts of New Zealand, the United States, and Canada. The Acts concerned were the New Zealand Military Service Act, 1916,[4] the United States Selective Service Act, 1917,[5] and the Canadian Military Service Act, 1917.[6]

In two particulars the provisions of these Acts were similar to those of the British Act: the only conscientious objection recognized was a conscientious objection to combatant service, and the right of conscientious objection was subject to the discretion of a judicial body established under the Act. But in two other particulars the provisions of these Acts were less generous than the British.

The New Zealand Military Service Act gave a man the right of appeal against military service on the grounds:

That he was on the fourth day of August, nineteen hundred and fourteen, and has since continuously been a member of a religious body the

[1] The Military Service Act 1916 (Session 2) (6 and 7 GEO 5, Ch. 15, 25 May 1916) extended liability of service to all men between 18 and 41; the Military Service (No. 2) Act 1918 (8 GEO 5, Ch. 5, 18 April 1918) raised the upper age limit to 51.

[2] 5 HC 78, col. 431, 19 January 1916.

[3] In a letter to Randall Davidson, 4 December 1916. Quoted in C. K. A. Bell, *Randall Davidson, Archbishop of Canterbury*, London, 1935, p. 821.

[4] Military Service Act (7 GEO 5, No. 8, 1 August 1916).

[5] Selective Service Act (65 Cong. Sess. I, Chap. 15, 18 May 1917).

[6] Military Service Act (7–8 GEO 5, Ch. 19, 29 August 1917).

tenets and doctrines of which religious body declare the bearing of arms and the performance of any combatant service to be contrary to Divine revelation, and also that according to his own conscientious religious belief the bearing of arms and the performance of any combatant service is unlawful by reason of being contrary to Divine revelation.[1]

The Act also provided that the Military Service Board—the judicial body to whom all appeals were to be made—should not allow any appeals on the ground of conscientious objection 'unless the appellant shall signify in the prescribed manner his willingness to perform such non-combatant work or services, including service in the Medical Corps and the Army Service Corps, whether in or beyond New Zealand, as may be required of him at such rate of payment as may be prescribed.'[2]

The United States and Canadian Acts also limited the right of conscientious objection to members of recognized non-combatant religious bodies and restricted the statutory exemption to an exemption from combatant duties only.[3]

The generosity of the British Act was not fortuitous. The British Cabinet had broadened the Australian conception of 'conscientious beliefs' to include objections of a non-religious nature, and had accepted the need for a clear statutory exemption from all military service. But the British law had the defect of its virtues: generous in theory, it also embodied the means whereby much of the generosity would be frustrated in practice. This discrepancy between theory and practice did not escape the Bill's critics outside Parliament. The leading Radical newspaper, the *Nation*, declared that the safeguards for conscientious objectors were 'practically worthless' and that 'the Government in drafting this Bill have shown no comprehension of this problem'.[4] It was a harsh but not undeserved criticism. Asquith's Liberalism and Long's impartiality had not been enough to guarantee that the intentions of the Cabinet were clear and consistent in law and that they would be correctly implemented in practice. The provisions of the other countries might have been narrow but they were unambiguous; and they did not leave the crucial role to bodies of locally elected

[1] New Zealand Military Service Act, 1916, 18 (I)(e).

[2] Ibid., 18 (4).

[3] See United States Selective Service Act, 1917, 4, and Canadian Military Service Act, 1917, II (I)(f).

[4] 22 January 1916.

men. In Canada the local tribunals were appointed by the Minister of Justice and consisted of only two members, one a County Court Judge, the other a layman sworn to 'faithfully and impartially perform his duties'.[1] The comparison indicates an essential weakness in the British law: it left too much responsibility for its interpretation to local tribunals few of whose members possessed the training or the expertise to fulfil this role. No doubt Walter Long was partly to blame; his background made him suspicious of anything in the nature of a specialist or expert tribunal, and his experience encouraged him to believe in the plain good sense of local councillors and Justices of the Peace. But the actual source both of the ambiguity of the law and of the need to leave its interpretation to the councillors and Justices, was the Prime Minister's approach to conscription. The political tactics that Asquith thought it necessary to adopt in order to secure 'general assent' for the Military Service Bill prepared the way for the 'utmost difficulty and complexity' that Long had hoped to avoid.

[1] Canadian Military Service Act, 1917, 6 (I)(3) and (5).

CHAPTER FOUR

THE CHANGE TO CONSCRIPTION

Once the Military Service Act had become law,[1] the War Office and the Local Government Board faced the problems of the organization of the call-up of single men and of the disposal of applications for exemption. The two men ultimately responsible were Lord Kitchener and Walter Long, though in practice Kitchener's responsibility devolved on the new Adjutant-General, Sir Nevil Macready.[2] The administrative preparations had to be consistent with Asquith's policy: both Macready and Long were obliged to make use of the arrangements that had been operating under the Derby Scheme. Members of the Government seem to have imagined that conscription was little more than an extension of voluntary recruiting (indeed this was precisely how Asquith wished them to look at it) and that the voluntary recruiting procedure could be adapted without undue difficulty to the needs of compulsion. Disillusionment was swift. The impact of conscription almost crippled the civilian and military organization, and M.P.s' postbags were filled with complaints of injustice and maladministration. For six months, from February to August 1916, the Local Government Board and the War Office struggled to impose on the individual parts of the machine—the recruiting offices, the tribunals, the medical boards—a degree of consistency of procedure, but by the time they were approaching success, the tribunals had already disposed of the great majority of applications for exemption.[3] The first encounter between a British Government and conscientious

[1] It became law on 27 January and came into operation on 10 February.

[2] His appointment dated from 12 February.

[3] By August, both single and married men called up under the Military Service Acts of January and May would have had their applications disposed of, so that the only applicants coming before the tribunals after August were men who became liable for service on reaching the age of eighteen and, in the final months of the war, men between forty-one and fifty-one.

objectors to military service took place during this period when conscription was a novelty and maladministration a commonplace.

For Walter Long and the Local Government Board the first step was to adapt the tribunal system of the Derby Scheme. Under the Act, the Board was responsible for ensuring that in constitution and operation the tribunals conformed to the requirements of the law.[1] In practice, however, the Board did not have the opportunity to exert a significant influence on the selection of tribunal members or on the way in which the members carried out their duties. The tribunal organization of the First World War was marked by an absence of central control. This was partly because it was necessary from the start to base the organization on the units of local government and partly because there was no practicable method of securing uniformity among a large number of tribunals without removing the discretionary power to decide cases on their merits.

The appointment of local tribunals illustrates the limitations of the Board's influence. Walter Long had assured the Commons that the tribunals would contain 'men who by their training and experience will give full and fair consideration even to those more extreme cases'. This assurance had done much to allay Liberal and Labour fears that the tribunals would be composed of prominent citizens who would be unsympathetic to applications from conscientious objectors or from members of the working class. But Long was never in a position to secure the appointment of any particular type of member. The Act required each local registration authority[2] to appoint a tribunal of not less than five and not more than twenty-five persons. The authorities had already appointed tribunals in the previous autumn so that the effect of the new law was to give statutory authority to the two thousand existing local tribunals.[3] In many cases additional members were appointed but the nucleus of the local tribunal under the Military Service Act

[1] Military Service (No. 2) Act, 1916, Second Schedule. In theory the Board's responsibility was limited to the local tribunals; in practice it covered the tribunals at all levels.

[2] Defined as 'the Common Council of London and the Councils of Metropolitan and Municipal Boroughs and of Urban and Rural Districts and the Council of the Scilly Isles'. See the National Register Act, 1915 (5 and 6 GEO V, Ch. 60, 15 July 1915), 2.

[3] 1,805 in England and Wales and 281 in Scotland. See 45th Annual Report of the L.G.B., Pt. I., p. 23, and SHHD 25478S/3171.

remained the same as that of the local tribunal that had been functioning under the Derby Scheme. Walter Long's opportunity to fulfil his assurance was thus limited to the appointment of new members. Even here he could do little more than advise; the only statutory requirements concerned the size of the tribunal and the need 'to provide for the adequate representation of labour in the district'.[1] Long did his best nevertheless. He circulated to the authorities a comprehensive list of recommendations:

> The functions of the Local Tribunal will be of a judicial nature. Persons should therefore be appointed who will consider the cases impartially, and will be guided in their conclusions by a full regard for the national interests of the country at the present time. . . . I desire in particular to refer to the representation of labour. The work of the Tribunals will closely concern the working classes, and it is imperative that they should be adequately represented on the Tribunals. . . . What is desired is that the Tribunals should contain a member or members of the working classes in whom the latter will have confidence. . . . Local Authorities should not hesitate to appoint suitable women on the Tribunals, if they think it desirable to do so. For obvious reasons it is considered undesirable that a man of military age should be a member of the Tribunal unless he has been attested or is unfit for military service. Local authorities should also be careful not to appoint on the Tribunals persons who have publicly expressed sentiments which would appear to make them unfair judges in cases which will come before Tribunals.[2]

These recommendations reflected Long's assurances to the Commons but they remained recommendations only; local authorities accepted some and ignored others. Even the statutory requirement to appoint a representative of labour was not invariably followed.

When a tribunal was appointed, its clerk sent to the Local Government Board a completed form R.37, giving details of the members of the tribunal and marking those who were also members of the local authority. These forms did not survive the general destruction of tribunal documents executed by the Ministry of Health in 1921 and 1922.[3] With the exception of those rare cases in which tribunal records have survived, the best evidence for the membership of the local tribunal is the minute book of the local

[1] SR&O, 1916, No. 53, Pt. I, I, 3, 3 February 1916.
[2] R.36, L.G.B. Circular to Local Registration Authorities.
[3] See Note on Sources, p. 259.

authority. Tribunal members were appointed at council meetings and the minutes often show not only the member's name but also his occupation, political affiliation, and—where it applied—the local interest he had been chosen to represent. This information, limited and impersonal though it is, suggests the background and experience of the men who would determine the applications for exemption.

Under the Derby Scheme the local tribunals had averaged five members, the number Long had recommended; under conscription the average rose to nine or ten, though in some urban areas the pressure of applications forced the local authority to increase the membership to the statutory maximum and even beyond. Large tribunals could split into two or more committees, the quorum for any hearing being three. Not surprisingly, council members were almost always in the majority, though few authorities went as far as the sixteen councillors of Beccles in Suffolk who appointed themselves *en bloc* as the local tribunal. The tribunal chairman, elected by the members, was usually an alderman or councillor; frequently this vital post went to the mayor. In this way, Alderman Neville Chamberlain became chairman of the Birmingham Local Tribunal, an experience that acquired significance when, as Prime Minister, he was responsible for introducing a new conscription Bill in 1939.

The membership of the local tribunals reflected the character of local government at the time.[1] Tradesmen predominated. For the butcher and baker, builder and estate agent, membership of the council was a means of protecting or furthering his own interests. There were exceptions in the rural districts where the tribunal was more likely to be dominated by farmers and landowners, and in the fashionable London boroughs where the professional men outnumbered the tradesmen. It was rare to find a local tribunal in any district without a lawyer, though this was not so much a recognition of Long's preference for men with judicial experience as a consequence of the active part played by solicitors in local affairs. By the same token, those groups that played little part in local politics, such as Anglican clergymen, schoolmasters, and retired officers, were seldom represented on the tribunals. The picture sometimes

[1] For an analysis of the membership of five local tribunals in 1916 see Appendix A.

drawn of the conscientious objector pleading his case before a battery of elderly colonels had little basis in fact. The gulf between the applicants and the tribunal members was essentially one of age. With very few exceptions, such as a man unfit for service, tribunal members were over forty-one.

Despite Long's suggestion, few women were appointed. This was not just a case of male prejudice; there was no reason to appoint women when all the applicants were men. Long's suggestion had been made in response to a proposal by Philip Snowden, who no doubt hoped that membership of the local tribunal would help the cause of women's suffrage. In the Second World War, more logically, the tribunals remained exclusively male until women became liable for national service.[1] In 1916, the absence of women was unlikely to have troubled the applicants; in the harassing of shirkers, women had exploited their sex as freely as the clergy had used their cloth, and as tribunal members, the few women who were appointed were regarded by John Graham as 'generally fiercer than the men'.[2] Paradoxically, one of the arguments put forward for excluding women was that they would be too sentimental and kind-hearted.[3]

In politics the tribunal membership tended to reflect the balance on the council. But practice varied. At Leeds, the council decided that each of the three parties should have equal representation on the tribunal.[4] On the other hand, Parliament's insistence on the appointment of a labour representative was not inspired by political considerations. It was hoped that the presence of a member of the working classes would help to dispel any suspicion that the tribunal was being used as an instrument of industrial conscription. On the whole, local authorities tried to fulfil both the letter and the spirit of this statutory requirement; it was common practice for the District Trades and Labour Council to be consulted before the appointment was made. But a working-class member was not always welcome among the middle-class councillors; at Harrow-on-the-Hill, the council refused to appoint a 'labouring man' on the grounds that he would be 'out of place', one councillor declaring that he did not accept the fashionable belief that a working man was

[1] SR&O, 1942, 22 January 1942.

[2] John W. Graham, *Conscription and Conscience: a history 1916–1919*, p. 65.

[3] See e.g. *Leeds Mercury*, 18 February 1916.

[4] Ibid.

as good as anyone else.[1] Local labour organizations were quick to protest if a bona fide labour representative was not appointed, but complaints were unlikely to be effective unless they were taken up by the Local Government Board itself. Even where a genuinely working-class representative was appointed, he was sometimes prevented from attending tribunal hearings during working hours. Claims for expenses for loss of earnings were not normally accepted by Command Paymasters,[2] and it is possible that a number of labour representatives would, like Mr. Sims, a compositor on the Camberwell Local Tribunal, have been able to attend the evening sessions only.[3]

Walter Long's faith in the competence and impartiality of magistrates was shared by the local councils, many of whose members were themselves on the Bench. On the tribunals, Justices were as numerous as Long could have wished and sometimes constituted half the membership. Their presence did not, however, inspire universal confidence. Their administration of the conscience clause in the Vaccination Act between 1898 and 1907, though defended by Long, had been bitterly criticized by others, notably by John Burns, the Liberal President of the Local Government Board in 1907. Burns had accused the magistrates of exceeding their powers, of rejecting applications without good reason, and of failing to achieve even a limited degree of uniformity in their decisions.[4] In 1916 Long may have believed that the appointment of magistrates was a guarantee that the tribunals would give 'full and fair consideration' to all cases, but Liberals who recalled John Burns's indictment would have been less sanguine.

The local tribunals in the First World War were civilian, middle-class, and public-minded. Their members represented above all the interests and attitudes of local government. Service on the tribunal was service for the country and there was no place for men who were not wholeheartedly behind the national cause. The appointment of a member who had expressed hostility to conscription would be challenged by the local military authorities, though Quakers served without opposition in 'a substantial number of

[1] See the Minutes of the Harrow-on-the-Hill Urban District Council, 14 February 1916, and *Harrow Observer*, 18 February 1916.

[2] ACI No. 431, 1916, 24 February 1916.

[3] Minutes of the Camberwell Local Tribunal, 17 February 1916.

[4] Burns's speech, 4 HC 174, col. 1275–84, 24 May 1907.

cases',[1] a comment on the military's almost reverent respect for the Society of Friends. Pacifism in the family was an embarrassment but not necessarily a disqualification; on one Yorkshire tribunal there were three members with sons who were conscientious objectors.[2] These were the exceptions. As a rule the tribunal members' patriotism was unsullied even by association. Though Walter Long had not exercised a direct influence on their selection, the members represented those groups in society—the councillors and magistrates—in whom he had confidence. These were, too, the 'responsible persons' he contemplated using for his food profiteering courts.[3] The elements of public service and judicial experience, together with the representation of labour, were also present in the higher tribunals. It would be wrong to suppose that Long aimed at a standard pattern, but these elements were the ones he thought it right to include wherever possible.

The appeal tribunals were not already in existence; under the Derby Scheme they had been discussed but never appointed.[4] It was now evident that they would be needed and the Local Government Board based their distribution on the counties in England and Wales and the sheriffdoms in Scotland.[5] Walter Long's approach to the selection of members was characteristic. He wrote to the Chairmen of County Councils and to the Mayors of County Boroughs, asking them to consult with 'such representative persons in the county' as they thought fit before submitting the names of seven to ten persons 'of judicial and unprejudiced mind and temperament' to serve on the appeal tribunal for the area. At least one member should have legal training and experience and 'a fair proportion of the members of the tribunal should be direct representatives of labour'. Long also suggested that women and representatives of chambers of commerce would be an advantage on the tribunal.[6]

Although the final appointments were confirmed by the Board, perhaps by Long himself, the actual selection of members was

[1] *The Friend*, 5 May 1916.
[2] *Leeds Mercury*, 9 March 1916.
[3] Long, *Memories*, pp. 228–9.
[4] See R.2, L.G.B. Circular to Local Registration Authorities, 19 November 1915.
[5] SHHD 25478S/3171. There were 85 appeal tribunals in all; a full list is given in the Report of the Central Tribunal, 1919, pp. 15–18.
[6] L.G.B. to Chairmen of County Councils, Lord Mayors, and Mayors, 31 January 1916. The letter is quoted in full in *The Justice of the Peace*, 5 February 1916.

made by the prominent men in the counties. If the records of the Bedfordshire Appeal Tribunal reflect a procedure that was commonly used, the chairman of the county council insisted on the inclusion of certain interests and left it to the clerk to the county council to find suitable men.[1] Certainly, the appeal tribunals were as representative of the shire hall and quarter sessions as the local tribunals were of the town hall and magistrates' bench. At both levels the tribunal members were public men, the difference being that on the appeal tribunals the members were generally of a higher calibre: King's Counsel rather than local solicitor, judge rather than Justice. This difference was the most marked in quality of chairmen. Whereas the chairman of the local tribunal had seldom had judicial experience outside the magistrates' court, the chairmen of appeal tribunals were often county court judges or chairmen of quarter sessions; in Scotland, fourteen out of fifteen appeal tribunal chairmen were King's Counsel.[2] The control exercised by lawyers of this standing was a safeguard against the irregular conduct of proceedings and in the Second World War became a statutory requirement.[3]

The Central Tribunal was first appointed in November 1915 as part of the appeal machinery of the Derby Scheme; in January 1916 it was given statutory authority with no immediate change of personnel.[4] Here at least the selection was certainly made by Walter Long and his advisers. The result was a blend of those elements—public service, legal experience, organized labour—that in Long's view were necessary to constitute the ideal tribunal. As the Tribunal's first Chairman, he appointed Lord Sydenham, a distinguished soldier and public man, who had been Secretary of the Committee of Imperial Defence and Governor of Bombay. In June 1916 Sydenham was succeeded by the Marquess of Salisbury, one of Long's former Cabinet colleagues. These two Chairmen steered the Tribunal through its most testing period when the provisions for conscientious objectors gave rise to difficult questions of interpretation and also imposed on the Tribunal the

[1] Correspondence of the Bedfordshire Appeal Tribunal, February–March 1916.

[2] SHHD 35478S/3171.

[3] Military Training Act, 1939 (2 and 3 GEO 6, Ch. 25, 26 May 1939), Second Schedule, Pt. II.

[4] For the membership of the Central Tribunal see Appendix B.

additional task of reviewing the cases of men who had been court-martialled in the army.

The members who served under Sydenham and Salisbury had to command confidence throughout the country: the law was represented by distinguished members of the bar, public service by men who had achieved prominence in government and politics (including current Members of Parliament), and organized labour by its acknowledged leaders in the unions and the Labour Party.

By the end of March 1916 the extension of the tribunal system was complete. The tribunal members would play a key role in the operation of the law, and Walter Long was no doubt satisfied that those who had been chosen were well qualified to do this. And yet, not since Lord Jeffreys's Bloody Assize have judicial bodies left to posterity a reputation so closely identified with bias and injustice. The bad reputation of the First World War tribunals is clearly shown in the Commons debate on the Military Training Bill in May 1939. M.P.s who remembered the difficulties and mistakes of 1916, were inclined to put the blame on the tribunals alone. Even a moderate critic, T. E. Harvey, told the House, 'the machinery of the old Act failed largely because of the prejudice, ignorance and inexperience of many members of the tribunals'.[1] Harvey's criticism was inspired chiefly by the handling of applications from conscientious objectors, and it was this aspect of the exemption procedure that was most frequently cited as evidence of the tribunals' ineptitude. It was argued that all would have been well if the members had been qualified to deal with matters of conscience, but this argument ignored the fact that there were four grounds for exemption not one; members had been chosen for their general qualifications not for their specialist knowledge. Even if Long had been empowered to appoint specialist tribunals, there were a limited number of alternatives to those elements he had already used. The experience of the Second World War indicated that it would have been difficult to constitute special conscientious objector tribunals without including those elements in which Long had confidence. The Military Training Act of 1939 authorized the Minister of Labour to appoint local tribunals whose sole function was to hear applications for exemption on conscientious grounds. The Minister, Ernest Brown, enjoyed many of the advantages denied to Walter Long: he was appointing a small number of

[1] 5 HC 346, col. 2182, 4 May 1939.

specialist tribunals and was in a position to concern himself personally with the choice of members. He told the Commons: 'Of all the duties I have had to undertake in the course of my ministerial life, I can honestly tell the Committee and the country that there has not been one about which I have taken more personal care.'[1] But this did not mean that Brown rejected his predecessor's preference for men with experience in the law, in public service, and in the trade unions; on the contrary these elements were always present, the only new element being a representative of the academic world in the person of a senior member of a university in the region. The essential difference lay not in the elements used but in the fact that Brown, because he was appointing a much smaller number of tribunals, was able to ensure that at local level the tribunal members were all of a high calibre. Long achieved a similar standard on his appeal tribunals, but below this he was forced to rely on thousands of local citizens who, though more fair-minded than their critics allowed, frequently lacked the training necessary to translate good intentions into practice.

The limitations of the local tribunal members in 1916 would not have mattered so much if the transition from voluntary recruiting to compulsion had not greatly increased the difficulties of operating the exemption procedure. The transition did not immediately eradicate attitudes that had been adopted during the voluntary period; on the contrary, as an extension of the Derby Scheme, the Military Service Act helped to keep them alive. One result was that the tribunals' attitude to the applications for exemption remained much the same as it had been under the Scheme. This attitude had been established by Walter Long's original instructions: 'It cannot be too much emphasized', he had written, 'that there are at this moment a very large number of men who could be spared from their present occupations;' it would be the duty of the local tribunal 'to assist the local Recruiting Authorities to secure these men for the Army'.[2] The tribunal members had thus been given two clear aims: to obtain as many recruits as possible and to cooperate with the military. When recruiting became compulsory and exemption a statutory right, these aims should have changed: the tribunals were now independent judicial bodies, not

[1] 5 HC 357, col. 1621, 22 February 1940.
[2] L.G.B. to Local Registration Authorities, 26 October 1915.

recruiting agencies, and their function was to determine claims for exemption, not to secure men for the army. Yet the original attitudes died hard. This was especially true where tribunal members had been involved in recruiting activities even before the Derby Scheme. The town council had been the centre of local patriotism and the councillors had been prominent on the recruiting committees that had been set up to co-ordinate the civilian and military recruiting efforts.[1] The same councillors were in many cases appointed to the local tribunals, with the chairman of the recruiting committee taking over the chairmanship of the tribunal as a matter of course. This happened in districts as far apart as St. Marylebone and Bristol and may well have been the rule rather than the exception.[2] It would have been surprising if these men had not found it difficult to adjust to a role that involved keeping men out of the army instead of encouraging them to enlist. The adjustment was not made easier by the aftermath of the Derby Scheme. Men who had attested in the autumn of 1915 were still coming before the tribunals in the spring of 1916, so that the tribunal members had to play two roles simultaneously; at the Camberwell and St. Marylebone Local Tribunals applications from attested men and conscripts were sometimes heard on the same day.[3]

A more formidable impediment to the impartial consideration of claims for exemption was the continuing close relationship between the tribunals and the military. The War Office Advisory Committees and Military Representatives appointed under the Derby Scheme continued to exercise an important influence on the tribunals' decisions. Long's original concept of the tribunals as bodies to facilitate recruiting probably remained uppermost in the minds of many tribunal members. No one appears to have

[1] There was no uniform system of recruiting committees. A Parliamentary Recruiting Committee established in September 1914 attempted to organize the appointment of local recruiting committees in each parliamentary division; these committees were composed largely of active members of the major political parties. But at various times in 1915 recruiting committees were appointed in local registration districts and it was these committees that usually provided the personnel for the local tribunal appointed under the Derby Scheme.

[2] See Minutes of the St. Marylebone Local Recruiting Committee, 5 February 1915, and of the Local Tribunal 18 February 1916; and George F. Stone and Charles Wells, *Bristol and the Great War, 1914–1919*, Bristol, 1920, pp. 108 and 115.

[3] Minutes of the Camberwell Local Tribunal, 24 February 1916, and Minutes of St. Marylebone Local Tribunal, 7 March 1916.

regarded it as inconsistent that the tribunals' expenses should have been met not by the Local Government Board but by the War Office.[1] Even when the responsibility for recruiting had passed to the civilian Ministry of National Service, local tribunals remained, in emotion if not in law, part of the War Office team; in October 1918 the tribunal at Camberwell sent warm congratulations to Foch and Haig on 'the magnificent results achieved in such a short period'[2] in much the same spirit as a local cricket club might send congratulations to the captain of an M.C.C. touring side.

The attitudes that the tribunal members inherited from the Derby Scheme, in particular the tendency to identify with the aims and organization of military recruiting, were bound to frustrate the wishes of Parliament at certain points. When this occurred, Walter Long was subjected to persistent questioning in the Commons. Long not only had to provide satisfactory answers, he was also responsible for guiding the tribunals towards a uniform procedure and a common interpretation of the law; thus much of the burden of the tribunals' transition to conscription fell on him personally. He remained at the Local Government Board until the fall of Asquith's Government in December 1916; by that time he had had enough of the procedure for exemption. His experience led him to advocate that in any future act 'exemptions should either not be inserted at all or, if this is impossible, they should be limited to very special cases in which conditions make it practically impossible for the man to be called up for service'.[3] It was a mark of Long's disillusionment and of his failure to understand the nature of the problem, that he should have believed in this method of avoiding a repetition of the difficulties he had had to face.

Long's task was hard and exasperating but it was probably less complex than the one that awaited Nevil Macready in February 1916. The new Adjutant-General was fifty-four. Although he had been hand-picked by Kitchener for this job, he had been in many ways an obvious choice. The position of Adjutant-General was the goal of ambitious staff officers and Macready had served the

[1] ACI No. 431, 1916. Command Paymasters were authorized to pay the general tribunal expenses on a scale tied to the number of applications decided per month; in this way the local authority could be out of pocket if the tribunal took too much time over individual cases.

[2] Minutes of the Camberwell Local Tribunal, 3 and 18 October 1918.

[3] Long, *Memories*, pp. 224–5.

classic apprenticeship as Director of Personal Services at the War Office from 1910 to 1914.[1] To the problems of conscription, Macready applied the gifts of a brilliant staff officer: intelligence, method, and an immense capacity for hard work. He knew how to choose men and how to inspire in them his own conviction that the interests of the army and of the individual soldier were best served by systematic and efficient organization at all levels. When he arrived at the War Office on 20 February, he succeeded Lord Derby as the man with overall responsibility for recruiting. To discharge this responsibility he assembled a team that included two outstanding administrators: Major Aukland Geddes and Colonel Wyndham Childs. Geddes, who was appointed Director of Recruiting, had been a Professor of Anatomy at Edinburgh and was to become Minister of National Service in Lloyd George's Government.[2] The creation of a manpower organization from the shambles bequeathed by the months of *laissez-faire* recruiting was—as Macready readily acknowledged—Geddes's achievement. Colonel Childs was Macready's friend and disciple; his appointment as Director of Personal Services, 'the discipline branch' of the War Office, was a predictable consequence of Macready's own promotion.[3]

The impact of this team on the organization of recruiting was not immediate: Geddes did not take up his duties until May 1916,[4] and Childs, though he followed his 'beloved chief' to the War Office in February, dealt only with those problems that arose after the conscripts had come under military law. For three months the attempts to build an effective recruiting machine were hesitant and confused. The task might have been less daunting if the Cabinet had authorized some form of preparatory study in 1915; as it was, the military had to a large extent to learn from their own mistakes. 'The work involved was herculean,' reported a Select Committee in the following year, 'and the War Office undoubtedly used the most strenuous efforts to perform it, but in fairness to

[1] For Macready's career see Sir Nevil Macready, *Annals of an Active Life*, 2 vols., London, 1924.

[2] Geddes's extraordinary career also included a period as President of the Board of Trade, 1919–20, and four years as Ambassador in Washington, 1920–24.

[3] For Childs's work as Director of Personal Services see Chapter 7 below. Childs was promoted Brigadier-General in 1916 and Major-General in 1917.

[4] Geddes joined Macready's staff in April and took up his duties as Director of Recruiting on 7 May.

Radio Times Hulton Picture Library

Fenner Brockway
(photograph taken in 1924)

Radio Times Hulton Picture Library

Wyndham Childs
(photograph taken in 1926)

Radio Times Hulton Picture Library

The 17th Earl of Derby

Walter Long

the military it must be said that they had undertaken a task of which they had no experience, for which they were unprepared, and for which by their very training and traditions they were totally unfitted.'[1]

Macready recognized at the outset that the War Office was not the best instrument to administer conscription, but his proposal that the job of calling up men should be given to a civilian department was rejected; Asquith's policy precluded such a fundamental change in the recruiting organization. It was August 1917 before recruiting came under the civilian control of a Ministry of National Service; until that date the War Office remained responsible for finding its own men. The machinery that Macready inherited to do this was based on the military pyramid of area, district, and command. At each area and district headquarters there was a recruiting officer. These men had not been chosen for their administrative ability; they knew how to conduct a recruiting rally but not how to operate a military register. Yet under conscription the register was the key to the call-up procedure. The Area Recruiting Officer held the alphabetical index to his section of the register; like the book catalogue of a library, the index was made up of white cards, one for each man in the area who was liable for service. For several weeks the operation of this register appears to have been little short of a farce. Men who did not wish to be called up found little difficulty in securing the removal of their white cards from the recruiting office, presumably by bribing the civilian clerks. Geddes later gave evidence that in one county (that was not London) forty thousand white cards had been removed from the register by 'deliberate vice'.[2] How many of these men the police were able to trace is not clear but the War Office was burdened with the additional task of prosecuting offenders all over the country.[3] Some of the men who avoided service were never caught; they kept on the move, away from the towns, or sought refuge in Ireland.[4] Recruiting officers were too busy to worry about these lost sheep; indeed the cards that disappeared were sometimes less of a problem than those that remained. The detail on each card was based on the information gathered during the National

[1] Report of the Select Committee on Military Service, 1917.

[2] Select Committee on Military Service, 1917, Geddes's evidence.

[3] Ibid.

[4] For some individual cases see 'Members in the Great War', *Socialist Standard*, September 1964.

Register, but this information was frequently found to be incorrect. In May 1916 Geddes estimated that the Military Register contained approximately one million errors.[1] In the face of this muddle and corruption, Macready's department strove to impose uniformity on the recruiting procedure. Recruiting officers accustomed to the free-for-all of voluntaryism now had to be kept within the law and the regulations. Macready bombarded them with Army Council Instructions and War Office Letters but it was not until the third week in August that Geddes was able to summarize all the essential instructions for recruiting officers in a single volume.[2] A measure of uniformity followed, but a year later the recruiting machinery was, in Geddes's view, still in the process of being built.

During this period of transition the military authorities were bound to make mistakes and the chances of this happening were greatly increased by the role that they were required to play in the recruiting procedure. The Military Service Bill did not, as some politicians had forecast, automatically provide the army with sufficient men; in terms of the numbers involved, the most important aspect of conscription was not that it made service compulsory but that it made exemption legal. During the first year of conscription, the number of exemptions granted was more than double the number of conscripts enlisted.[3] The military authorities, who might have expected that the new law would relieve them of any anxiety about the monthly recruiting figures, discovered that on the contrary they now had to compete for their share of the available manpower not only against the demands of the civilian departments but also against legitimate personal claims for exemption. In these circumstances it was unrealistic to expect the military to take an objective view of applications to the tribunals. War Office representatives at every level believed, almost to the point of obsession, that if they did not take a tough line on claims for exemption, the army would be cheated of the recruits it needed. This belief was strengthened, illogically, by the knowledge that thousands of shirkers were finding it easy to evade service by 'deliberate vice'. Military representatives almost invariably opposed applications for exemption on those grounds that, in

[1] Select Committee on Military Service, 1917, Geddes's evidence.

[2] *Registration and Recruiting*, War Office, 21 August 1916.

[3] See above p. 4, note 3.

their view, were most likely to be abused—ill-health and conscientious objection. Such automatic opposition was not in the spirit of the Act, nor was it in the army's best interests: it provoked criticism and created unfamiliar and exasperating problems for the units to which these recruits were sent. Yet the attitude of the military authorities was not, as their enemies claimed, a manifestation of Prussianism in Britain: it was a consequence of the competitive role they were required to play. If the recruiting procedure had been in civilian hands, the military would have had to be content with the men allotted to them; by making the War Office responsible for obtaining its own recruits, the Cabinet encouraged the sort of aggressive, even unscrupulous, tactics that the military used. Wherever the blame lay, the tactics were bound to be a decisive factor in the treatment of conscientious objectors before the tribunals and under military law.

The change to conscription resulted in one further impediment to the rational treatment of conscientious objectors. The Military Service Act did not place the responsibility for conscription on a single department of state. The War Office organized the call-up and the Local Government Board supervised the exemption procedure; by the summer of 1916 the Home Office and the Board of Trade had been drawn in by the need to find employment for conscientious objectors. This splintered responsibility led to interdepartmental friction which in turn made administrative improvements in the treatment of conscientious objectors difficult to achieve. Even when the Ministry of National Service was given control over civilian and military manpower in 1917, it did not have the authority to extricate those conscientious objectors who had been trapped by the muddle of the previous year. The fate of these men still rested with the individual departments, so that changes in policy were frequently referred to the Cabinet itself: a question of additional privileges for conscientious objectors in prison had to be decided by a Cabinet Committee, individual cases became the subject of Cabinet Papers, and the release of conscientious objectors whose health was deteriorating was only secured by the active intervention of members of Lloyd George's War Cabinet.[1] In this way, the treatment of conscientious objectors, a peripheral problem, occupied the time and attention of men already overburdened with the conduct of the war.

[1] See Chapter 10 below.

CHAPTER FIVE

THE CONSCIENTIOUS OBJECTORS

In the First World War, people spoke of conscientious objectors—or more commonly of 'conchies'—as though there existed a clearly defined group of men to whom the term could be applied. In practice the term's usage embraced some men whose claim to be considered conscientious objectors was tenuous, while excluding others whose decision to refuse combatant service was evidently inspired by conscience. The exemption procedure produced numerous anomalies. It was not uncommon for a man to seek exemption on three or four grounds simultaneously. The Lothian and Peebles Tribunal heard an appeal from a man who claimed exemption on the grounds that he was the sole support of his widowed mother, that he suffered from acidity of the stomach, that the rabbits he destroyed would spoil a considerable acreage of crop if he was enlisted, and that he had a conscientious objection to military service.[1] The tribunal indicated that it accepted his plea of conscience by granting him exemption from combatant duties only. Legally—and statistically—this man would have been classified as a conscientious objector, though the nature of his application at least leaves room for doubt.

Some doubt must also exist with regard to a group of men who were classified as conscientious objectors in 1918. By this date a well-known procedure existed for transferring to civil prison men who claimed to be conscientious objectors at their court martial; in most cases the men were allowed to do work of national importance out of prison on the Home Office Scheme. Such a procedure was an understandable temptation to the men who were called up during the final phases of the war. The temptation was particularly acute after February 1918 when the Cabinet authorized the 'clean cut' whereby men in all occupations below a certain age

[1] Lothian and Peebles Appeal Tribunal, Box 'March/April, 1916', No. 28.

were made available for the forces. Coal-miners, metal-workers, and farm labourers who had been protected for so long in their essential industries faced the prospect of immediate enlistment. As the 'clean cut' became effective the monthly average of men committed to prison and alleging conscientious objection rose sharply, and the Central Tribunal noted that nearly all these men had previously been protected in essential industries.[1] At the same time there was a sharp increase in the number of men who claimed to be conscientious objectors at their court martial but who had never been before a tribunal. In 1916 only 4 per cent of court-martialled conscientious objectors had not been before a tribunal; in 1918 the figure rose to 30 per cent and to 50 per cent for men from the coalfields of South Wales and Lanarkshire.[2] Men who had no intention of serving at the front discovered that the most direct route to civilian employment under the Home Office was via a court martial rather than a local tribunal. All these men were classified as conscientious objectors though there would appear to have been justification in the Central Tribunal's claim that some 'did not scruple to allege such objections as a last resort to avoid combatant service'.[3]

The absence of a tribunal hearing could have the opposite effect, of denying the status of conscientious objector to men whose conscience did not allow them to undertake combatant service. This denial could occur in different ways. A man who joined a non-combatant organization, such as the Red Cross or the Friends Ambulance Unit, before 1916, was not necessarily required to subject his views to a tribunal when conscription was introduced. In the autumn of 1915, the F.A.U. in France and Belgium was 'for the most part composed of those who were prepared to make a definite stand on the question of military service',[4] but in the following year only a few members chose to return to England to obtain individual exemption from a tribunal; the remainder were exempt by a special agreement between the Unit's Committee and the Army Council,[5] and were not included in the official statistics as conscientious objectors.

[1] Report of the Central Tribunal, pp. 26–7. [2] Ibid. [3] Ibid.

[4] M. Tatham and J. E. Miles, *The Friends Ambulance Unit 1914–19*, London, 1919, pp. 186–7.

[5] 'The certificate which we obtained for you', members of the Unit were told, 'is the best that is obtainable under the Act.' See a letter to members of the F.A.U., 17 May 1916, Arnold Rowntree 'C.O. Papers 1916–1919', Box I.

There were also individuals whose conscientious objection was tacitly acknowledged by the authorities but never confirmed by a tribunal hearing. The novelist E. M. Forster, in his own words, 'developed a conscientious objection' while serving with the Red Cross in Alexandria; though arrangements were made for him to return to England to face a tribunal, he was never sent and continued to serve in the Middle East until 1919.[1] Forster was prepared to go before a tribunal and should probably be classified as a conscientious objector. Siegfried Sassoon's position was less unequivocal. Having made a public protest against 'the political errors and insincerities' for which soldiers were being sacrificed, Sassoon allowed himself to be declared a victim of shell-shock and placed out of harm's way in a military hospital.[2] Other officers who came to reject the war resigned their commissions and were either court-martialled and discharged (as was the case with Max Plowman[3]) or sent before a tribunal.[4] To complicate matters still further there was a traffic in the other direction of men who had been classified as conscientious objectors and who subsequently renounced their objection and accepted combatant service.[5]

It is all these variations on the theme of conscientious objection that make it difficult to provide a satisfactory definition of the class of men who should be regarded as the conscientious objectors of the First World War. Though imperfect, the most useful definition is the one that came to be accepted by the governments of the day: conscientious objectors were men whose bona fides was established by a tribunal, or who, having failed to satisfy or appear before a tribunal, still refused combatant service on conscientious grounds. Despite the destruction of many of the records of the First World War tribunals[6] the number of men coming within this definition of conscientious objection can be calculated from other sources. Chief among these is the unpublished Supplementary Report of the Central Tribunal which gave the figures for conscientious objectors affected by the disfranchisement clause in the Repre-

[1] E. M. Forster to the author, 13 February 1963.

[2] See Siegfried Sassoon, *Memoirs of an Infantry Officer*, London, 1930, pp. 289–334. Sassoon believed that the alternative was to be shut up in an asylum for the rest of the war.

[3] Plowman's court-martial statement is quoted in Max Plowman, *Bridge into the Future*, Letters edited by D.L.P., London, 1944, p. 772.

[4] E.g. Lt. H. S. Buss, whose case is reported in *The Friend*, 10 May 1918.

[5] Report of the Central Tribunal, p. 22.

[6] See Note on Sources, p. 259.

sentation of the People Act of 1918.[1] The report gave two separate totals: the number of conscientious objectors exempted from all military service, and the number of men court-martialled in the army who claimed that the offence was the result of a conscientious objection to military service. The first total was given as a best estimate based on tribunal returns to the Local Government Board from all but 'a small number of tribunals'. It was estimated that 5,111 exemptions from all military service on the grounds of conscientious objection had been granted up to September 1918 and were still in force on that date. To these should be added the 1,400 Christadelphians whose certificates of exemption from all military service were issued by the Army Council.[2] The second total was known from the Central Tribunal's own records to be 5,944.[3] The only conscientious objectors outside these two totals were those who were given and who accepted exemption from combatant duties only. The maximum strength of the Non-Combatant Corps was 3,319.[4] About 400 should be subtracted for the officers and NCOs who were not conscientious objectors,[5] leaving a total of 2,919. A further 1,000 to 1,500 men were exempt from combatant duties only but did not serve in the Corps or suffer court martial.[6] Though minor adjustments would be necessary to subtract the men who joined the Non-Combatant Corps after court martial and to add the direct enlistments into the RAMC, the total number of conscientious objectors would remain approximately 16,500. As a proportion of the total number of men recruited voluntarily and compulsorily during the war,[7] 16,500 conscientious objectors represented 0·33 per cent.

Numerically insignificant, the conscientious objectors nevertheless commanded attention. There can have been few months between January 1916 and August 1919 when the problem of the conscientious objector did not present itself to Parliament, to the government departments, or to the Cabinet. Though the principal

[1] Supplementary Report of the Central Tribunal, 1922, MH 47/3.

[2] Report of the Pelham Committee, 1919, p. 5; and see p. 115 below. The Minutes of the Central Tribunal, 14 May 1918, indicate that these Christadelphians were not included in the total of 5,111.

[3] Supplementary Report of the Central Tribunal.

[4] *Military Statistics, 1914–1920*, p. 226.

[5] Under ACI No. 551, 1916, the establishment of a Non-Combatant Corps Company was one officer and thirteen NCOs to ninety-four privates.

[6] See below, p. 131.

[7] 4,970,902. See Cmd. 1193, 1921, p. 9.

reason for this was the initial failure to make comprehensive provisions for dealing with conscience, a contributory reason was the widespread ignorance of the sources from which conscientious objectors would be drawn. The task of describing and classifying these sources has long been neglected; neither Graham nor Boulton made any serious attempt at it, perhaps because they represented the Quaker and socialist viewpoints respectively and were disinclined to recognize the importance of other sources of conscientious objection. In recent years the ideology of pacifism and the sociology of two of the non-combatant sects have been the subject of detailed research.[1] There remains the need to classify all the sources of conscientious objection in the First World War in the light of the legal and administrative measures that were made for them.

The tribunals were the key to the successful execution of the Government's policy for conscience. Tribunal members could divide the sources of conscientious objection into two broad groups. The first contained those religious bodies in whose teaching refusal of military service was explicit or implicit, and which were therefore predictable sources of conscientious objection in any human situation. When an applicant was a member of one of these bodies there was prima facie evidence for believing him to be a conscientious objector. The second group of sources, though they may have inspired convictions of equal sincerity, provided no prima facie evidence of conscientious objection. These sources were the broad areas of religious, moral, and political belief, from which were drawn large or small numbers of conscientious objectors (or no conscientious objectors at all) according to the nature of the war or the character of the government. In this sense they were *unpredictable* sources of conscientious objection.

The best known of the predictable sources was the Society of Friends. The Quaker attitude to war was well established if not always perfectly understood. When conscription was introduced, it was widely recognized that provision would have to be made for Quakers who were not prepared to undertake active service. Before the tribunals, the Quaker seldom failed to win acceptance (though not always the form of exemption he wanted), and among those

[1] D. A. Martin, *Pacifism: an historical and sociological study*, London, 1965, and B. R. Wilson, *Sects and Society: a sociological study of three religious groups in Britain*, London, 1961.

absolutists who refused any compromise with the law, the Quaker Stephen Hobhouse came to be regarded by the members of Lloyd George's administration as the embodiment of sincere convictions.

The popular view that a member of the Society of Friends was *ipso facto* a genuine conscientious objector, was based on a misunderstanding of the Quaker position: because the Society had traditionally witnessed against war, it was assumed that one of the Society's fundamental tenets was conscientious objection to military service. But the Quaker objector was inspired by his belief in the authority of the Inner Light, not by his adherence to a pacifist tenet. The Inner Light illuminated the human conscience but was not synonymous with it; conscience was subject to the distorting influence of instinct or casuistry, whereas the Inner Light was a source of Divine inspiration. Traditionally this inspiration had led Quakers to reject 'all outward wars and strife and fighting with outward weapons',[1] but such rejection was entirely a matter for the individual. It was not the case that all, or even the majority, of Quakers of military age became conscientious objectors; the Society's own statistics show that only 45·4 per cent of members of military age became conscientious objectors, while 33·6 per cent enlisted in the armed forces.[2] There is a certain irony in the contrast between the universal respect for Quaker pacifism and the proportion of young Quakers who were prepared to fight, but the figures do not necessarily reflect the fickle or superficial nature of Quaker loyalties. The Society of Friends was not a religious sect rejecting contemporary life and imposing a party line on its members; its pacifism was traditional rather than doctrinal. Many of the young Quakers who joined the armed forces would have been birthright members—that is to say, those who had been born into Quakerism—whose tenuous adherence to the pacifist tradition was snapped by the surge of patriotic feeling at the outbreak of war.

Deviation on this scale did not occur in the religious sects that emphasized group rather than individual conscience. The degree of regimentation varied. The British Union Conference of the Seventh Day Adventists advised members of military age on the

[1] From the Society's Declaration presented to Charles II in 1660 and quoted in *Peace Among the Nations, being the Testimony of the Society of Friends on War*, London, September 1915.

[2] *Extracts from the Minutes and Proceedings of the London Yearly Meeting of Friends*, London, 1923, pp. 231–2.

correct action, but for members of the Jehovah's Witnesses (also known in the First World War as the International Bible Students Association) the element of individual choice was practically eliminated. As sources of conscientious objection, the most important of these sects were the Christadelphians, the Plymouth Brethren, and the Jehovah's Witnesses. Though there were differences of detail between these sects, their beliefs all centred upon an expectation of the early return of Jesus Christ to the world. Their eschatological beliefs differed radically from the conventional eschatology of the majority of Christians. The Kingdom of God was not a heavenly after-life but a Kingdom to be established upon earth after the forces of evil had been defeated at Armageddon. As citizens of this future Kingdom the members of the sects could not owe allegiance to any earthly ruler, nor could they become involved in the affairs of the world through which they were passing. Their rejection of military service in the armies of this world was, like their disinclination to exercise the franchise, a logical consequence of their apocalyptic beliefs.

The Christadelphian objection was expressed in their petition to Parliament in February 1915. It emphasized both that they were looking for the 'early advent of Christ to set up a Divine Government over all the earth' and that they were 'conscientiously opposed to bearing arms, on the ground that the Bible, which they believe to be the word of God, commands them not to kill'.[1] Their literal biblicism did not however make them pacifist; they were not opposed to war as such, only to fighting in the armies of this world. Their position was essentially passive, not pacifist; they did not wish to become involved.

The position of the Plymouth Brethren was more complex. In 1849 the sect had split into two main groups, the Open and the Exclusive Brethren, and had suffered further schisms before the First World War. In all cases the Brethren's objection to military service would appear to have been based on three essential elements: their apocalyptic expectations, their conviction that to take human life was contrary to the commands of Christ, and their consciousness of the fact that in killing another human being they would be responsible either for taking the life of a Christian Brother or for thrusting an unsaved sinner into eternal damnation.

Between the different groups the precise nature of the objection

[1] Jannaway, op. cit., pp. 32–5.

varied. The Open Brethren were the least explicitly non-combatant and some of their members joined the armed forces. The Churches of God, the strictest branch of the Open Brethren, emphasized, in their memorial to the Government in 1915, the incompatibility of fighting with the teaching of Christ.[1] The Exclusive Brethren particularly emphasized their unwillingness to be 'unequally yoked with unbelievers' in the army.

The Jehovah's Witnesses' objection to military service differed in one important respect from that of the Christadelphians and the Brethren. Whereas the non-pacifist nature of the latter's objection was not emphasized and indeed was partly obscured by its association with biblical sanctions against killing, the objection of the Jehovah's Witnesses was aggressively non-pacifist. In relation to the wars of this world they were neither pacifists nor patriots. Such an objection might have been expected to raise acute difficulties before the tribunals, but these difficulties were experienced in the Second World War rather than the First: in 1916, the sect was not well known and had not yet aroused the almost universal hostility that was to be directed against it twenty-five years later.

Of the other predictable sources, only the Seventh Day Adventists and the Pentecostal Churches produced a significant number of conscientious objectors. Both these groups expressed their unswerving loyalty to the Government and were anxious that their refusal of combatant service should not be misinterpreted. In this they differed radically from those conscientious objectors who emphatically rejected loyalty of this nature for political or eschatological reasons.

The Seventh Day Adventists based their objection to combatant service on a literal reading of the Commandments. In 1916 the Adventists reminded Asquith's Government of the sect's historic position:

> As a Christian Church, believing in the undiminished authority and perpetuity of the moral law, given by God himself in the Ten Commandments, we hold that we are thereby forbidden to take part in combatant service in time of war.[2]

[1] *Report of the Conference of Representative Overseers of the Churches of God in the British Isles and Overseas*, 1935, p. 24.

[2] Quoted in F. McL. Wilcox, *Seventh Day Adventists in Time of War*, Washington, D.C., 1936, p. 256.

This was a fundamental tenet, and although the decision to become a conscientious objector was left to the individual, very few members joined the armed forces.[1]

In the various Pentecostal Churches rejection of combatant service was a logical consequence of membership, but once again the decision to do so was left to the individual. The modern Pentecostal movement[2] developed in the early years of the twentieth century, initially drawing its members from other Churches, particularly from the Baptist and Methodist, and later establishing Churches of its own. Its character was evangelical and fundamentalist, with special emphasis on the Pentecostal gift of speaking with tongues. In the Assemblies of God and the Apostolic Church refusal of military service was encouraged; in other Pentecostal bodies, literal biblicism and sectarian withdrawal from the conflicts of society provided a general, but not universally accepted, basis for conscientious objection.

Among the predictable sources of conscientious objection only the Society of Friends possessed a tradition that would have been familiar to most tribunal members. The other non-combatant groups were not necessarily unknown: when a sect was strong in a particular area, such as the Christadelphians in Birmingham, its organization and beliefs could not have remained totally obscure; and other sects, such as the Seventh Day Adventists and Plymouth Brethren, though not strong in one locality, would have been known to some tribunal members. But the predictable sources of conscientious objection did not end here: there were a number of smaller religious groups in whose teaching refusal of military service was implicit, but whose very existence was a surprise to the authorities.[3] To the members of the local tribunal, a Muggletonian and a Dependent Cokler were equally mysterious. That the applicants from these sects did not cause greater difficulty was principally because their conscientious objection was based on characteristics—literal biblicism, sectarian withdrawal, apocalyptic expectations—that were shared with the larger and better-known

[1] Wilcox, op. cit., pp. 258–9.

[2] For its development see Wilson, op. cit., pp. 30–36.

[3] Cf. the U.S.A., where the conscientious objectors included 'an astonishing number of different sects and denominations, many unfamiliar to the average layman': W. G. Kellogg, *The Conscientious Objector*, New York, 1919, p. 33.

non-combatant groups. Thus the applicants from the Church of Christ,[1] Dowie's Church,[2] Dependent Coklers,[3] and the Peculiar People,[4] expressed an objection primarily in terms of a literal reading of selected biblical texts. Muggletonians[5] and Christian Israelites,[6] though literal biblicists, were more likely to base their objections on their expectations of an early advent of Jesus Christ. A desire to be 'separate from the multitude' and to reject secular and political life inspired the Sandemanian objectors.[7]

There are no comprehensive statistics of the number of conscientious objectors coming from each of the predictable sources. Such figures as are available indicate that the most prolific sources were the three large apocalyptic sects—the Christadelphians, the Plymouth Brethren, and the Jehovah's Witnesses—in whose objection to military service pacifism did not play a significant part. There were not less than 1,716 Christadelphian objectors, probably the largest group from any source,[8] whereas only 750 Quakers became conscientious objectors.

Incomplete though these statistics are, they help to correct those accounts that concern themselves almost exclusively with the experiences of Quakers and socialists. The fact that these two groups provided the dynamic for the opposition to conscription, has encouraged the view that other conscientious objectors, particularly those who were remote from worldly affairs and uninterested in the establishment of an earthly utopia, were un-

[1] Also known as Campbellites and Disciples of Christ; a movement founded in the U.S.A. in 1811 and initially associated with the Baptist Churches. See James Hastings (ed.), *Encyclopaedia of Religion and Ethics*, IV, Edinburgh, 1911, p. 713 and XI, 1920, pp. 328–9.

[2] The followers of John Alexander Dowie, a Congregational minister and faith-healer who founded churches in Australia and Chicago in the 1890s. See W. W. Sweet, *The Story of Religion in America*, New York, 1950, p. 378.

[3] A small Sussex sect founded about 1850 with strong literal biblicist faith.

[4] An evangelical Christian community founded in 1838, originally called the Plumstead Peculiars, now associated with the Union of Evangelical Churches.

[5] A seventeenth-century sect, the followers of John Reeve and Lodowicke Muggleton, who claimed to be the two witnesses of Revelation xi. See Hastings, op. cit., VIII, 1915, p. 871.

[6] Members believed themselves to be descendants of the lost tribes of Israel. The Pelham Committee listed one conscientious objector from the Christian Israelite schism, the New and Latter House of Israel.

[7] A sect founded about 1730; also known as Glasites. See Hastings, op. cit., VI, 1913, p. 230.

[8] See Appendix C.

important.[1] During the war itself, the activist objectors not infrequently dismissed the sectarians as 'cranks' and were inclined to disown the Christadelphians altogether because the members of this sect were prepared to work on munitions. Yet, unpalatable though it may have been to the young idealists of the I.L.P. and the Society of Friends, a large number of those who refused combatant service on the grounds of conscience were motivated by neither pacifist nor political principles.

Somewhere between the predictable and unpredictable sources of conscientious objection was the cult of spiritualism. One spiritualist pleaded his case before Neville Chamberlain at Birmingham. He was accompanied by an older spiritualist who told the tribunal members: 'We spiritualists get our training with the spirit world through mediums. We could not take life under any circumstances. We could not go into the spirit world with such a thing on our consciences.'[2] It is not clear how far this statement was representative of spiritualists as a whole, but the Birmingham Tribunal accepted it as a ground for conscientious objection and granted exemption to the man concerned.

In religious terms the unpredictable source of conscientious objection was a Christian pacifism that was unsupported by a specific teaching of the applicant's Church. With the exception of the Roman Catholics, these Christian pacifists expressed their objection as a subjective interpretation of the Christian ethic: war was contrary to the spirit of Christ, service in the armed forces irreconcilable with His teaching. Within their several Churches these conscientious objectors were a dissenting minority. They applied to the tribunals as individual Christians but they found that their Church leaders' attitude to the war was an important factor in the tribunal's decision. In this the Anglican pacifists were particularly vulnerable. In the past the Anglican communion had not accepted a pacifist interpretation of scripture and showed no inclination to do so in 1914. Though the picture of a belligerently patriotic clergy has been exaggerated[3] the public was left in no doubt that the Established Church was in favour of the

[1] See, e.g., G. S. Spinks, *Religion in Britain since 1900*, London, 1952, which discusses conscientious objectors in the First World War without mentioning the eschatological sects.

[2] *Birmingham Gazette*, 29 March 1916.

[3] For an attempt to redress the balance see Roger Lloyd, *The Church of England in the Twentieth Century*, London, 1946, pp. 233–9.

war. The attitude of a few influential churchmen was unashamedly jingoistic. The Bishop of London, A. F. Winnington-Ingram, promoted the allied cause as the struggle of 'the Nailed Hand against the Mailed Fist';[1] he was much in demand as a preacher to the troops and, as an enthusiast for recruiting, he advocated the restriction of ordination to men unfit for military service.[2] More moderate views—such as those of three other prelates, Randall Davidson of Canterbury, Charles Gore of Oxford, and E. L. Hicks of Lincoln—commanded less attention, and it is hardly surprising that the tribunal members tended to regard the Bishop of London as the authentic voice of Anglicanism. In this context, the Anglican pacifist seldom found it easy to establish the merits of his case.

The applicant from one of the Free Churches[3] was less open to the charge of being out of step with his leaders. Though the main body of members in each Church supported the war, nonconformity had never been committed to a definite position on military service. The Churches were thus able to adopt an attitude that to many Anglicans would have seemed inconsistent. The Congregational Union accepted the war as the only course 'consonant with national righteousness' but declared its respect for those members who sincerely embraced pacifism.[4] The strongest pacifist minorities were Methodist; a Wesleyan Methodist Peace Fellowship, founded in October 1916, had a membership of ninety ministers and a thousand laymen by the end of the war.[5] Both the Anglican and Free Churches produced men whose objections had political overtones. An Anglican theological student provided the test case of whether an essentially political objection could be regarded as conscientious within the meaning of the Act;[6] and it was the Methodist, S. E. Keeble, whose Christian Socialism

[1] See *The Times*, 8 October 1915; see also the Bishop's contribution to *The Times Recruiting Supplement*, 3 November 1915.

[2] *The Times*, 3 May 1916.

[3] This designation includes associated groups that produced conscientious objectors, such as the Beeston Brotherhood, a Wesleyan Methodist organization that flourished in Beeston, Notts.

[4] R. Tudur Jones, *Congregationalism in England, 1662–1962*, London, 1962, p. 356.

[5] M. Edwards, *Methodism and England: a study of Methodism in its social and political aspects during the period 1850–1932*, London, 1943, pp. 197–9.

[6] Minutes of the Central Tribunal, 2 May 1916.

inspired rejection of the war as 'the greatest enemy of social reform'.[1]

The Roman Catholics who came before the tribunals were Christian pacifists in a restricted sense. The traditional teaching of Roman Catholic moral theology was that the Just War must fulfil certain conditions.[2] In theory this doctrine admitted the possibility of a conscientious objection to a particular war: in practice the hierarchy had never made up its mind, and it was not open to a layman to decide that a war was unjust. This did not prevent a handful of British Catholics in the First World War from refusing military service on the theologically tenuous ground that Pope Benedict was appealing for peace. Their association, known as the Guild of the Pope's Peace, was small in numbers but run with style by its secretary, Francis Meynell.[3] Surprisingly, the Catholic objectors do not appear to have invoked the sixteenth-century theologian Francisco de Vitoria, who had added to the Thomist conditions for a Just War a further condition that the methods by which the war was fought must in themselves be just.[4] This omission may, however, only reflect the absence of any accurate information about the true nature of the fighting in France.

There were a number of applicants to the tribunals who should probably be classified as religious objectors if only because they were listed as members of specific Churches or Christian organizations. The character of their objection to military service remains obscure. They belonged to such diverse bodies as the Salvation Army, the Russian Orthodox Church, and a total-abstinence organization known as the Independent Order of Rechabites.[5]

[1] Edwards, op. cit., pp. 196–7.

[2] St. Thomas Aquinas established three conditions: (a) that the war had to be fought with the authority of the sovereign (*auctoritas principis*); (b) that there was a just cause (*justa causa*); and (c) that there was a rightful intention whereby military action would tend to produce beneficial results (*recta intentio*). See F. L. Cross (ed.), *The Oxford Dictionary of the Christian Church*, London, 1957, p. 1438.

[3] The Guild does not appear to have kept formal records but it had a committee (which included two priests) and published leaflets. This information comes from a former member, Mr. Charles France of Welwyn Garden City.

[4] See Cross, loc. cit.

[5] Others included the Church Army, Jewish Christian Church, Lutheran Church, Greek Orthodox Church, the Universalists, Ethical Church, Swedenborg Society, Theosophists (including Liberal Catholics), and the Church of Jesus Christ of Latter Day Saints. In the case of the last three groups, it is possible that conscientious objection was inconsistent with membership though the groups do not appear to have made a statement on military service.

"PERCY'S" PROGRESS IN THE ARMY.

"Percy," the Conscientious Objector, who refuses to wear khaki, is making progress. He has had his hair cut—unwillingly, even forcibly, it is true—and has put his feet into Army boots. They may make a soldier of him yet!
— (Photograph exclusive to the *Daily Sketch*.)

From the front page of the *Daily Sketch*, 15 April 1916

Radio Times Hulton Picture Library

Lord Curzon and Lord Milner

Elliott & Fry

Stephen Hobhouse

A few conscientious objectors described themselves as members of a religious or quasi-religious body that denied that refusal of service followed from its teaching. Not much was known about the bodies concerned and it is possible that the inconsistency was not always recognized by the tribunal members. Thus while the Central Tribunal ruled that in Christian Science there was 'no evidence of conscientious objection within the meaning of the Military Service Acts',[1] at least five Christian Scientists were granted exemption by lower tribunals.[2] On balance, the tribunal members' ignorance of fringe religion probably resulted in the acceptance of spurious claims rather than in the rejection of genuine ones.

Finally, there were a few applicants who were described as members of religious groups that have not been identified. The names used by these groups suggest that they may have been branches of sects and Churches that have already been discussed.[3]

The tribunals did not hear many applications from men who had no religious or political affiliation. The free-lance pacifist, so common in 1940, was comparatively rare in 1916. 199 men working under the Pelham Committee are described simply as 'moral' objectors.[4] In the majority of cases, their objection to war would not have differed radically from that of the Christian pacifists working alongside them. But a more individual moral objection was put forward by those intellectual opponents of the war who belonged to the close group of friends known collectively (and by their critics, derisively) as 'Bloomsbury'. Not all the members of the Bloomsbury Group who were of military age became conscientious objectors although the philosophic and aesthetic views to which they subscribed provided a possible basis for refusing service. 'All Bloomsbury believed in reason, and this belief was leavened or balanced by sensitiveness and a love of beauty.'[5] 'Reason' and 'beauty' recoiled from a conflict that appeared ugly

[1] Minutes of the Central Tribunal, 20 July 1916.

[2] See Appendix C; for the Christian Science position on military service see Wilson, op. cit., p. 178.

[3] Bible Students (probably Jehovah's Witnesses), Church of Faith, Faithist, Church Invisible, Radiant Livers, Nazarites (not Nazarenes), Testimony of Jesus, Brotherhood Church, Fellowship of Christ, Company of Believers.

[4] See Appendix C.

[5] J. K. Johnstone, *The Bloomsbury Group*, New York, 1963, p. 17.

and irrational, but this did not prevent Maynard Keynes from helping the government or E. M. Forster from joining the Red Cross. Those who did become conscientious objectors included Clive Bell, Duncan Grant, David Garnett, and James Strachey. James's brother, Lytton, applied for exemption on conscientious grounds but was excused on the grounds of ill-health. The moral or intellectual objection of these men owed something to their membership of Bloomsbury, though not—according to the survivors—to the specific teaching of G. E. Moore.[1] David Garnett adopted a somewhat different objection to that of his friends in that he insisted that it was always wrong to delegate one's private judgement by agreeing to obey orders without question.[2]

In 1916, a Central Tribunal ruling differentiated between a religious or moral objection to war in all circumstances and a political objection to participating in a particular conflict.[3] In practice, it was rare to find an objection that came within this definition of 'political'. There were numerous applicants whose objection had been inspired by socialist views. At the end of the war, the N.C.F. published an analysis of the 1,191 'socialist' objectors for whom it had particulars.[4] As there would have been few socialist objectors who had not joined the N.C.F. and as the N.C.F. was extremely efficient in tracing and checking the particulars of its members, it is safe to assume that this figure represents somewhere near the total number of socialists who became conscientious objectors during the war.

It was characteristic of the majority of these men however that their socialist views were inseparable from a belief in the brotherhood of man and a rejection of war as a means of settling international disputes. The tribunal statements of the so-called 'political' objectors reflect this fusion of the political and the moral: socialist opposition to militarism, to restrictions on personal freedom, to undemocratic diplomacy, and to the capitalist interests invested in the war, was expressed within the context of a moral

[1] Moore's influence has been 'blamed' by *inter alios* R. F. Harrod, *The Life of John Maynard Keynes*, London, 1951, pp. 211–19. Moore's influence on conscientious objectors from Bloomsbury was denied in letters to the author by Leonard Woolf, David Garnett, James Strachey, and Duncan Grant.

[2] David Garnett to the author, 6 March 1965.

[3] Minutes of the Central Tribunal, 25 July 1916.

[4] *The No Conscription Fellowship: a Souvenir of its work during the years 1914–1919* (*N.C.F. Souvenir*), London, 1919, pp. 37–8.

concern for the sanctity of human life.[1] The political objectors included, therefore, both men who made no bones about their willingness to fight for a cause of which they approved and men who regarded fighting as immoral in all circumstances. So long as this is understood, the designation 'political objection' is a convenient shorthand for those applications in which there was a clear element of politics.

The most fertile source of political objection in the First World War was the Independent Labour Party. The majority of I.L.P. members opposed the war[2] and this opposition crystallized on the issue of compulsory military service; in the jargon of the Party, conscription was 'the thin end of the wedge of Czarism'.[3] Party members organized the N.C.F. and campaigned against the introduction of compulsory service. When, in November 1915, the Derby Recruiting Scheme was drawing to its close and conscription appeared imminent, the Party's National Administrative Council adopted a resolution that provided the rationale for political resistance to a compulsory service Act:

> This meeting of the National Administrative Council of the I.L.P. reaffirms its unabated opposition to any form of compulsory military service, and expresses its conviction that, as it is practically impossible for a conscript system to become effective in this war, the motive behind the movement to impose such compulsory service can only be for the purpose of obtaining a powerful reactionary weapon which would continually menace the future industrial and political developments of democratic institutions. It would also enable the governing class to pursue a foreign policy which would inevitably lead to further wars. The N.A.C. further declares that such compulsory service would gravely imperil the foundations of British civil and political liberty, which constitutes the main difference between the British and continental nations. The N.A.C., therefore, calls upon members of the Party to resist to the utmost every attempt to impose Conscription. If, in spite of our efforts, the system is imposed, the members of the N.A.C.

[1] See the statements quoted in *What are Conscientious Objectors?*, Dulwich N.C.F., July 1917.

[2] The seven M.P.s who sat under I.L.P. auspices divided five to two against the war. The five were Hardie (until his death in 1915), Ramsay MacDonald, Snowden, Jowett, and Richardson. The two who supported the war, Parker and Clynes, owed their election to trade union support and followed the unions' pro-war line. See G. D. H. Cole, *A History of the Labour Party from 1914*, London, 1948, pp. 20–21. In 1914, the I.L.P. membership was about 30,000.

[3] Minutes of the City of London Branch of I.L.P., 9 March 1916.

pledge themselves to resist its operations, and, while recognizing the right of every individual member to act as his or her conscience dictates, the N.A.C. will do all in their power to defend those members who individually refuse to submit to such compulsion.[1]

Political objection was by no means restricted to members of the I.L.P., but the latter were the best organized and most active group. Among other socialist and radical organizations that produced conscientious objectors the British Socialist Party was the most prominent, though here there had been a bitter conflict between the opponents and supporters of the war.[2]

Conscription crystallized left-wing opposition to the war; it also presented socialists with a dilemma. Socialist theory was not easily reconciled with resistance to a law that embodied both the will of the majority and the principle of state control. One young I.L.P. member, Arthur Creech Jones,[3] explained this dilemma to Dr. Salter, a veteran pacifist whose advice he was seeking:

There are several aspects of non-resistance [to the Germans] which I find a little difficult to reconcile with my Socialist principles, or rather it occurs to me that the application of the non-resistance ideal in the present state of society involves the sacrifice of much which is essential to the social development of a state and also of Socialism. I mean that by maintaining the highest law of all—the sanctity of human life—there is a danger to encourage individualism and weaken collective action.[4]

Creech Jones evidently resolved the dilemma to his own satisfaction because he became a conscientious objector, but he was unlikely to have shared the optimism of his I.L.P. colleague, Clifford Allen. On the eve of his own arrest, Allen wrote: 'I expect to be handed over to the military authorities to-morrow. . . . This, I hope, will be the proudest experience of my life. I am glad we Socialists have been involved in this business; it has given the Socialist Movement its great chance.'[5] To many socialists, Allen's

[1] Ibid., 11 November 1915.

[2] See Henry Pelling, *The British Communist Party: a historical profile*, London, 1958, p. 3. Smaller groups of objectors came from the Socialist Labour Party, Socialist Party of Great Britain, Industrial Workers of the World.

[3] Secretary of State for the Colonies in Attlee's 1945–50 Labour Government.

[4] Arthur Creech Jones to Dr. Salter. An undated copy in Creech Jones's Papers; the reply is dated 18 February 1915.

[5] Clifford Allen to H. Bryan (Secretary of the I.L.P.), 10 August 1916, City of London I.L.P./V/109.

leadership of the N.C.F. was an invitation to anarchy, not an inspiration to socialism. After attending the N.C.F. convention in April 1916, Beatrice Webb wrote: 'These men are not so much conscientious objectors as a militant minority of elects, intent on thwarting the will of the majority of ordinary citizens expressed in national policy. . . . The social salvation of the twentieth century is not coming by the dissidence of dissent. Democracy means either discipline or anarchy.'[1] The conflict on this question within the socialist movement was not simply a reflection of the division between the opponents and supporters of the war; it also reflected the more fundamental dichotomy between power and idealism, between the need for solidarity and the claims of individual conscience. The introduction of conscription was not the last occasion when this conflict divided the left wing of British politics; the disagreements of 1916 were re-echoed in the clash between Ernest Bevin and George Lansbury in 1936 and more recently in the differences within the Labour Party on unilateral nuclear disarmament.

In the N.C.F.'s analysis of socialist objectors, twenty-seven are described as anarchists. As a source of conscientious objection anarchism took different forms. A few objectors were pacifist anarchists; their inspiration was Leo Tolstoy and some described themselves as 'Tolstoyan' at the tribunal hearing. There was a larger group of men whose refusal of military service sprang from a rejection of authority. To the militant individualist, conscription epitomized the authoritarian invasion of personal freedom. Beatrice Webb claimed that among the members of the N.C.F. were 'not a few professional rebels, out to smash the Military Service Act, because it was the latest and biggest embodiment of authority hostile to the conduct of their own lives according to their own desires'.[2] The very prospect of being under discipline was intolerable to some men. 'I will not be compelled—that is quite definite in me,' wrote D. H. Lawrence when he became liable for service, 'I will not be compelled to anything.'[3] Lawrence was not put to the test, but others who shared his horror of com-

[1] Beatrice Webb Diaries, 8 April 1916. (All quotations are taken from the unpublished version, vols. 28–38, in the British Library of Political and Economic Science.)

[2] Ibid.

[3] Quoted in Aldous Huxley (ed.), *Letters of D. H. Lawrence*, London, 1932, p. 403.

pulsion became conscientious objectors; in prison and on the Home Office Scheme they set out to undermine authority by hooliganism or strike action or good-humoured ingenuity.[1]

Anarchism in this sense was seldom the *declared* ground of an application. There were other undeclared sources of conscientious objection, though there is no conclusive evidence that cowardice (which loomed so large in the popular imagination[2]) was one of them. The use of the word 'coward' was rare—a minor victory for good form over prejudice—but the euphemisms were unambiguous: conscientious objectors were 'worms' and 'the white-feathered crew'; their civilian jobs were referred to as 'funk holes'. It would have been surprising if fear had not been a contributory motive in some applications, but there is nothing to indicate that it was a significant source of conscientious objection. Paradoxically, it was aggression rather than fear that was seen as a source of conscientious objection by the psycho-analysts of the post-war era. The analysts never claimed that any one hypothesis was applicable to all conscientious objectors but they did give special emphasis to the view that refusal to take part in war could be the result of a reaction-formation against a strong individual aggressiveness; and that pacifist activity becomes both a guarantee of peace of mind and a channel for releasing aggression in vigorous propaganda against the militarist establishment.[3] There were conscientious objectors who displayed a marked degree of aggression, and not only against the authorities, but individual cases of sublimated aggression are naturally enough difficult to identify. The evidence of James Strachey is therefore of particular interest:

> If you had asked at the time, I expect I should have given you a lot of rational reasons for the decision. . . . But only a couple of years after the end of the war I spent two years in Vienna working with Freud, and that gave me a good deal deeper view of what my dominant motives had been. Put very crudely, it might have been argued that my conduct was the product of an excessive quantity of sadism combined with a violent reaction against it.[4]

[1] See Chapter 8 below.

[2] Caroline Playne quotes a lecturer of 1916: 'The number in whom conscientious objections are only a name for cowardice and indifference is, I fear, distressingly large.' See C. Playne, *Society at War*, London, 1931, pp. 201–2.

[3] This hypothesis was particularly associated with Dr. Edward Glover; see E. Glover, *War, Sadism and Pacifism*, London, 1933, pp. 60–61.

[4] James Strachey to the author, 16 March 1965.

The deeper psychological insight did not, however, alter Strachey's view that in certain circumstances pacifism was morally right.

The psychology of pacifism merits a separate study. For the tribunal members of the First World War there was neither the time nor the incentive to probe beneath the declared ground of an application. Even the desire to unmask 'shirkers' seldom got beyond the stage of clumsy insinuation.

Once the ground of an application had been established, the tribunal members had to select the right form of exemption. This meant that they had to discover not only the source but also the extent of a man's objection to military service. In relation to the extent of their objection, the conscientious objectors fell into three categories: those who would accept non-combatant service under the military; those who would accept alternative service under civilian authority; and those who were unwilling to undertake any form of service as a condition of their exemption.

The non-combatants did not object to being part of a military organization or to wearing military uniform. But the extent of their objection could not be described as being to combatant duties. There were some non-combatant duties, particularly those associated with the support of combat troops, that they refused to accept. In this they had no common policy but adopted individual positions, so that whereas nearly all non-combatants would refuse to handle ammunition, some would also refuse to stand guard over it, and some again would refuse to construct roads or railways that might be used to convey military supplies. The different attitudes posed administrative problems that somewhat offset the advantage to the authorities of having to deal with men whose objection did not extend to all military service. The tribunals were unable to guarantee that those posted to the Non-Combatant Corps would necessarily be employed on strictly non-combatant duties, and the military authorities found it difficult to select tasks that were at once useful to the prosecution of the war and inoffensive to scruples of the men. In this the Seventh Day Adventists presented a special problem. In one respect the members of this sect were model objectors: 'They were willing to serve their country in any way that did not call for the taking of life, or any direct participation in the work of slaughter. If the Government offered genuine non-combatant service, they felt that the Scriptures authorized and called them to render such service.'[1] But while they were willing to do non-combatant duties, the Adventists insisted that their Sabbatarian beliefs should be respected. Such beliefs, though recognized in subsequent legislation,[2] were not recognized in the Military Service Act, and the responsibility for trying to accommodate them fell primarily upon the military.

When Asquith introduced the Military Service Bill to the Commons, the official and popular idea of a conscientious objector was of a man who would be willing to do non-combatant work in the army. The Cabinet quickly accepted a broader definition, though the military and the public were reluctant to follow this example. In practice, fewer than one in five conscientious objectors were prepared to come under military control.[3] As the Quaker M.P.s, T. E. Harvey and Arnold Rowntree, had forecast, the majority of conscientious objectors believed that civilian service was the acceptable alternative to combatant duties. Two out of every three conscientious objectors adopted this position either at the tribunal or after court martial and imprisonment.[4] These alternativists objected to coming under military authority,[5] but were prepared, however grudgingly in some cases, to undertake work under civilian direction. Like the non-combatants they had no common policy; the majority refused to do jobs, such as the manufacture of munitions, that facilitated the taking of life, but were willing to fulfil roles in which the contribution to the war effort was either minimal or disguised. In many cases this meant some form of agriculture. A unique alternativist position was adopted by the Christadelphians: they were willing to work directly for the suc-

[1] Wilcox, *Seventh Day Adventists in Time of War*, pp. 258–9.

[2] The Factories Act, 1937 (1 EDW 8 and 1 GEO 6, Ch. 67, 30 July 1937), 91 (1).

[3] About 3,000 out of 16,500. In the Second World War the ratio was almost exactly the same. See J. M. Rae, 'The development of official treatment of conscientious objectors to military service, 1916–1945' ('Conscientious Objectors 1916–1945'), Ph.D. thesis, University of London, 1965, p. 137.

[4] About 11,500 out of 16,500. For the number of men who accepted conditional exemption initially see p. 132, below; for the number who accepted after court martial and worked on the Home Office Scheme (4,126) see *Military Statistics 1914–1920*, p. 673.

[5] Some men objected to taking the military oath, but under conscription this objection was groundless. The Army Act of 1881 provided that recruits should be deemed to have been enlisted when they had taken an oath of allegiance, but under the Military Service Act a man was deemed to have been enlisted from an appointed date and no oath was required of him.

cessful prosecution of the war, even in a munitions factory, as long as they did not come under military authority.[1] Their attitude was not as inconsistent as their critics claimed: they were not pacifists but their eschatology prevented them from joining the armies of this world.

The absolutists refused to undertake alternative service as a condition of exemption. If they were unable to obtain unconditional relief, they resisted all attempts to induce them to accept a less absolute form of exemption. About one in every twelve conscientious objectors took this position.[2] They included both suffering and fighting absolutists. Brigadier-General Childs explained to the War Cabinet in 1917: 'The absolutists, again, presented two types: those who adopted an attitude of resistance to every attempt to make them work, and those who not only refused to undertake any service for the state, but were increasingly busy in their endeavours to induce their fellow citizens to defy the Government.'[3] The suffering absolutists were not merely obstructionist; their attitude sprang from a desire to witness against war and militarism by refusal to come to terms with the machinery of conscription. A characteristic view was expressed at a court-martial hearing:

> The longer I remain in prison the more convinced I am that all war is contrary to the Spirit of Christ's teaching. . . . With a firm belief in these truths, I can accept nothing but absolute exemption from all the working of the Military Service Acts. I feel that all the alternative service of whatever kind, is merely a compromise with the spirit of force to which I am opposed.[4]

The fighting absolutists wanted not only to witness against conscription but also to undermine the Military Service Acts. In the majority of cases they did not hesitate to make use of the machinery of the tribunals; whether their application for absolute

[1] See Report of the Pelham Committee, 1919, p. 6; and Wilson, *Sects and Society*, pp. 256–7.

[2] About 350 received absolute exemption, and about 1,000, having failed to obtain this exemption, resisted all attempts to make them accept conditions. For these totals see below, p. 130 and p. 167.

[3] CAB 23/2/142.

[4] Quoted in *The Absolutists' Objection to Conscription*, Friends Service Committee, London, May 1917, p. 20.

exemption was granted or rejected, they would be striking a blow against conscription. In 1917, an absolutist wrote from prison:

> No Government can face permanent imprisonment of admittedly good citizens. They would be a thorn in the flesh, or a nucleus always stimulating opposition which would ultimately prevail. Unconditional exemption would equally carry with it the seeds of ultimate, even if not immediate, destruction of conscription.[1]

Nearly all the fighting absolutists would have been members of the N.C.F., which had the avowed aim of forcing the Government to repeal the Military Service Acts.

There remain those conscientious objectors whose objection extended to the tribunals and who, therefore, refused to apply for exemption. The Central Tribunal found that of 2,288 conscientious objectors interviewed in prison in 1916, 73 or 4 per cent had not applied to a tribunal on the grounds of conscientious objection.[2] It is not clear how many of these applied on other grounds in the first instance and how many refused to apply at all because an application implied a recognition of the legality of the conscription arrangements. The extreme absolutism of the latter was specifically discouraged by the N.C.F.[3]

The extent of an objection was in some cases dictated by religious conviction, but it was probably true of the majority of objectors that they did not have a preconceived idea of how far they would be prepared to cooperate with the authorities. Few had faced the implications of conscientious objection before compulsory military service became imminent, and for several weeks after the Act had been passed, Asquith's Government did nothing to clarify the nature of the options open to men who had been exempt from combatant duties. This uncertainty on the part of the conscientious objectors and the Government was exploited by the N.C.F.

The N.C.F. made no secret of its aims: from its inception in the autumn of 1914 until the end of 1915, it campaigned against the introduction of compulsory military service; after January 1916, it tried to force the Government to repeal the Military Service Act. The leaders who pursued these aims were not primarily interested in the fair and rational treatment of conscientious

[1] Ibid., p. 13. [2] Report of the Central Tribunal, p. 27.
[3] N.C.F. Letter to Members, 31 January 1916.

objectors; on the contrary, they wanted the provisions for conscience to fail because they believed that this would force the Government to reconsider the principle of compulsion. If the rank and file could be dissuaded from accepting any form of alternative service the law would be a dead letter. These aims were reflected in N.C.F. tactics.

In the spring of 1915, the N.C.F. built up its membership on the basis of a statement of principles that declared: 'The No-Conscription Fellowship is an organisation of men . . . who will refuse from conscientious motives to bear arms, because they consider human life to be sacred, and cannot, therefore, assume the responsibility of inflicting death.'[1] In July the objection was extended to include not only 'any employment that necessitates taking the military oath', but also 'the production of any material the purpose of which is the taking of human life'.[2] The Fellowship's Committee recommended that this objection should be made clear when members registered under the National Register, and it was this objection that was expressed in the Fellowship's Manifesto to the Cabinet in September 1915.[3] At the Fellowship's first National Convention on 27 November 1915, the objection was extended once again. The existing statement on war work was deleted and replaced by the following resolution:

> That members of the Fellowship will refuse to engage in any employment which necessitates taking the military oath. Whilst leaving the decision open to the individual judgement of each member, the Fellowship will support members who conscientiously resist compulsory alternatives to military service involving a change in occupation.[4]

This resolution indicated that the majority of members would refuse both combatant and non-combatant service under military authority, but that only a proportion would go further and refuse any compulsory direction to alternative civilian employment. This remained the position of the Fellowship while the Military Service Bill was being debated in Parliament.

Once the Military Service Act had become law, the aim of the N.C.F. was to 'cause the removal of Conscription from the life of

[1] N.C.F. Statement of Principles, 1915.
[2] N.C.F. Report, July 1915.
[3] N.C.F. Letter to Members, 25 September 1915.
[4] N.C.F. Letter to Members, 9 December 1915.

this country of free traditions'.[1] This could not be achieved unless members were encouraged to demand nothing less than absolute exemption. There can be little doubt that the National Committee of the Fellowship expected many of these applications to be rejected by the tribunals, and that it was not altogether dismayed at the prospect. On 31 January 1916 the Committee wrote to members: 'When members cannot accept the decisions of the Tribunals, and have to suffer, we shall have an unanswerable case to advance. We can show how our men faced every ordeal, and how those who failed to convince the Tribunals with words are now proving their sincerity by deeds.'[2] In urging members to go before the tribunals and claim absolute exemption, the Committee recognized that the extent of the objection was a matter for the individual conscience, but emphasized that deviation from official policy would not further the aims of the Fellowship. On 6 February the Committee wrote to members: 'We advise that members (who must, of course, be guided by their own convictions) should apply for absolute and complete exemption, and should maintain that claim, for thus we can advance our real objection and make our testimony effective in the country.'[3]

During March and April, the policy of the National Committee was to exhort its members to hold out for absolute exemption, and at the same time to convince the Government that schemes for providing civilian alternative service would inevitably fail. Until the third week in March this policy was encouraged by the absence of administrative machinery for placing conscientious objectors in alternative service. When, on 23 March, Walter Long announced that this machinery was in the process of being established,[4] the N.C.F. reacted at once. The Government's action was condemned in *The Tribunal* as a deliberate attempt to divide and weaken the corporate resistance of the conscientious objectors;[5] and on the day of Long's announcement, the National Committee wrote to all members recommending that where certificates of conditional exemption were granted by the tribunals, they should be handed back as unacceptable.[6] Two weeks later, on 8 April, an Emergency

[1] N.C.F. Letter to Members, 31 January 1916. [2] Ibid.
[3] N.C.F. Letter to Members, 6 February 1916.
[4] R.70, L.G.B. Circular, 23 March 1916.
[5] *The Tribunal*, 23 and 30 March 1916.
[6] N.C.F. Letter to Members, 23 March 1916.

National Convention of the Fellowship was called to demonstrate the solidarity of the membership against alternative service. At the Convention, 1,500 delegates, representing 15,000 members throughout the country, decided by 'an almost unanimous vote' to reject alternative service, and this decision was reported to the Prime Minister in a letter from the National Committee.[1]

The 'almost unanimous' absolutism of the Convention was not carried over into the tribunal hearings. Even if all the 1,350 conscientious objectors who consistently refused alternative service were members of the N.C.F., the figure represents only 9 per cent of the declared membership. The N.C.F. leaders were no more successful in forcing the withdrawal of conscription than they had been in preventing its introduction, but the tactics they adopted in the spring of 1916 exacerbated the difficulties inherent in the Government's inexperience and in the ambiguities of the law. By encouraging men to exaggerate the extent of their objection, the N.C.F. not only created obvious difficulties for tribunals and the military, but also discredited attempts to provide alternative service for those objectors who were willing to accept a conditional exemption. In these circumstances the Fellowship's complaint to the Prime Minister that the arrest and court martial of its members bore 'a grave resemblance to religious persecution'[2] was somewhat disingenuous.

[1] N.C.F. Letter to the Prime Minister, 15 April 1916. [2] Ibid.

CHAPTER SIX

THE TRIBUNALS AT WORK

(i)

When Asquith's Cabinet accepted the need to make legal provisions for conscientious objectors, it was assumed that the problems of administering the law could be left to the tribunals. A similar assumption characterized the debates on the Military Service Bill despite the doubts of those who recalled the magistrates' handling of the Vaccination Acts. It was on the tribunals therefore that men fixed the blame when the working of the conscience clause created more difficulties than it resolved. Both sides—the Government and the military on one hand, and the conscientious objectors on the other—found it convenient to place the responsibility for maladministration on the tribunals alone; by doing so they disguised their own contribution to the muddle. History has tended to endorse this face-saving manoeuvre; in those accounts of the First World War that touch on the subject of conscientious objectors, the implication is that an enlightened section of the law was frustrated by the bias or incompetence of the tribunal members.[1] The evidence does not support this interpretation. There is no doubt that the tribunal members made errors of judgement and administration, and that these errors were sometimes inspired by prejudice, but when the work of the tribunal is seen in the context of conscription as a whole, the limitations of the tribunal members seem relatively unimportant.

The tribunals' work was to a large extent shaped by the experience and legacy of the Derby Scheme under which men willing to attest had been called up in Groups according to age and marital status. This hangover from the days of voluntary recruiting caused numerous misunderstandings even before the tribunal hearing took place. One misunderstanding is particularly worth consider-

[1] See e.g. A. J. P. Taylor, *English History, 1914–1945*, London, 1965, p. 54.

ing because it illustrates so well the inclination to misinterpret each other's motives that characterized relations between the conscientious objectors and authorities from the earliest days.

A form of application for exemption (R.41) was available at the local tribunal or recruiting office. A few conscientious objectors, when asking for a form, were led to believe that exemption could not be claimed until a man had voluntarily attested his willingness to serve. This was correct procedure under the Group System of the Derby Scheme but not of course under the Military Service Act. There was good reason for the mistake. The Group System was still open and men inquiring about exemption might have been volunteers or conscripts. Under the Group System an attested man could express a preference for non-combatant duties,[1] so that a man asking about such duties might be told that he would have to attest first. Similarly, if a man wrote for an application form but did not make it clear that he came under the Military Service Act, the tribunal clerk might send a form for use under the Group System which contained the phrase: '. . . further proceedings can only be taken on the application if the man concerned has been voluntarily attested.'[2]

Of all applicants the conscientious objector stood to lose most by being led to believe that he should attest first before applying for exemption. Attested men shared with conscripts a statutory right to apply to the tribunals, but not on the ground of conscientious objection. The War Office view was that, prima facie, a man who had volunteered for the army could not claim to object to military service;[3] and Walter Long informed tribunals that 'applications on the ground of conscientious objection ought not to arise in the case of men who have voluntarily become attested'.[4] The conscientious objector who attested in error was thus denied his statutory right to apply for exemption. Not surprisingly he suspected that he had been tricked by the military, while on their part the military believed that the men in question had thought better of their decision to volunteer and were trying to escape by using the conscience clause. Mutual suspicion increased the difficulty of finding a formula that would enable these claims to conscientious objection to be heard. In April the War Office was

[1] Derby, *Group and Class Systems*, p. 15. [2] R 54.
[3] H. J. Tennant's statement, 5 HC 80, col. 674, 23 February 1916.
[4] R.36, L.G.B. to Local Registration Authorities.

finally persuaded to allow the cases to be referred to local tribunals, but the military made it clear that this was being done 'as a matter of grace' and not as an admission of error.[1]

The great majority of conscientious objectors were not misled in this way, but the procedure for application and appeal included other, less easily avoided hazards, some of which were interpreted as a violation of the statutory right of conscientious objection. When the applicant returned his form to the clerk of the tribunal, the duplicate was forwarded to the local Military Representative, who in turn sought the advice of his Advisory Committee. It will be remembered that the War Office had appointed Military Representatives and Advisory Committees to watch over its recruiting interests under the Derby Scheme. The Military Service Act had recognized the role of the Military Representative; the Advisory Committee had remained without statutory authority but with considerable influence. Both the Military Representatives and, in many cases, the tribunals continued to accept the recommendations of the Committees as they had been in the habit of doing under the Scheme. At the end of the war the Chairman of the St. Marylebone Local Tribunal paid a tribute to the way in which the Tribunal, the Advisory Committee, and the Military Representative had 'worked together, hand in hand, as a band of brothers with one object in view—to do our duty'.[2] Such fraternalism was not appreciated by the applicant who felt that the Advisory Committee, with no statutory authority, was usurping the function of the local tribunal, and that, as War Office appointments, the Committee members were automatically opposed to conscientious objectors.

Both the applicant and the Military Representative enjoyed an unrestricted right of appeal against the decision of the local tribunal. The notice of appeal form was sent through the local tribunal so that the tribunal members were given an opportunity of commenting on the applicant's reasons for appealing. Walter Long advised local tribunals to indicate those cases in which an appeal was being made 'on wholly inadequate grounds' in order that the case might be 'promptly dealt with' by the higher tribunal.[3] This procedure also enabled the Military Representative to add his

[1] Minutes of the Central Tribunal, 10 April 1916.
[2] Minutes of the St. Marylebone Local Tribunal, 19 November 1918.
[3] R.70, L.G.B. Circular, 23 March 1916.

own comments on the appeal. It is not clear how far the Military Representative used this opportunity, but the papers of the Lothian and Peebles Appeal Tribunal throw an interesting light on the character of their comments. One appeal form of a man who claimed exemption on conscientious grounds carried this comment by the Military Representative of the local tribunal:

> This man would make a splendid soldier. He has a fine physique and just wants the nonsense knocked out of him. When the Tribunal's decision was given to him he walked out of the room in a towering rage and slammed the door after him, so that I think his Christianity is not very sincere. I think his appeal should be rejected.[1]

On another appeal, the military comment was:

> This is a case of a clever man who has argued himself into a certain frame of mind and it would do him a world of good to see service. . . . His fellow workmen all want to see him go.[2]

Under the Military Service Act, an appeal to the Central Tribunal required the permission of the appeal tribunal concerned. The Local Government Board had advised appeal tribunals to allow such an appeal only in those cases 'in which some definite, clear broad principle was raised'.[3] The practice of appeal tribunals differed widely. 38 per cent of all appeals allowed to the Central Tribunal came from 8 of the 85 appeal tribunals. The Gloucester Appeal Tribunal allowed 266 cases to go forward whereas the Nottinghamshire allowed only 2.[4] These figures cover appellants on all grounds but they indicate how far a conscientious objector's chances of raising a 'clear, broad principle' might depend on the area in which he lived.

All these aspects of the application and appeal procedure helped to place under military law a number of men who later established a conscientious objection to all military service. But the real test of the Government's provisions came at the tribunal hearing itself. If the hearing resolved the conflict between the individual conscience and the legitimate demands of the state, the provisions

[1] Lothian and Peebles Appeal Tribunal, March/April, 1916, No. 6.

[2] Ibid., No. 11.

[3] R.76, Notes of Conference of Chairmen of Appeal Tribunals, 27 March 1916.

[4] Report of the Central Tribunal, pp. 15–18, gives the statistics of the sources of appeals.

could be said to have succeeded; if however the hearing failed to resolve this conflict in a significant number of cases, the Government would be faced with new administrative problems for which it had not prepared.

The tribunals had to hear applications on four different grounds and from attested as well as from conscripted men. The total number of applications on the ground of conscientious objection is not known (the tribunals only recorded the certificates granted) but some indication of the proportion that were on conscientious grounds may be obtained from the statistics of the Middlesex Appeal Tribunal. Of the 8,791 men who appealed to this tribunal, only 577 or about 6½ per cent appealed on the ground of conscientious objection.[1] The small proportion meant that few tribunals acquired any worthwhile experience of dealing with questions of conscientious objection; and when the chairman of one appeal tribunal tried to obviate this difficulty by suggesting that one committee of the tribunal should hear all appeals on conscientious grounds, his suggestion was rejected by his colleagues.[2]

If the number of applicants on conscientious grounds was small, the number on the other three grounds was very large indeed. Between January and July 1916, three-quarters of a million men applied for exemption[3] so that during these six months the tribunals were under heavy pressure. In urban areas there was time for only the briefest consideration of each case. The Battersea Local Tribunal allowed five minutes for the hearing of each application,[4] and this was in line with Long's instruction that tribunals 'should rigorously check any tendency to protract the proceedings'.[5] At Leicester the local tribunal sittings sometimes lasted nine to ten hours;[6] and at Camberwell the tribunal sat in relays from 11.0 a.m. to 9.30 p.m., often four times a week.[7] The City of Glasgow Local Tribunal disposed of more cases in a single month than the majority of tribunals disposed of in six years in the Second World War.[8]

[1] Middlesex Appeal Tribunal, Statistics of Cases, MH 47/143.

[2] Minutes of the County of London Appeal Tribunal, 6 March 1916.

[3] *Military Operations, France and Belgium 1916*, London, 1932, p. 152.

[4] Letter Books of the Battersea Local Tribunal, 2, p. 126.

[5] R.36, L.G.B. Circular to Local Registration Authorities.

[6] F. P. Armitage, *Leicester 1914–1918: the war-time story of a Midland town*, Leicester, 1933, p. 169.

[7] See Minutes of Camberwell Local Tribunal for February 1916.

[8] 6,145 in July 1916. See SHHD 25478S/981. The tribunal must have sat in two or more divisions, but the number of cases disposed of is still formidable.

In these circumstances no case was more likely to go by default than that of the conscientious objector. Raising issues that were provocative yet subtle, not dealing exclusively with facts but concerned also with intuitive feelings, the application on conscientious grounds was not susceptible of hasty treatment. The lack of time did not necessarily mean that the tribunal failed to recognize a conscientious objection, but rather that it was unable to take sufficient care in selecting a form of exemption that would meet the case.

Though brief, the tribunal hearing was subject to specific regulations.[1] Beyond these the procedure was determined by the tribunal members themselves. In practice the pattern varied little from one tribunal to another. Hearings were held in public (usually in the Town Hall) but the chairman had the power to exclude spectators in special circumstances. There was no ban on the press and verbatim reports of tribunal hearings both filled the columns and stimulated the circulation of the local newspapers. The crowded public gallery was seldom hostile to the applicant. The hearing was no Revolutionary Tribunal with a mob crying for victims and a Military Representative, as a local Fouquier Tinville, despatching young men to certain death. The public who took the trouble to attend were usually friends of the applicant and this was particularly true when the application was on conscientious grounds. In industrial areas, with strong socialist loyalties, an I.L.P. applicant would be accompanied by a vociferous group of supporters. Tribunal members were interrupted and jeered, and it was a commonplace for 'The Red Flag' to be sung at the hearing.[2] Trade union and Labour Party men who had agreed to sit on the tribunal were the object of special scorn: at the Leeds Local Tribunal these members were on one occasion greeted with cries of 'Renegades' and 'Down with the treacherous Labour Members'.[3] Rowdyism of this sort encouraged some tribunals to exclude the public, a move which in turn brought protests from the conscientious objectors and their friends.

The applicant was entitled to be represented by a friend or by counsel, though for a short time in 1918 the right of legal repre-

[1] Unless otherwise stated the regulations appear in SR&O, 1916, 53, 3 February 1916.

[2] See e.g. the *Glasgow Herald*, 16 March 1916, and the *Leeds Mercury*, 24 March 1916.

[3] *Leeds Mercury*, 28 March 1916.

sentation was withdrawn; the withdrawal was announced on 25 April as the last great German offensive reached its climax and the right replaced a week later when the German offensive had clearly shot its bolt.[1] In practice, legal representation was rare; Long instructed tribunals to discourage it[2] and the N.C.F. advised its members not to be represented by a friend and certainly not by a solicitor.[3] Conscience was not transferable. While representation was rare, it was common for a witness to be called to testify to the length of time the applicant had held his views on military service. The witnesses were members of the applicant's Church, close relatives, or friends whose testimony would carry weight with the tribunal. Edward Marsh, Winston Churchill's Private Secretary, testified to the 'unimpeachable courage and complete sincerity' of the Roman Catholic objector, Francis Meynell,[4] a task which Maynard Keynes performed for James Strachey.[5] In other cases the applicant provided a written testimonial of his bona fides or a certificate to establish his membership of Church or sect.[6]

In hearing witnesses, the tribunal was not bound by the normal rules of evidence: hearsay and opinion were admissible. This was to the applicant's advantage in that it allowed his friend to express an opinion on the strength or sincerity of his convictions. But it cut both ways. The tribunal could also accept opinion hostile to the applicant or evidence that was irrelevant to the issue. The Battersea Local Tribunal received a number of anonymous letters hostile to applicants,[7] and in the Commons Philip Snowden alleged that one tribunal had rejected an application on the strength of an anonymous letter alone.[8] At another tribunal, the Military Representative was allowed to introduce evidence that an applicant on conscientious grounds ill-treated his wife and children.[9] These incidents appear to have been isolated rather than typical despite Beatrice Webb's savage comment that the tribunals were 'a

[1] Withdrawn by SR&O, 1918, 495, 25 April 1918, I, 12(2) and replaced by R.191, L.G.B. Letter to tribunals, 2 May 1918.

[2] R.36, L.G.B. Circular to Local Registration Authorities.

[3] N.C.F. Letter, 6 February 1916.

[4] See Playne, op. cit., p. 278.

[5] Harrod, op. cit., p. 211.

[6] A number of these appear in the papers of the Lothian and Peebles Appeal Tribunal.

[7] Letter Books of the Battersea Local Tribunal, 3, p. 521.

[8] 5 HC 80, col. 2069, 15 March 1916.

[9] Selected Case Papers of the Central Tribunal, 17, 282 MH 47/3.

scandalous example of lay prejudice—another proof that if you have a law you must have a lawyer to administer it'.[1]

For the conscientious objector by far the most significant regulation governing the hearing was that which gave the Military Representative the right to appear as a party to every application. The War Office view was that their representative was a party in the legal sense with the same authority as counsel in court. The original selection of these military counsel for the prosecution had been made by the GOC of the District from 'officers and retired officers of the regular army and territorial forces and gentlemen of business capacity and influence'.[2] At local tribunals they acted 'voluntarily and without remuneration'; at appeal tribunals they received 'pay and allowances appropriate to their military rank'.[3] The Representatives ranged in rank from Lieutenant to General, and they included a Member of Parliament, various party candidates, solicitors, and even clergymen.[4] The presence of the latter, though curious in retrospect, was consistent with the Church's conscious identification with the national cause; and a clergyman was regarded by the military as having special qualifications for contesting applications on conscientious grounds: he was a priest called in to refute a heresy. All Military Representatives received their initial instructions from the Director-General of Recruiting, Lord Derby; after February 1916 they were instructed by the Adjutant General, Sir Nevil Macready. It was Derby who explained that while the individual was protected by the law 'the duty of the Military Representative is to protect the nation by obtaining as many men as possible for the Army'.[5] Sympathy for hard cases was, in the War Office's view, misplaced:

> . . . a Military Representative should recognize that, so far as military interests are concerned, he is the pivot of the machine and if he allows his decision to be influenced by any other consideration than that of the national interest, he cannot be held to be fulfilling the duty for which he was appointed.[6]

As a party to each application, the Military Representatives had the right to question an applicant, though they were instructed

[1] Beatrice Webb Diaries, 9 March 1916.

[2] *The Recruiting Code*, Ministry of National Service, January 1918, sec. 181.

[3] Ibid.

[4] There were clergymen at Sutton (Surrey) and Newcastle (Staffs.) Local Tribunals.

[5] Derby, *Group and Class Systems*, p. 5.

[6] Loc. cit.

to 'confine themselves to the presentation of evidence and the elucidation of facts relevant to the decision of the case'.[1] They were also instructed to 'avoid expressing an opinion on controversial political and religious questions, which are not relevant to the matter to be decided by the Tribunal'.[2]

Despite these instructions there were numerous allegations that Military Representatives were bullying applicants—particularly those on conscientious grounds—and denying them the right of a fair hearing. In reply to the widespread criticism of the Military Representatives' conduct, Major Lionel de Rothschild, the Military Representative at the City of London Local Tribunal, gave a Personal Explanation to the House of Commons in which he denied that Military Representatives were 'trying to evade the wishes of Parliament and to drag men into the army by bullying and improper action'.[3] The evidence indicates, however, that bullying and improper action were not uncommon. Both the War Office and, later, the Ministry of National Service found it necessary to warn Military Representatives that they had no right to remain with the tribunal while its decision was being discussed if the applicant had been excluded.[4] The Ministry also found it necessary, when it assumed responsibility for recruiting, to tell Representatives that they 'should refrain from adopting a browbeating and domineering tone in cross-examination. . . . it must be remembered that in applying for exemption an applicant is only exercising his rights'.[5] The confrontation between the Military Representative and the conscientious objector was unlikely to have been characterized by mutual understanding. The former wore uniform (if entitled to do so) and came to the hearing well armed with warrior texts; the latter was suspicious of the Military Representative's motives and unimpressed by his knowledge of the Old Testament. It is hardly surprising that many conscientious objectors saw this uniformed prosecutor as the enemy who, more than any other, was responsible for the fact that they did not receive the exemption they wanted. The Military Representative did not always contest an application on conscientious grounds; he was instructed not to 'press opposition against applications for exemption of conscien-

[1] Ibid., p. 29. [2] ACI No. 1300, 1916.

[3] 5 HC 80, col. 1214–16, 2 March 1916.

[4] Derby, *Group and Class Systems*, p. 32; *The Recruiting Code*, 1918, sec. 190. SR&O, 1918, No. 495, I, 7, made such procedure illegal.

[5] *The Recruiting Code*, 1918, sec. 187.

tious objectors where the applicant was well known to hold religious scruples against war before the passing of the Military Service Act, 1916'.[1] Nor was his attitude invariably belligerent. At the Barrhead Local Tribunal, James Maxton found the Military Representative 'extremely fair' in that he 'maintained an attitude of complete impartiality throughout the entire sitting'.[2] But in the majority of cases the Military Representative had to challenge applications on conscientious grounds and to appeal against awards of absolute exemption. This was his job. His attitude was an inevitable consequence of the role he was asked to play. He had been instructed to win men for the army; if he had left uncontested the applications for exemption on the grounds of conscientious objection he would have been failing in his duty. This did not prevent him being blamed when a large number of conscientious objectors whose applications had been unsuccessful were arrested and eventually court-martialled. In the War Cabinet of 1917, W. Hayes Fisher, who succeeded Long at the Local Government Board, accused the Military Representatives of preventing the exemption of genuine conscientious objectors.[3] In its public report, however, the Board took a different line emphasizing that the Military Representative's right of appeal against an exemption was a safeguard against 'any laxity on the part of the local tribunal'.[4] In the Cabinet, Hayes Fisher was trying to shift the responsibility for maladministration on to the War Office, but it was both unfair and illogical to blame the Military Representative for fulfilling his instructions. Only when he became part of the civilian recruiting machinery of the Ministry of National Service was he instructed to have regard not only for the needs of the army but also for other urgent national requirements.[5]

Whether bullying or considerate, it was the Military Representative who linked the tribunal most firmly to the War Office's recruiting machinery. Though he appeared as one party to an application, he was the friend and colleague of the members of the tribunal. It was not unknown for him to sit with the tribunal members and

[1] ACI No. 1300, 1916.
[2] John McNair, *James Maxton: the beloved rebel*, London, 1955, p. 58.
[3] CAB 23/4/246 (I)(d).
[4] 46th Annual Report of the L.G.B., 1916–1917, I, pp. 19–22.
[5] R.158, L.G.B. Circular, 3 November 1917.

to refer to the body as 'my tribunal'.[1] In some cases members might have resented his domineering attitude, but it is probable that the sentiments expressed by the Chairman of the St. Marylebone Local Tribunal were indicative of the true relationship between the Military Representative and the tribunals. The Military Representative was 'our friend and colleague, to whom we all are most deeply indebted for his never failing courtesy and urbanity, for his sound judgement, for his forbearance and prudence, for his reasonableness and sympathy, which have endeared him to us all'.[2]

The procedure of the Central Tribunal did not allow the military authorities to play a decisive role.[3] When the case papers of an appellant were received from the appeal tribunal, appellants on conscientious grounds were required to complete a written questionnaire.[4] From the answers and from other relevant material, a responsible official of the Central Tribunal made a summary of evidence. This was studied, together with the case papers, by two members of the Tribunal, the summary of evidence being sent to the other members only two days before the hearing. At the hearing one of the members who had studied the evidence as well as the case papers, presented the case for the appellant. Apart from a few cases selected as typical of the various classes of appellant, the Tribunal did not hear appellants in person. This procedure was criticized and was the subject of a High Court action brought against the Tribunal by an appellant on conscientious grounds. The High Court ruled that under the Second Schedule of the Military Service (No. 2) Act, 1916, the Tribunal had the right to regulate its own procedure.[5] A War Office Assessor was attached to the Central Tribunal, but he only acted as a representative of the military authorities when the appellant appeared in person; in other cases he attended but took no part in the proceedings. There would appear to have been no complaints of the role of this military representative.

[1] *The Tribunal*, 8 March 1916.

[2] Minutes of the St. Marylebone Local Tribunal, 19 November 1918. See also similar votes of thanks from the Lanark and Stirling Local Tribunals, SHHD 254785/3162.

[3] The procedure is described in the Report of the Central Tribunal, pp. 13–14.

[4] See Appendix D.

[5] Rex v. Central Tribunal *ex parte* Parton, King's Bench Division, 18 April 1916. Quoted at length in *The Justice of the Peace*, 13 January 1917.

(ii)

The ever-present military reinforced the inclination of the lower tribunals to adopt a negative approach. Implicit in the Board's instructions was the need to restrict exemptions to the minimum. Walter Long's advice to tribunals on the treatment of conscientious objectors was a fair and accurate expression of the wishes of Parliament, but contained the phrase, 'While care must be taken that the man who shirks his duty to his country does not find unworthy shelter behind this provision every consideration should be given to the man whose objection genuinely rests on religious or moral convictions.'[1] The character of the tribunal hearings suggests that the members were more receptive to the first half of Long's injunction than the second. At local level, the cross-examination of an applicant on conscientious grounds was seldom more than a crude attempt to test consistency of behaviour. There was no time either to make an assessment of the man's integrity or to clarify the exact nature of his objection. It was all very well for the Central Tribunal to circulate a list of carefully thought-out questions; the local tribunals, with only a few minutes for each applicant, had to rely on more rough-and-ready methods. If a man could prove that he had joined a non-combatant Church or sect before the war, his application was almost always successful; if not, his chances of obtaining exemption depended largely on his ability to answer—or at least to parry—questions designed to expose the inconsistencies in his position. For many tribunal members, inconsistency was synonymous with insincerity. An applicant who would use force in one situation could not object to doing so in another; a man who contributed—however indirectly—to the war effort, had no grounds for refusing service; a pacifist interpretation of Scripture was invalidated by inability to explain a text condoning war. This narrow concern with the logic of the applicant's position was probably inevitable. It inspired clashes of text and counter-text, and hypothetical questions some of which have passed into the folk-lore of the period. 'What would you do', the applicant was asked, 'if a German soldier was about to rape your mother?' However wicked the jack-booted Prussian, his

[1] R.36, L.G.B. Circular to Local Registration Authorities.

virility was never in doubt. The same question appeared in a variety of forms. At the Middlesex Appeal Tribunal it was expressed in more decorous terms: 'Would you fight to save your property or women-folk at home from attack?'[1] In Hereford it was given racial overtones: 'What would you do if you saw a nigger assaulting one of your relatives?'[2] And at Harrogate the tribunal preferred a more homely setting: 'Suppose a lot of roughs came down the street and surrounded your house and started breaking windows and smashing your home up, would you let them do it?'[3]

If the tribunal members hoped that this question would elicit clear-cut evidence that the applicant's conscientious objection was bogus, they were disappointed. The answers proved nothing and the tribunal members did not understand why. This exchange at the Bradford Local Tribunal illustrates the inconclusive nature of this line of questioning:[4]

Member: What would you do if a German came to you with a bayonet fixed?
Applicant: I shouldn't know what to do.
Member: No, I don't think you do but I have a pretty fair idea. What would you do if a German attacked your mother?
Applicant: If possible I would get between the attacker and my mother: but under no circumstances would I take life to save life.
Member: If the only way to save your mother were to kill a German, would you still let him kill her?
Applicant: Yes.
Member: You ought to be shot. If a man came and violated your sister would you not give evidence against him?
Applicant: No, I would not.
Member: If you saw a man shoot your mother would you tell a magistrate you saw him shoot her?
Applicant: I should have to or tell a lie.

The exchange of biblical texts was equally inconclusive though it could give colour to routine proceedings. T. E. Harvey recorded an exchange at the Hampstead Local Tribunal that might have

[1] Middlesex Appeal Tribunal, Questions for Conscientious Objectors, MH 47/144.

[2] *Hereford Journal*, 11 April 1916.

[3] *Leeds Mercury*, 3 March 1916.

[4] *Bradford Daily Telegraph*, 16 March 1916.

been spoken by an early follower of George Fox and a Cromwellian recruiting sergeant:[1]

Mil. Rep.: I'd be glad if you would explain Numbers 32, verse 6, 'Shall your brethren go to war and shall ye sit here?'

Applicant: I can't explain it without knowing the context.

Mil. Rep.: You say you know the bible and I'd be glad to know. What about 'Vengeance is mine'?

Applicant: Yes, vengeance is mine saith the Lord, not man's. Whatever you or the tribunal say, nothing can alter God's law, 'Thou shalt not kill'.

Mil. Rep.: God's law be damned, go and fight.

Not all cross-examination was as irrelevant as this. Serious attempts were made to probe the alleged objection more deeply but these were almost always cut short either by the pressure of work or by the limitations of the participants. It was characteristic of the hearing that the tribunal members and the applicant seldom succeeded in making contact with each other or with the subject in which they had, momentarily, a common interest. The reported hearings have an unsynchronized, Pinteresque quality, so that the questioning was inconsequent rather than unfair, the examination of the applicant's views perfunctory rather than prejudiced. It is easy to dismiss the tribunals' approach as sterile; it is less easy to say with certainty how the councillors and their colleagues should have filled the few minutes during which they were face to face with the applicant on conscientious grounds. It was not until June 1916, when the tribunals had been functioning for nearly four months, that Walter Long circulated detailed suggestions, together with the list of questions used by the Central Tribunal.[2] It is possible that the standard of investigation at the lower tribunals improved during the summer as a result, but such an improvement would have affected only a minority of conscientious objectors.

Although Long may have been slow to advise tribunals on the evidence they should consider relevant, he was quick to respond to criticism of the tribunal members' behaviour. In March 1916, he wrote to all tribunals:

Some tribunals are alleged to have subjected applicants to a somewhat harsh cross-examination with respect to the grounds of their objection.

[1] Notes on the hearing of Lawrence Deller's case, T. E. Harvey Papers.

[2] R.84, L.G.B. Circular, 1 June 1916. See also Appendix D.

It is of course necessary that the tribunal should satisfy themselves of the *bona fides* of an applicant and of the precise grounds and nature of his objection, but it is desirable that enquiries should be made with tolerance and impartiality.[1]

Many of these allegations had been made in the Commons by a group of members[2] who were known to be sympathetic and who were supplied with details by individual conscientious objectors and by organizations that sent observers to the tribunal hearings. Philip Snowden and Edmund Harvey received a large correspondence from applicants on conscientious grounds who claimed to have been unfairly treated by the tribunals or the military. Snowden estimated that in one year he received over 30,000 letters from conscientious objectors;[3] citing a number of cases of alleged ill-treatment, he made a comprehensive indictment of the tribunals' behaviour in two speeches to the Commons in March and April 1916. The speeches were published as a pamphlet under the title *British Prussianism: the Scandal of the Tribunals.*[4]

Snowden's criticisms were echoed in the liberal and radical press. The organs of the N.C.F. and I.L.P.—*The Tribunal* and *The Labour Leader*—exposed every week the alleged irregularity and unjudicial behaviour of the tribunals. But it was not only the obvious champions of the conscientious objectors who spoke out. In *The Times* the Bishops of Oxford and Lincoln both called for more respectful treatment of applicants on conscientious grounds.[5] In private the criticism of the tribunals was often sharper. 'Their contemptuous approach', William Temple wrote to a friend, 'remains a reproach to our civilization.'[6]

Though there was a formidable sum of public and private criticism, the contemptuous approach was not, as Graham sug-

[1] R.70, L.G.B. Circular, 23 March 1916.

[2] Notably Philip Snowden of the I.L.P., T. E. Harvey and Arnold Rowntree, Quaker Liberals, and R. L. Outhwaite and Philip Morrell, Liberals.

[3] Snowden, *An Autobiography, 1: 1864–1919*, p. 406.

[4] Published by the National Labour Press, Manchester, 1916. Snowden's speeches: 5 HC 81, cols. 261–78 and 1443–52, 22 March and 6 April 1916.

[5] *The Times*, 14 March 1916 and 4 April 1916. The Bishop of Oxford, Charles Gore, wrote privately, 'The real mistake was in not originally directing the tribunals how to behave.' Quoted in G. L. Prestige, *The Life of Charles Gore*, London, 1935, p. 389.

[6] F. L. Iremonger, *William Temple*, London, 1948, pp. 187–8. Temple, Gore, and E. L. Hicks, Bishop of Lincoln, had all been prominent sympathizers with the cause of women's suffrage.

gests,[1] typical of the tribunals as a whole. Allegations of misconduct were almost always based on statements attributed to tribunal members and quoted out of context. In the full-length reports of tribunal hearings the contemptuous treatment of applicants is evident only in a minority of cases. A striking insult, however, was accorded wide publicity. It was seized upon not only by the journals sympathetic to conscientious objectors but also by the national and provincial press, for whom a vitriolic outburst made a good headline. Thus when the Chairman of the Nairn Appeal Tribunal in Scotland described conscientious objectors as 'the most awful pack that ever walked the earth', he was reported not only in the national and 'conscientious objector' press, but also in provincial newspapers as far away as Cornwall.[2] In this way contempt and insult were made to appear the norm.

A minority of tribunals were contemptuous in their treatment of conscientious objectors. Tired and irritable in the face of continuous criticism, Walter Long claimed that complaints were invariably based on an incorrect version of the facts,[3] but his successor told the War Cabinet in 1917, 'I am not concerned to defend all tribunals. Some may have been harsh or unwise. . . .'[4] Hostility to conscientious objectors was implicit in the bellicose attitudes of the civilian population, and that some members should have been offensive is less remarkable than that many others acted with restraint. At the time, the tribunals' critics did not hesitate to pay tribute to those members who tried to administer the Act judicially. Philip Snowden and R. L. Outhwaite acknowledged that 'many' tribunals had 'tried to do their duty sincerely' and had been 'most anxious to administer the Act in a fair and impartial way'.[5] *The Friend* made a similar acknowledgement; 'Many tribunals have been most considerate and patient,' it reported, 'particularly some of the appeal tribunals, and that such has been the case redounds to their lasting credit.'[6] Individual tribunals were noted for their impartiality. The N.C.F. considered that the Guildford Local Tribunal was conducted on model lines,[7] and few conscientious objectors could have complained of the aims of the County of London Appeal Tribunal, as stated by the Chair-

[1] Graham, op. cit., Ch. III. [2] *Cornwall County News*, 8 March 1916.
[3] 5 HC 81, col. 1453, 6 April 1916. [4] CAB 23/4/246(I)(d).
[5] 5 HC 82, cols. 1044 and 1046, 11 May 1916.
[6] *The Friend*, 5 May 1916. [7] *The Tribunal*, 8 March 1916.

man, Sir Donald Maclean: 'I am quite sure that what we will aim at is to be judicial, not in the merely legal sense, but in the proper sense—the fair-minded, impartial administration of an Act of Parliament, which is conveyed to us by means of Regulations by which we are bound.'[1]

The good intentions of the tribunal members could be dispelled by sheer exhaustion or—more commonly—by an increasing impatience with the attitude of the conscientious objectors themselves. Judge Mellor, who doubled as chairman of an appeal and a local tribunal, admitted that although he started out with sympathy for the conscientious objector, 'the result of six weeks sitting is to take my sympathy away altogether.'[2] The judge was not alone in his experience. Like many people who are persuaded to make a generous gesture against their better judgement, the British public accepted the principle of conscientious objection to military service with bad grace, and were swift to express righteous indignation if the conscientious objectors appeared arrogant or dissatisfied rather than grateful. The Government in particular found it hard to stomach criticism of the way in which the conscience clause was being implemented. In an uncharacteristically vehement comment, Walter Long blamed the applicants for the shortcomings of the tribunals. 'They come before the tribunal,' he told the Commons, 'they lecture it, they assume an air of superiority, and they claim that they have some sort of divine right to assume a position superior to that adopted by the great majority of their fellow citizens. It is not extraordinary that in these circumstances the tribunals often deal with their cases in a peremptory manner. . . .'[3] Sympathy for the conscientious objector was also alienated by the practice of preparing applicants for the tribunal hearing. The use of 'coaching' and mock tribunals was seen as an attempt to manufacture conscientious objectors. The issue was not unfamiliar. In 1907, Sir Henry Craik had raised it in the Commons: 'Let the really conscientious objector have the courage of his opinions, and not place himself in the hands of agents of anti-vaccination societies who know how to work up adherents to their cause.'[4] In the case of military service, it was the N.C.F. that was accused of working up adherents. The Fellowship's activities were strongly

[1] Minutes of County of London Appeal Tribunal, 6 March 1916.
[2] Quoted in *Manchester Guardian*, 11 May 1916.
[3] 5 HC 82, col. 1038, 11 May 1916.
[4] 4 HC 174, col. 1286, 24 May 1907.

resented by the tribunals, and in May 1916 the Chairman of the Middlesex Appeal Tribunal, Herbert Nield, the Conservative Member for Ealing, felt that it was time to write to the Home Secretary:

> The No Conscription Fellowship is responsible for much of the trouble the Tribunals are having—as a rule the objectors are quite young men 18–22 and they appear to me to be carefully coached and induced to oppose the working of the Act. I venture to hope that you will have these men very carefully watched and that you will not hesitate to proceed against them directly you have proof of their activities.[1]

In reply, Herbert Samuel stated the view that was accepted both by the Cabinet and by the War Office: it was not illegal to encourage men to claim exemption on the ground of conscience but it would be illegal to advocate refusal to obey the law.[2] To the tribunal members such a distinction would doubtless have seemed mere hair-splitting; they continued to regard with suspicion any applicants who admitted to being members of the N.C.F.

Coaching and mock tribunals did not prevent a large number of weak applications; the Fellowship of Reconciliation complained that some applications on conscientious grounds were 'trivial and shallow to the last degree'.[3] But spurious claims to exemption were not restricted to the field of conscience. 'Hardship' and 'essential employment' produced their share of claims that were shallow, even ludicrous; more than one man applied for exemption on the ground that he was the only person in his firm who knew the secret formula for making a certain product.[4] If applications on conscientious grounds were sometimes as weak, they were seldom as blatant, indeed the weakness was more likely to result from the limitations of the applicant than from his insincerity. Few conscientious objectors seem to have been able to state their position clearly and to defend it in cross-examination,[5] and this was not

[1] HO 45/10801/307402. [2] Ibid.

[3] See the Fellowship's journal, *The Venturer*, 7 April 1916.

[4] At the Lothian and Peebles Appeal Tribunal. Unfortunately the appellant did not identify the product, though certain liqueurs, including Drambuie, are produced from 'a secret formula' and might just have provided the means to fool an unsuspecting tribunal.

[5] Cf. the comments in R. S. W. Pollard, 'Conscientious Objectors in Great Britain and the Dominions', *Journal of Comparative Legislation*, 28 (1946), pp. 72–81. Pollard found that in the Second World War 'the majority of COs are quite unable to state their views logically and coherently'.

solely due to the conditions of the tribunal hearing. The Pelham Committee found that of 3,701 conscientious objectors engaged on work of national importance, only 124 had attended university; a further 707 had received a secondary education, while the remaining 2,870 had not been educated beyond the Elementary stage.[1] For the less educated man, the task of communicating the dictates of conscience was extraordinarily difficult. In a less hectic atmosphere his inarticulateness might not have mattered, but before the tribunals of 1916 it left him hopelessly vulnerable to the prosecution of the Military Representative. While the applicant groped for the correct words, he was harassed by biblical texts and hypothetical questions. And as the Quaker journal, *The Friend*, pointed out, the applicant himself was in many cases

> wholly inexperienced, often and quite naturally one-sided in his view, passionate and idealistic, sometimes over-stating his case and sometimes mis-stating it, sometimes apparently impracticable, confused by varying impulses—religious, political, economic, social—desirous of being loyal to his highest conceptions and continually embroiled in irrelevant discussions about the lowest, and always surrounded by the immense difficulties of a just and reasonable interpretation of his own convictions.[2]

There were some conscientious objectors—including the Quakers—for whom the presentation of their case was probably less important than the source of their objection. This was because the tribunals tried to adopt a uniform policy where a large number of applicants were drawn from a common source. The policy was implicit in the attitude of the tribunal members or imposed by a decision of the Central Tribunal; its impact on the way in which applications were disposed of varied, but was most marked in the case of the three largest groups of applicants—the Quakers, the Christadelphians, and the socialists.

The Military Service Act did not attempt to define conscientious objection, but Walter Long encouraged the tribunals to recognize only genuine religious or moral convictions. This definition, which was later reinforced by the decisions of the Central Tribunal, was regarded as too broad by the military, who wanted religion to be recognized as the only basis for conscientious objec-

[1] Report of the Pelham Committee, 1919, Schedule 5.
[2] *The Friend*, 5 May 1916.

tion, and as too narrow by the N.C.F., who wanted political convictions to be included. But all parties—the tribunals, the military, and the N.C.F.—agreed that *par excellence* the acceptable conscientious objector was a member of the Society of Friends. The Society itself tried to avoid preferential treatment and sought to identify with the cause of all objectors, but the high quality of the Quaker applications and the weight of the long witness against war were bound to win swift recognition. The Society's statistics show that only 11 per cent of the members who applied to the tribunals failed to establish the ground of their application.[1] Of those who were successful, the majority were exempt on the condition that they joined the Friends Ambulance Unit or the Unit's General Service Section; and although the Central Tribunal ruled that membership of the Society did not entitle an applicant to absolute exemption as of right,[2] there is little doubt that the Quakers held all but a few of those absolute exemptions that were granted.[3] The tribunal members do not appear to have been influenced by the fact that so many young Quakers had already joined the armed forces, and Military Representatives were, in effect, instructed not to oppose Quaker applications.[4] If a Quaker refused to accept the tribunal's decision, it was almost certainly because he chose this method of witnessing against compulsory military service.

The success of the Quaker applications owed something to the popular misconception that refusal of military service was a fundamental tenet of the Society. But for the Christadelphians, the tribunals' failure to understand the true nature of the sect's objection resulted in rejection rather than acceptance. It was precisely because Christadelphians were prepared to work in munitions factories that the tribunals' initial response was one of hostility. Once again it was the inconsistency that jarred; and the tribunal members were not alone in finding this difficult to under-

[1] *Extracts from the Minutes and Proceedings of the London Yearly Meeting of Friends*, 1923, pp. 231–2.

[2] R.77, L.G.B. Circular, 27 April 1916.

[3] In March and April 1916, out of 355 Quakers applying to local tribunals, 77 or about 22 per cent received absolute exemption. See *The Friend*, 12 May 1916.

[4] ACI No. 1300, 1916, instructed Military Representatives not to press opposition to applications from men who had held religious scruples against war before 1916.

stand. Before he resigned his commission, Max Plowman wrote from France:

The soldier in the trenches understands the position of the CO in prison. He doesn't understand the position of the CO who helps to provide the means for keeping soldiers in the trenches while he (the CO) is out of range.[1]

The loose organization of the Christadelphian sect did not permit a united effort to explain the sect's position to the authorities, but a prominent member of the South London Ecclesia, F. G. Jannaway, took the initiative in opening negotiations with the tribunals and the War Office. On 4 April 1916 Jannaway attended a meeting of the Central Tribunal to explain that members of the sect were willing to do work of national importance but could not accept non-combatant work within the army.[2] Two days later the Central Tribunal had worked out a formula to meet the Christadelphian objection:

The Tribunal, having satisfied themselves that the appellant is a *bona fide* Christadelphian who joined that body before the outbreak of war and that the basis of faith common to Christadelphians forbids them to take service under military authority, grant the appellant exemption from combatant service only, subject to the proviso that if within twenty-one days he undertakes work which, not being under military control, is nevertheless *useful for the prosecution of the war* under conditions approved by the Tribunal, he shall be exempt from non-combatant service so long as he continues to carry out such work under such conditions. The work proposed to be reported to the Tribunal for approval. Power is reserved to the Tribunal to extend the period of twenty-one days or to vary this order if the appellant establishes to their satisfaction that he had done his best to comply with the condition.[3]

Military Representatives and local and appeal tribunals were informed of the Central Tribunal's decision,[4] but there was no guarantee that the formula would be used. The Middlesex Appeal Tribunal decided to treat Christadelphians in accordance with the Central Tribunal's example,[5] but the County of London Appeal

[1] Plowman, op. cit., p. 104.
[2] Minutes of the Central Tribunal, 4 April 1916.
[3] Minutes of the Central Tribunal, 6 April 1916.
[4] War Office Letter to GOsC, 11 April 1916, MH 47/144; R.77, L.G.B. Circular, 27 April 1916.
[5] Minutes of Middlesex Appeal Tribunal, 19 April 1916.

Tribunal decided that each Christadelphian appeal must be considered on its individual merits.[1]

In order to safeguard the Christadelphian position still further and to obtain the release of those who had been enlisted and court-martialled, Jannaway continued to negotiate with the Army Council. He compiled a register of bona fide Christadelphians of military age, to whom the Army Council eventually agreed to grant a special 'Christadelphian Certificate of Exemption from Military Service'.[2] In August 1916 the War Office and the Central Tribunal arranged for all Christadelphian cases to be referred direct to the Pelham Committee on Work of National Importance. As a result about 1,400 Christadelphian objectors were granted exemption by the Army Council rather than by the tribunals.[3]

The exemption of the Christadelphians showed the system at its best; both the Central Tribunal and the War Office were prepared to be flexible in order to accommodate an objection that was unpopular and, at first sight, inconsistent. The Christadelphian objection may have been distasteful to the strict pacifist but it did involve a rejection of military service in all pre-apocalyptic situations, and it was this rejection for all 'time' that enabled the authorities to accept it as conscientious within the meaning of the Act. The same criterion—that the rejection of military service was for all human circumstances—was used to test the acceptability in law of other objections, and was the one clear contribution towards the definition of conscientious objection made by the Central Tribunal. The definition was logical though it barred a sincere objection to a particular conflict. It was also convenient in that it

[1] Minutes of County of London Appeal Tribunal, 17 May 1916.

[2] The Certificate stated:

> This is to certify that . . . residing at . . . a Christadelphian and a recognised conscientious objector to Military Service will not be called upon to join the Army provided he is engaged in Work of National Importance such as Agriculture, Forestry, Mining, Transport, Education, Public Utility, or such other work as may be approved of by the Committee on Work of National Importance, 26 Abingdon Street, Westminster; and that he notifies in writing that he is so engaged, on the first of every month to the undersigned, at the undermentioned address. If the holder of this certificate cease to be engaged in work such as stated above, this certificate will not be valid and he will then be called up for Military Service.

See Jannaway, op. cit., p. 199.

[3] Report of the Pelham Committee, p. 5. The Army Council Certificates were subsequently called in, and new certificates were issued by the Pelham Committee.

excluded the militant socialist objector whose recognition by the tribunals would have provoked the strongest possible protest from the War Office.

How far the intense hostility to political objectors expressed by the military leaders influenced the tribunals is not clear. From the first, Kitchener, Macready, and Childs had set their face against any suggestion that political convictions should be regarded as a ground for exemption. To the military, the socialist who refused to fight and who sought to undermine recruiting through the activities of the N.C.F., was both unpatriotic and dangerous; to grant him exemption would be to make a mockery of conscription. This view was explicit in the attitude of the Military Representatives but it is doubtful if the tribunals needed prompting; the young militants of the I.L.P. had few sympathizers among the middle-aged and elderly tribunal members. In the reaction of the tribunals and the military there was an element of political prejudice and a sense of outrage that the motives for the war should be questioned. But there was also the rational objection to socialist applications that was stated by the Central Tribunal.

The Tribunal did not give a ruling on political objections until May 1916, but this was the climax of a process of inquiry during which the Tribunal had heard orally several appellants on political grounds and interviewed representatives of socialist organizations. In the case that was the subject of the ruling, the Tribunal accepted that the appellant's views were sincere but argued that a political conviction that participation in a particular war was wrong could not be recognized as conscientious within the meaning of the law.[1] This decision was circulated to the lower tribunals on 14 June and confirmed them in their disinclination to recognize political objectors as conscientious. But by placing the emphasis on the political nature of the objection rather than on the fact that it was not an objection to war in all circumstances, the Central Tribunal had barred those objections in which political convictions were associated with moral sanctions against taking human life. Some tribunals did attempt to differentiate between the political and the politico-religious objection. In Lanarkshire, the Appeal Tribunal recognized as genuine appellants who had been educated at a Socialist Sunday School, but rejected those whose opinions derived from socialist propaganda. The Sheriff of Lanark

[1] Minutes of the Central Tribunal, 2 May 1916.

recommended this curious formula to the Central Tribunal.[1] In July the Central Tribunal modified its original decision by differentiating between applicants whose political objections were associated with 'a genuine belief that the taking of human life in any circumstances is morally wrong' and who should be given exemption, and applicants whose objection was purely political. Of the latter the Tribunal wrote:

In some the objection alleged is based on opposition to the present war; in others on disapproval of the present organisation of society, which the man considers not worthy of defence, though he would fight in defence of a State organised in a way he approves. These opinions, however genuinely and strongly held, do not, in the view of the Central Tribunal, constitute conscientious objection within the meaning of the Military Service Acts.[2]

This decision, though challenged by the organizations representing conscientious objectors,[3] remained the official interpretation of the law.

It is doubtful, however, whether this Central Tribunal ruling had any significant effect on the practice of the lower tribunals. The ruling came too late: the majority of political objectors were young, single men who had been called up long before July; and by this date the tribunals were anyway firmly wedded to their reluctance to recognize a political objection as conscientious, however closely it was associated with religious or moral convictions.

(iii)

Once the tribunal was satisfied that the ground of an application had been established, it decided what form of exemption should be granted. This decision was based not so much upon what was considered the right exemption for a particular applicant, but upon the tribunal's interpretation of its powers under the Military Service Acts and upon the Local Government Board's guiding principle that 'The exemption should be the minimum required to

[1] Minutes of the Central Tribunal, 7 July 1916.

[2] Minutes of the Central Tribunal, 25 July 1916. This decision was not circulated to tribunals until 23 August, in R.96, L.G.B. Circular.

[3] Joint Advisory Committee of the Service Committee of the Society of Friends, the Fellowship of Reconciliation and the No Conscription Fellowship, to the President of the Local Government Board, 1916: MH 47/144.

meet the conscientious scruples of the applicant.'[1] During the first three months of the tribunals' working in 1916, the exemption of conscientious objectors raised two related and overlapping problems: whether an applicant on conscientious grounds could be granted an absolute exemption, and whether he could be granted any form of exemption other than one from combatant duties only.

The tribunals' attitude towards the granting of absolute exemption was governed by the wording of the principal Act. The addition of provisions for conscientious objectors to the draft Bill had made the sub-section on exemptions ambiguous, and this ambiguity had not been entirely removed by amendments to the draft. The wording the tribunals had before them is worth repeating:

> Any certificate of exemption may be absolute, conditional, or temporary, as the authority by whom it was granted think best suited to the case, and also in the case of an application on conscientious grounds, may take the form of an exemption from combatant service only, or may be conditional on the applicant being engaged in some work which in the opinion of the Tribunal dealing with the case is of national importance.[2]

This wording was taken by some tribunals to mean that absolute exemption could not be granted to conscientious objectors.[3] At the same time the fact that the only conscientious objection recognized in the Act was to combatant service, encouraged the majority of tribunals to believe that exemption from combatant service only was the maximum that ought to be granted to applicants on conscientious grounds.

These interpretations of the law were quite different from those accepted by the conscientious objectors, who understood that the law allowed a conditional or unconditional exemption from all military service. The clash between the contradictory interpretations was bound to raise difficulties; the policy of the N.C.F. ensured that these were not confined to isolated cases.

Among the records of the Middlesex Appeal Tribunal are two explanatory notes on the exemption of conscientious objectors,

[1] R.36, L.G.B. Circular to Local Registration Authorities, 3 February 1916.

[2] Military Service (No. 2) Act, 1916, 2 (3).

[3] For specific cases, see Memorandum drawn up for Philip Kerr (Lloyd George's Private Secretary) by Hugh Thornton (Milner's Private Secretary), 19 July 1917: Lothian 139/5. Kerr was preparing a dossier on the problem of conscientious objectors for the Prime Minister.

probably drawn up by the Chairman, Herbert Nield. They express an interpretation of the Act that was held by numerous tribunals. One of the notes read:

> With regard to sub-section (d) it will be observed that the objection is limited to 'undertaking combatant service'. In view of this limitation, the ground of objection would be fully met by the granting of exemption from combatant service, and it would appear that the tribunal would not have the power under the section to grant an exemption from anything but combatant service. In other words the tribunal can grant total exemption on either of the grounds (a) (b) or (c) but when a claim is made under (d) the power to grant exemption is limited to combatant service because the ground of application is objection to combatant service.[1]

This interpretation of the law was not consistent with the Government's intentions, and on 23 March the Local Government Board wrote to all tribunals to emphasize that any of the statutory forms of exemption could be granted to applicants on conscientious grounds,[2] but Nield warned his colleagues that letters from the Board were not always accurate and if they differed from the Act and the Regulations, they were *ultra vires* and not binding on the tribunal.[3]

On 27 March, Long held a conference of appeal tribunal chairmen at which he made it clear that absolute exemption could be granted to applicants on conscientious grounds.[4] But though Long could explain and advise he could not dictate. Two days after the conference, the Middlesex Appeal Tribunal resolved that 'as a rule the maximum exemption to be granted to conscientious objectors be exemption from combatant service unless the appellant is already engaged in work which the tribunal consider to be of national importance and then so long only as he remains in that work'.[5] This resolution excluded the possibility of granting absolute exemption and the tribunal followed this guiding principle throughout the war.[6]

The organization representing conscientious objectors had no

[1] Middlesex Appeal Tribunal, MH 47 Box 144.

[2] R.70, L.G.B. Circular, 23 March 1916.

[3] Memorandum of Middlesex Appeal Tribunal, MH 47/144.

[4] R.76, Notes of Conference of Appeal Tribunal Chairmen, 27 March 1916.

[5] Minutes of the Middlesex Appeal Tribunal, 29 March 1916.

[6] The tribunal gave no absolute exemptions to conscientious objectors: Middlesex Appeal Tribunal: Statistics of Cases, MH 47/143.

doubt that tribunals such as the Middlesex were flouting the law. The N.C.F. wrote to Asquith: 'Conscientious objectors, who have every desire to remain law-abiding citizens, are now being driven outside the law, and are becoming liable to persecution simply because the provisions of the law are not being put into operation.'[1] In May, *The Friend* commented: 'The misinterpretation of the right of absolute exemption is an astonishing instance of perversity and ignorance.'[2]

When, in April, the High Court ruled that the tribunals had no power to grant absolute exemption to applicants on conscientious grounds,[3] it was evident that unless the law itself was amended, the Government's intentions would continue to be misinterpreted. In the following month, the special section in the Military Service Act (Session 2) stated unequivocally that all statutory forms of exemption could be granted to conscientious objectors.[4] But if the conscientious objectors hoped that this section would encourage tribunals to grant absolute exemption more freely, they were to be disappointed. There was no noticeable change in tribunal policy. In reply to an inquiry from an appeal tribunal, the Central Tribunal insisted that the circumstances would still have to be very exceptional for a conscientious objector to be unconditionally exempt from all military service.[5] When, in the following year, the Lord Chancellor, Lord Findlay, expressed the view that the two Military Service Acts made it clear that a conscientious objector who established the ground of his application should be granted a certificate of absolute exemption, his opinion bore little relation to the manner in which the law was being interpreted in practice.[6]

The tribunals' extreme reluctance to grant absolute exemption to conscientious objectors led to the arrest and eventual court martial and imprisonment of those applicants who refused to

[1] N.C.F. Letter to the Prime Minister, 15 April 1916.

[2] *The Friend*, 5 May 1916.

[3] Rex v. Central Tribunal *ex parte* Parton, King's Bench Division, 18 April 1916. Quoted at length in *The Justice of the Peace*, 13 January 1917.

[4] It is hereby declared that the power to grant special certificates of exemption in the case of an application on conscientious grounds under subsection (3) of section two of the principal Act is additional to and not in derogation of the general power conferred by that Act to grant an absolute, conditional, or temporary certificate in such cases.

Military Service Act, 1916 (Session 2), 4 (3).

[5] Minutes of the Central Tribunal, 6 July 1916.

[6] CAB 23/2/142.

accept any other form of exemption. These men remained a complex administrative problem for the remainder of the war. The War Office did not hesitate to put the blame on the tribunals. In 1917 Lord Derby, the Secretary of State for War, reported to the War Cabinet: '. . . it was recognized by the military authorities that there were many hundreds of men who were forced into the Army through the ineptitude of the tribunals who should have been clearly given exemption by the tribunals when acting in their statutory capacity.'[1] From inside the War Cabinet, the criticism was no less scathing; Lord Milner told his colleagues that the 'plain intention of Parliament and of the Government of the day as expressed in the Military Service Acts has been frustrated by the action of the tribunals' and that the latter's policy 'has, in fact, resulted in reversing the whole policy designed by the Government to meet cases of this kind'.[2] But it was not until January 1918 that Hayes Fisher wrote to the tribunals to ask whether there had been 'any men who claimed exemption on the grounds of conscientious objection and who were refused absolute exemption, not because the tribunal considered that such exemption was not justified in the cases in question, but because the tribunal were under the impression that they had no power to grant absolute exemption in such cases'.[3]

When the Camberwell Local Tribunal received this letter it resolved to inform the Local Government Board that the Tribunal had been 'thoroughly cogniscant (*sic*) of its powers' and that the Tribunal's policy had been to award a conditional exemption to conscientious objectors in certain cases, but never absolute exemption.[4]

Many other tribunals had decided that absolute exemptions should not, as a matter of policy, be given to conscientious objectors. The Central Tribunal itself had followed a policy similar to that of the Camberwell Tribunal:

> The Central Tribunal were never in doubt as to their power to grant absolute exemption; they were however very strongly of the opinion that in granting exemption on the condition that the man took up work of national importance to their satisfaction, they were granting it in a form which, in the words of the Act, was 'best suited to the case'.[5]

[1] CAB 23/4/246(I)(a). [2] CAB 23/4/246(I)(b).
[3] R.168, L.G.B. Letter to local and appeal tribunals, 1 January 1918.
[4] Minutes of the Camberwell Local Tribunal, 3 January 1918.
[5] Report of the Central Tribunal, p. 12.

There were, however, other tribunals that had refused to grant absolute exemption to conscientious objectors because they had been under the impression that they had no power to do so. One of these was the Middlesex. But when it received the Local Government Board's letter, it resolved to reply 'that the Tribunal had always held that it had power to grant absolute exemption in these cases'.[1] The Tribunal's records show that this had not been the case, and Herbert Nield, who had been Chairman in 1916, refused to accept the resolution because, he claimed, 'in the early days of the tribunal they had held the contrary opinion and had given decisions to this effect'.[2] Despite Nield's integrity, the other members were not inclined to admit that the Act had been misinterpreted. They resolved to tell the Local Government Board that all cases of conscientious objection had been considered on their merits, and to make no reference to the Tribunal's views on its powers to grant absolute exemption.[3]

The Middlesex Appeal Tribunal was not alone in its disinclination to admit an earlier misunderstanding of the law. Even when a tribunal was prepared to do so, such as the Denbigh Appeal Tribunal, whose clerk wrote that the majority of members 'were not aware that they had the power of granting absolute exemption in this case',[4] the confession was not made public. The Local Government Board and the Scottish Office were both able to report that their inquiries had not disclosed any case in which a man had been refused absolute exemption because the tribunal had been under the impression that it had no power to grant such exemption.[5]

Here this remarkable history of legal and administrative confusion ended. Its seeds had been sown in the manner in which the provisions for conscientious objectors had been grafted onto the draft of the Military Service Bill. Hurried drafting had left the law open to different interpretations by tribunals on one hand and applicants on the other. The fact that it was the law itself that was ambiguous meant that the problem was not susceptible of administrative solutions. At the same time the ambiguities of the law were the means by which the tribunals were able to rationalize their

[1] Minutes of the Middlesex Appeal Tribunal, 2 January 1918.

[2] Ibid., 16 January 1918. [3] Ibid.

[4] WO 32/2051/3319.

[5] See 47th Annual Report of the L.G.B. 1917–1918 (Cd. 9157), Pt. IV, p. 51, and SHHD 25478S/2447A.

reluctance to give total exemption to conscientious objectors in time of national crisis. This reluctance was reflected not only on the tribunals and the King's Bench, but also in the Cabinet and the War Office. Walter Long, though most scrupulous and persistent in clarifying the Government's intentions to the tribunals, nevertheless made it clear that he did not believe that absolute exemption ought to be given. Officially, he had always insisted that a case would have to be 'very exceptional to justify exemption free from conditions',[1] and he gave his personal view in a speech to the Commons in May: 'Are we to assume', he asked, 'that men are to get exemption on conscientious grounds and be allowed to do nothing for the service of the state? If that is the condition, I am not going to waste a moment of time considering it.'[2] On this issue General Childs's view was unequivocal, and when the opportunity arose, he urged it on the King; to George V's Assistant Private Secretary, Childs wrote, 'the day that *absolute* exemption is granted to anybody whether his objection be based on religious or on other grounds we are beaten.'[3]

The three conflicting views had existed side by side. The Government had intended that absolute exemption should be given only in very exceptional cases; the conscientious objectors believed that it should be given in any case where a man could not accept alternative service; the military and the majority of tribunals thought that it ought not to be, or could not be, given at all. These conflicting interpretations caused increasing bitterness, both among those conscientious objectors who believed that they were being denied their legal rights, and among those tribunal members, senior officers, and members of the Government who believed that the conscientious objectors were exploiting the already generous provisions of the law.

The difficulties surrounding the award of a conditional exemption were hardly less complex. When in January 1916 the power to grant an exemption conditional on the applicant being engaged in work of national importance was inserted in the draft Bill, it was clear that the Cabinet had given little thought to how the exemption would work in practice. The Act contained no definition of work of national importance and in both Act and Circulars the

[1] R.84, L.G.B. Circular, 1 June 1916.

[2] 5 HC 82, col. 1042, 11 May 1916.

[3] RA GV5910/2. The Private Secretary was Lt. Col. Clive Wigram.

matter was left to 'the opinion of the tribunal'.[1] Herbert Samuel had explained to the House how he thought this form of exemption would be applied in practice:

A man may come forward and say, 'I am a bootmaker, and want to go on making boots.' The tribunal may say, 'There are a sufficient number of bootmakers already, and really it is more important that you should become a soldier than remain a bootmaker.' Therefore the man is sent to be a soldier. But if he comes forward and states, 'I am a conscientious objector and I do not want to fight; I come under paragraph so-and-so of the Act, and I am engaged in making boots, which is work of national importance. As such I shall do useful work for the nation.' The tribunal may reply: 'While this is not a work of national importance, if you say you are a conscientious objector, and object to becoming a soldier, you will obtain your exemption.'[2]

The tribunals were criticized for not following Samuel's guidance, but the law spoke of 'work of national importance', not of work that became of national importance by virtue of being performed by a conscientious objector. The Government had issued no list of occupations that were of national importance nor had it created machinery for placing conscientious objectors in such occupations. The creation of machinery for this purpose had been discussed in January by representatives of the War Office and the Friends Ambulance Unit, but the War Office had been discouraged from taking the matter further by the reported hostility to alternative service of the young Quakers and members of the N.C.F.[3]

The tribunals' reluctance to grant conditional exemption[4] was fortified by the same arguments that were used to insist that there was no power to grant any exemption other than from combatant duties only. Those conditional exemptions that were granted during March would have been in most cases to Quakers who could find work of obvious national importance in one of the organizations associated with the name of the Society of Friends.

[1] Military Service (No. 2) Act, 1916, 2 (3); R.36, L.G.B. Circular to Local Registration Authorities, 3 February 1916.

[2] 5 HC 78, col. 451, 19 January 1916.

[3] Memorandum respecting negotiations with Lord Derby, by Sir George Newman, 15 February 1916, Rowntree 'C.O. Papers 1916–1919', Box 2.

[4] There were exceptions, including the Camberwell Local Tribunal whose policy was to grant to applicants on conscientious grounds a conditional exemption or nothing: Minutes of the Camberwell Local Tribunal, 3 January 1918.

The War Office had encouraged the extension of the Friends Ambulance Unit to take Quaker conscientious objectors and had instructed Military Representatives not to oppose those Quaker applicants who were willing to join.[1]

When the problem of conditional exemption was debated in the Commons on 22 March, the Government was urged to draw up a list of occupations that conscientious objectors could be allowed to undertake.[2] The following day Walter Long informed tribunals that the Government was engaged on the appointment of a committee 'to whom a tribunal may refer for advice as to what service of national importance an applicant for exemption on the ground of conscientious objection should undertake. . . .'[3] On 28 March it was announced that the Board of Trade had appointed the Committee on Work of National Importance under the Chairmanship of the Hon. T. H. W. Pelham, an Assistant Secretary at the Board of Trade.[4] But it was not until 14 April, two months after the tribunals had started functioning under the Act, that the Committee circulated a list of occupations that could be considered of national importance.[5] By this date many single applicants had been before the local tribunals and some had had their appeals rejected by the higher tribunals. Although it was possible to apply for a variation of a certificate of exemption, few tribunals would have been willing to grant one and the Central Tribunal decided that the appointment of the Pelham Committee was not sufficient ground for reviewing a tribunal's decision.[6]

The value of the Committee was also limited by the fact that it had no real authority: it could only make recommendations and could not help in a particular case unless the applicant was referred to it by the tribunal. The tribunals were slow to make use of the Committee. On 18 April H. J. Tennant told the Commons: 'I am afraid there has not been recourse to that Committee as largely as one could have hoped.'[7] The Middlesex Appeal Tribunal first

[1] R.70, L.G.B. Circular, 23 March 1916.

[2] By Mr. J. W. Wilson, 5 HC 81, col. 328, 22 March 1916.

[3] R.70, L.G.B. Circular, 23 March 1916.

[4] Report of the Pelham Committee, 1919, p. 1. Pelham's colleagues were the Quaker M.P., T. E. Harvey, the Labour M.P., C. Fenwick, and a Mr. C. P. Spicer. For the work of the Committee see Chapter 9, below.

[5] Committee on Work of National Importance, Preliminary List of Occupations, 14 April 1916, Pelham Committee Papers.

[6] Minutes of the Central Tribunal, 5 June 1916.

[7] 5 HC 81, col. 2258, 18 April 1916.

referred a case to the Committee at the beginning of May,[1] and on 11 May Pelham reported that the total number of applicants referred to the Committee in the first six weeks was only 265.[2]

The machinery for granting conditional exemption faced other difficulties besides the delayed appointment and limited authority of the Pelham Committee. One arose over the wording used on the certificate of exemption. Both the Lancashire (Salford) and Middlesex Appeal Tribunals were in the habit of marking certificates 'Exemption from combatant duties only conditional on the applicant being engaged on work of national importance'.[3] This wording was clearly an attempt to reconcile the limited nature of the conscientious objection recognized in law with the statutory exemption from both combatant and non-combatant service. Though intended as a conditional exemption, the first part of the wording led to the arrest of some applicants as deserters from the Non-Combatant Corps. In the Salford case it was the War Office that instructed its Military Representative to make the difference between the two forms of exemption clear to the Tribunal's Chairman, Judge Mellor, and some of the cases were subsequently reheard.[4] It is clear that other tribunals used this ambiguous wording in granting conditional exemption, for in August 1916 the Local Government Board had to urge tribunals not to confuse the two exemptions and to be clear which form of exemption they were giving.[5]

A further difficulty arose as a result of a sub-section in the principal Act which stated: 'No certificate of exemption shall be conditional upon a person to whom it is granted continuing in or entering into employment under any specified employer or in any specified place or establishment.'[6] The sub-section had been inserted as an amendment to the draft Bill as a safeguard against any form of industrial conscription,[7] but it was at variance with the other amendment specifying work of national importance as a

[1] Minutes of the Middlesex Appeal Tribunal, 8 May 1916.

[2] Minutes of the Central Tribunal, 11 May 1916.

[3] For Salford see the Minutes of the Pelham Committee, 16 May 1916, and for Middlesex see the Minutes of the Middlesex Appeal Tribunal, 10 May 1916.

[4] The details of the Salford case are given in the Minutes of the Pelham Committee, 16–24 May 1916.

[5] R.97, L.G.B. Circular, 26 August 1916.

[6] Military Service (No. 2) Act, 1916, 2 (3).

[7] 5 HC 78, col. 989, 24 January 1916. Originally proposed by Sir John Simon.

condition of exemption. This further instance of faulty drafting was subsequently amended so that the sub-section no longer applied to exemptions granted on the ground of conscientious objection.[1]

Underlying the tribunals' reluctance to exempt a conscientious objector from all military service, whether absolutely or on conditions, was the conviction that the proper role for the man who objected to fighting was the performance of non-combatant service in the army. During the long national debate on conscription, it had been widely assumed that while a sincere pacifist might abhor the business of killing, he would be prepared to undertake ancillary military duties, particularly if these involved the care and safety of the wounded. This assumption was reinforced by Asquith's speech introducing the Military Service Bill and by the wording of the law which appeared to recommend an exemption from combatant duties only for conscientious objectors. The result was that for the first two months of conscription—from mid-February to mid-April 1916—all but a few exemptions took this form; and even when the granting of a conditional exemption was facilitated by the work of the Pelham Committee, non-combatant work in the army remained the right exemption in the eyes of many tribunals.

The tribunals' enthusiasm for non-combatant duties was not shared by the applicants. The exact number who rejected this form of exemption at the tribunal hearing is not known; they are swallowed up in the total of those who left the hearing with no exemption at all. Others expressed their rejection in action rather than words. They failed to report when summoned to join the Non-Combatant Corps and were arrested. Of the 4,888 men awarded certificates of exemption from combatant duties only, 1,969 had to be arrested and were subsequently court-martialled.[2] When the Central Tribunal reviewed the cases of these men, it decided that over four-fifths of them were 'men who should undoubtedly be treated as having a conscientious objection to all military service'.[3] Though the Central Tribunal adopted a less stringent attitude in reviewing the cases of conscientious objectors who had been court-martialled, its findings indicate the extent

[1] Military Service Act, 1916 (Session 2), 5.

[2] See p. 132, below.

[3] Report of the Central Tribunal, p. 25. See also Appendix E.

to which the lower tribunals had been granting exemption from combatant service only to men who could have established their claim to exemption from all forms of military service.

Asquith's Cabinet were not unaware of what was happening. They had agreed to the appointment of the Pelham Committee, and their decision on 29 April to extend compulsion to all men of military age[1] provided an opportunity to clarify the law. The clarification was attempted,[2] but it might have been more effective if Asquith had had his way. On Sunday 30 April, Asquith had lunch with Gilbert Murray, the Regius Professor of Greek at Oxford and an advocate of a more rational and humane treatment of conscientious objectors. At lunch, Murray produced statistics from the Quaker journal *The Friend* to show the Prime Minister the extent to which the tribunals were refusing to go beyond an exemption from combatant duties only for conscientious objectors. Asquith's response was to suggest an amendment to the new Bill emphasizing alternative civilian work and giving up the non-combatant work under the military.[3] That Asquith found time to consider the matter at all is remarkable, though his critics might well have said that it was characteristic; the week-end was one of crisis, not only over the new conscription Bill but also in Ireland, where the Easter Rebellion had been defeated only two days previously, and in Mesopotamia where General Townshend's division had just surrendered to the Turks. It is not surprising that neither the Cabinet nor the War Office was in a mood to accept further concessions to the conscientious objectors; and Asquith was no longer strong enough politically to press the amendment on his colleagues.[4]

Whatever form of exemption was granted, the applicant knew that it was not final. The certificate could be varied by a higher tribunal or by the issuing tribunal on its own initiative. In theory this gave the conscientious objector protection against the lack of uniformity in local decisions; in practice, it enabled the military to keep a tight rein on local tribunals that were inclined to be generous. Even the Local Government Board regarded the appeal

[1] CAB 37/146/24. [2] See p. 120, above.

[3] This meeting is reconstructed from two letters: Gilbert Murray to T. E. Harvey, 30 April 1916, T. E. Harvey Papers, and Philip Morrell to Gilbert Murray, 2 May 1916, Gilbert Murray Papers, 2.

[4] For the difficulties of Asquith's position at the time see Jenkins, op. cit., pp. 391–4.

procedure as a safeguard for the military rather than for the applicant.[1] The chances of a conscientious objector himself obtaining a 'better' form of exemption by appealing were small. The Middlesex, one of whose 'guiding principles' was that it should hesitate before upsetting the decisions of a local tribunal, dismissed 70 per cent of the appeals by conscientious objectors.[2] The Central Tribunal took a less negative view, but only those cases in which the conscientious objection raised a question of principle reached this level.

Military Representatives also used the variation procedure to pull back ground lost at the tribunals. A Christadelphian who was fined by the Rotherham magistrates for knocking out a horse's eye while working on a farm, provided the Military Representative with an opportunity to apply to the South Yorkshire Appeal Tribunal for a variation of the man's certificate on the grounds that cruelty to animals was inconsistent with conscientious objection to military service.[3] The power to vary a certificate was so deeply resented by conscientious objectors that one of the first questions put to Neville Chamberlain in 1939 when he reintroduced conscription, was whether men granted exemption by the tribunals would be free from interference from the military.[4]

The practice of variation might have complicated the task of analysing the tribunal decisions but fortunately the statistics refer in almost every case to certificates of exemption that were 'still in force' at a late stage in the war. Despite the existence of these statistics, however, no official or unofficial analysis of tribunal decisions has been published. This omission has resulted in the popular assumption that the majority of conscientious objectors were refused exemption.[5] Though a completely accurate analysis

[1] 46th Annual Report of the L.G.B. 1916–1917, I, pp. 19–22.

[2] Middlesex Appeal Tribunal: Statistics of Cases, MH 47/143.

[3] *The Justice of the Peace*, 26 January 1918.

[4] The question was put by George Lansbury, 5 HC 346, col. 2099, 4 May 1939; this point was met in the National Service (Armed Forces) Act, 1939, 5 (8).

[5] The assumption is implicit in a number of discussions and statements on the treatment of conscientious objectors in the First World War. See e.g. Graham, op. cit., p. 69; Denis Hayes, *Challenge of Conscience: the story of the Conscientious Objectors 1939–1949*, London, 1949, p. 71; Stephen Hobhouse, *Forty Years and an Epilogue: an autobiography, 1881–1951*, London, 1951, p. 155; and Ernest Bevin's statement in the Commons, 5 HC 381, col. 912–13, 9 July 1942.

cannot be made, there is enough evidence to show that this assumption is incorrect.

Not all conscientious objectors were the subjects of tribunal decisions. 1,400 Christadelphians were granted certificates of exemption by the Army Council[1] and a further 1,234 men did not apply to the tribunals on the grounds of conscientious objection.[2] Thus of the approximate total of 16,500 conscientious objectors, only about 13,866 were the subjects of tribunal decisions. The Central Tribunal estimated that to September 1918 the number of exemptions from all military service issued on conscientious grounds by the tribunals and still in force was 5,111.[3] Of these 4,729 had been granted by tribunals in England and Wales, 250 by tribunals in Scotland, and 132 by the Central Tribunal itself. These certificates were of three types: absolute, conditional on the applicant being engaged in work of national importance, and 'other certificates'. The latter would have been forms of conditional exemption, granted, in most cases, to men who had applied both on conscientious grounds and on the grounds that their work was in the national interest or that hardship would ensue if they were enlisted.

The exact number of absolute exemptions is not known. In August 1917 Lord Derby reported to the War Cabinet that between four and five hundred absolute exemptions had been granted to conscientious objectors,[4] and in April 1919 a Government spokesman gave the total as 600.[5] In neither case was any indication given whether the total included the absolute exemptions granted to members of the Friends Ambulance Unit by the Army Council. It is known, however, that to 28 April 1917 the tribunals in England and Wales had issued 270 absolute exemptions that were still in force[6] and that the figure for Scotland to 30 November 1917 was 44.[7] It is probable, therefore, that no more than 350 absolute exemptions were granted and allowed to remain in force.

[1] See Report of the Pelham Committee, 1919, pp. 5–6.
[2] Report of the Central Tribunal, p. 25; see also Appendix E below.
[3] Supplementary Report of the Central Tribunal, 1922.
[4] CAB 23/4/246(I)(a).
[5] Viscount Peel, 5 HL 34, col. 162, 3 April 1919.
[6] See Appendix F.
[7] SHHD 25478S/2384. The Scottish figures are less reliable because they are based on tribunal returns that have not been officially correlated and may not be complete.

It has been shown that approximately 2,919 men were granted a certificate of exemption from combatant service only and served in the Non-Combatant Corps.[1] A further 1,969 were granted this form of exemption and, refusing to serve, were court-martialled in the army.[2] These two groups give a total of 4,888. But in England and Wales 5,617 certificates of exemption from combatant service only were still in force on 28 April 1917,[3] and a further 624 were still in force in Scotland on 30 November 1917.[4] These figures suggest that between 1,000 and 1,500 men were given a certificate of exemption from combatant duties only, but did not serve in the Non-Combatant Corps or suffer court martial in the army. Under Army Council Instruction 551 of 1916, all men holding these certificates were to be posted to the Non-Combatant Corps, but at no time could the Corps have included these extra men. If, on the other hand, these men had renounced their conscientious objection and undertaken combatant service, their certificates would not have been 'still in force'. The only satisfactory explanation for these extra certificates of exemption from combatant service only, is that these were the cases in which the tribunal granted an exemption from combatant service only conditional on the applicant being engaged in work of national importance. It has been shown that in 1916 a number of tribunals were in the habit of granting this hybrid exemption, and it is probable that in the return of tribunal statistics this was entered as an exemption from combatant service only. In practice, however, it was a conditional exemption from all military service and in an analysis of the tribunals' decisions should be counted as such.

With the help of these figures it is possible to analyse the position of the conscientious objectors in relation to the tribunals.

The figures (see table, p. 132) indicate the two most important conclusions that can be drawn from the work of the tribunals in the First World War. The tribunals granted some form of exemption to over 80 per cent of those conscientious objectors who were the subjects of their decisions. The figure may be consistent with the view that the tribunals' investigation of claims was perfunctory; it is not consistent with the view that the majority of tribunals allowed prejudice or intolerance to dictate their decisions. On the

[1] See p. 71 above.
[2] Report of the Central Tribunal, p. 25; see also Appendix E.
[3] See Appendix F.
[4] SHHD 25478S/2384.

Tribunal decisions

1. Exempt from all military service:	
(a) Absolutely or conditionally	5,111
(b) 'From combatant service only conditional on being engaged on work of national importance'	1,000–1,500
2. Exempt from combatant service only:	
(a) Served in the Non-Combatant Corps	2,919
(b) Refused to serve and court-martialled	1,969
3. Refused exemption by the tribunal	2,425
Number of conscientious objectors that were the subjects of tribunal decisions	approx. 13,700
Others	
1. Conditionally exempt by the Army Council	1,400
2. Did not apply for exemption on the grounds of conscientious objection	1,234
3. Miscellaneous[1]	224
	2,858
Total number of all conscientious objectors	approx. 16,500

other hand, the tribunals failed to satisfy the 1,969 men who refused to serve in the Non-Combatant Corps, and the 2,425 who were refused exemption; a further 92 conscientious objectors received other certificates of exemption that they were unable to accept or that expired with the lapse of time.[2] Thus, of the 13,700 who were the subjects of tribunal decisions, 4,486 left the tribunals dissatisfied and determined to resist coercion. The machinery of conscription ensured that the problem of what to do with these men passed from the tribunals to the military.

It was a measure of the tribunals' success that they were able to grant a form of exemption to so many conscientious objectors; it was a measure of their failure that there were nevertheless a large number of cases in which they were unable to match the form of exemption to the objection of the applicant. Both the success and the failure have to be seen in the context of the

[1] The Central Tribunal reviewed the cases of 224 men after 31 December 1918, and these cases do not therefore appear in the analysis in the Report of the Central Tribunal, p. 25. In the analysis given here, they would be distributed between 2(b) and 3 under '*Tribunal decisions*' and 2 under '*Others*'.

[2] Report of the Central Tribunal, p. 25.

tribunals' difficulties. The tribunals' role in the military recruiting organization, the uncompromising policy advocated by the N.C.F., the pressures of time, and the limitations of the Government's provisions, all made it hard for the members to avoid coming to decisions that were unacceptable to some applicants. In 1916 the Local Government Board reported:

> . . . the admirable manner in which the work has on the whole been done is no small tribute to the high standard of local government attained in this country, and to the public spirit of the members of the tribunals.[1]

While the tribunals may not have earned this glowing testimonial, neither did they deserve the harsh criticism that was directed against them both by the military and by the conscientious objectors, and that became the judgement of posterity.

[1] 45th Report of the L.G.B., 1915–1916 (Cd. 8331), Pt. I, pp. 22–4.

CHAPTER SEVEN

OBSTINATE MULES AND RAMPANT GRIFFINS

Some of the conscientious objectors are obstinate mules but the military authorities are like rampant griffins and I think there is a good deal of unnecessary friction and suffering.

Gilbert Murray to Herbert Samuel, 19 April 1916[1]

The tribunal decision divided the conscientious objectors into two groups: those who accepted the decision and raised few subsequent problems, and those who, in rejecting the decision, forced the government of the day to take further legal or administrative measures to deal with them. The former, though no less important as conscientious objectors, must occupy a subordinate place in this part of the story; their post-tribunal experiences are described in a single chapter.[2] It is in the treatment of those men who refused to accept the tribunal's decision that the conflict between conscience and politics was most acute and most revealing; and it is with this aspect of the conflict that the remaining chapters are primarily concerned.

There were 5,944 conscientious objectors who either refused to accept the tribunal's decision or failed to apply to a tribunal on the ground of conscientious objection.[3] All these men had been 'deemed . . . to have been duly enlisted' by the Military Service Act and were liable for service for the period of the war. If they failed to comply with a notice paper calling them to the colours,[4] they were arrested by the civil police and charged as deserters; a court of summary jurisdiction fined them and placed them in military custody.[5] The conscientious objectors went quietly; they

[1] Gilbert Murray Papers, 2. [2] Chapter 9 below.

[3] The total is given in Supplementary Report of Central Tribunal, 1922.

[4] Army Form W.3236. The form gave the time and place at which the recruit was to report; if he failed to report, a second form was sent, but any subsequent failure was reported to the civil police.

[5] The procedure is described in *Registration and Recruiting*, pp. 13–15.

were already subject to military law but (with very few exceptions) they did not choose to disobey an order until they were physically as well as legally in the army's power. Once they had passed through the gates of the castle or barracks that served as the Area Headquarters, they soon made it clear that they were determined to resist all attempts to make them soldiers: they refused to undergo a medical examination, to sign documents, to put on uniform. The Headquarters permanent staff had received no special instructions on how to respond to this challenge; they had no authority to relax the letter of the law or to waive those parts of the reception procedure that provoked disobedience. Asquith and his Cabinet colleagues had not anticipated this confrontation between the inflexibility of military discipline and the uncompromising resistance of men for whom obedience would have been a breach of faith. The official view was that only the insincere applicants would leave the tribunals without a certificate of exemption and once they were inside the barrack gates their bluff would soon be called by the realities of military life. This view underestimated both the difficulties of the tribunals and the courage of the individual objector; by the beginning of May the number of soldiers refusing orders on the grounds of conscientious objection had already reached one hundred and was increasing rapidly.[1] Faced with this threat to the discipline of the army, the Adjutant-General wrote a memorandum for Lord Kitchener which the latter circulated to the Cabinet on 15 May. Macready's document could have left the Cabinet members in no doubt of the military point of view:

> It cannot be too clearly understood that once a man is handed over by a decision of a tribunal to the military authorities as a soldier, it is not for the military authorities to consider the reasons such a man may have for refusing to do his work. It is the clear duty of every commanding officer to do his best with the legitimate means at his disposal to make every man who is handed over to him an efficient soldier.[2]

It was now imperative that the Cabinet should agree a policy that would prevent not only the undermining of military discipline at a time when the army was calling up thousands of conscripts but also the ultimate consequences of the use of 'legitimate means' to force obedience to military law. Discussions between the War

[1] *The Tribunal* gives the total as 102 on 1 May and 689 on 26 May. See the issues for 4 May and 1 June 1916 respectively.

[2] CAB 37/147/35.

Office and members of the Government began at once. Whatever policy emerged, however, the Cabinet could not prevent conscientious objectors coming under military law unless Parliament agreed to alter the basis of the Military Service Act, and there was no chance of this agreement being sought or given. The problem of the treatment of conscientious objectors in the army might be mitigated but could not be eliminated altogether. This had been evident to Macready from the outset and he had already established a new branch of the Directorate of Personal Services—to be known as AG3(CO)[1]—with special responsibility for soldiers whose acts of disobedience were inspired by conscientious objection. The Directorate's primary concern was the discipline of the army, so that this was a logical extension of its work. Macready had had a further reason for choosing this sub-division of his own department: the Director of Personal Services, Brigadier-General Childs, had shown on previous occasions that he was capable of handling a challenge to military authority with a combination of firmness and finesse rarely demonstrated by regular officers. Childs, who remained Director of Personal Services until 1921, thus became the man who, more than any other, both dictated and personified the army's policy for the treatment of conscientious objectors.

Borlase Wyndham Childs was an unusual soldier. As a young law student articled to his father's practice in Liskeard, he had volunteered for service in the South African War, and had been offered a regular commission, a privilege normally reserved for the cadets of Woolwich and Sandhurst. His military experience had been almost entirely as a staff officer; he had quelled mutinies and dispersed riots but had never held a command on active service. In 1916 he was thirty-nine, and despite his narrow experience, had risen from the rank of captain to that of brigadier-general in the space of five years. In his accelerated promotion an important factor had been his close association with Nevil Macready. The two officers had met fourteen years earlier in circumstances that were calculated to make a lasting impression on the future Adjutant-General. As Chief Staff Officer of Cape Colony, Macready received a telegram informing him that a mutiny had occurred at Stellenbosch, an 'ashbin' camp thirty miles to the north where soldiers awaiting embarkation were dumped sometimes for weeks

[1] The records of AG3(CO) are in WO 32/2051–5.

on end. Macready travelled north at once, but when he arrived he found the mutiny put down, two of the mutineers killed, and the remainder under close arrest. The young officer responsible was Second Lieutenant Childs.[1] A few months later Macready offered Childs the post of Garrison Adjutant at Cape Town. It was the start of a working friendship between the two officers that lasted until 1918. When Macready became Director of Personal Services he chose Childs as his Staff Captain; when he went to France as Adjutant-General to the BEF, Childs followed as his assistant; in 1916 they returned to the War Office together. 'It was to him . . .', Childs wrote later, 'that I owe everything in my military life.'[2] To Childs, Macready was always 'my beloved chief': to Macready, Childs was known simply as 'Fido'.

Childs had been trained as a lawyer and his approach to the problems of discipline in the army was characterized by a respect for the supremacy of the law and a dislike of any person or movement that smacked of subversion or anarchy. He was intelligent and urbane, ruthless in his pursuit of irregularities, but charming in his negotiations with the leaders of discontent. This ability to combine a firm hand with a conciliatory approach earned him a reputation for duplicity, but it was a quality that made him an indispensable member of Macready's team. In 1910, Childs accompanied Macready to the Rhondda Coalfield where twelve thousand miners were on strike.[3] There had been looting in the Tonypandy and Aberdare valleys and the colliery owners were demanding a show of military force. Macready thought otherwise. He instructed Childs to make contact with the miners' leaders and discover their complaints. With tact and skill Childs won the confidence of the strike committees so that the militant young marxists of the Tonypandy Plebs Club soon preferred to trust him rather than the civilian spokesmen. Childs was equally skilful in his dealings with those who complained of the army's treatment of conscientious objectors, but on this issue he found it more difficult to inspire trust; however sympathetic, he was still regarded as a member of the opposition whereas at Tonypandy he had been able to adopt a neutral role. Childs recognized an ambivalence in his own

[1] Macready, op. cit., I, p. 128.

[2] Major-General Sir Wyndham Childs, *Episodes and Reflections*, London, 1930, p. 68.

[3] Childs's role is described in Macready, op. cit., pp. 139–49.

attitude: 'I used to find myself torn between conflicting emotions—contempt for the Conscientious Objector in the main, and intense sympathy which I could not keep within bounds when I came across specific cases of Conscientious Objectors who were brutally treated, as I am sorry to say was sometimes the case.'[1] The conflict between sympathy for the individual and dislike of the movement as a whole was not always easy to resolve, and it sometimes led Childs to go further in conversation with the friends of conscientious objectors than he was prepared to go in practice. 'He was an able man,' wrote John Graham, 'and among the qualities which constituted his ability was an affable and courteous attitude towards the friends of the persecuted. He was always accessible, agreeable and reasonable. But beneath the velvet glove was the iron hand, and with all the mutual courtesies there were many disappointments.'[2] Others who were concerned for the welfare of conscientious objectors found less to admire in the Director of Personal Services. To Clifford Allen, the Chairman of the N.C.F., Childs was an 'arch rascal', a trimmer who was prepared to suit his policy to the whims of his political masters;[3] and Margaret Hobhouse, campaigning for the release of her son, Stephen, found Childs 'a painstaking and well-disposed man but narrow, red-tapey and quite unable to appreciate the psychology of the CO. . . .'[4]

It was to be expected that as head of AG3(CO) Childs should be mistrusted by those he was trying to help: suspicion of his motives was inherent in the relations between the conscientious objectors and the military. The policy that he adopted—and that Kitchener and Macready endorsed—was unquestionably fair in theory: he argued that a conscientious objector who was subject to military law must have the same protection against ill-treatment and unauthorized punishments as any other soldier. 'My attitude', he wrote after the discovery of a particularly bad case of victimization, 'has always been and will be as long as I hold my appointment, that British soldiers will be treated in accordance with the law.'[5] The success of this policy was neither immediate nor unqualified.

[1] Childs, op. cit., p. 152. [2] Graham, op. cit., p. 64.

[3] Clifford Allen's Diary, 6 February 1918, Clifford Allen Papers.

[4] Margaret Hobhouse to Tom Jones, 21 June 1917, Lothian 139/5. Tom Jones was Assistant Secretary to the Cabinet and confidant of Lloyd George.

[5] Childs to Lt.-Gen. the Rt. Hon. Sir J. G. Maxwell, 17 August 1917, WO 32/2054/1654.

As the number of conscientious objectors arrested and handed over increased, Childs complained to Macready that he was being 'inundated with letters of every kind and description from irresponsible people' alleging that these objectors were being ill-treated.[1] Childs's policy was to ignore those letters that he regarded as general and irresponsible, and to follow up specific complaints with enquiries to the District Commander; '. . . but to date,' he claimed in mid-May, 'the result of enquiry has in every case proved that the allegations have either been entirely unfounded or grossly exaggerated.'[2] A year later Childs took a different view: 'In the early days of the problem of the conscientious objector there was a considerable amount of ill-treatment to the extent of attempting by physical means to enforce compliance with orders and it was one of the problems I had to tackle.'[3] Childs's inclination to play down the charges brought against the military in the spring and early summer of 1916 was not an attempt to suppress the truth. The sheer number of trivial complaints tended to discredit authentic allegations of ill-treatment; and where the latter were concerned, Childs shared with other soldiers a tolerance of what was euphemistically described as 'horseplay' that encouraged him to underestimate the effect on liberal and pacifist opinion of even the most lighthearted attempts to turn conscientious objectors into soldiers. The argument that a little horseplay between soldiers was to be expected was for some weeks used by Kitchener and his Under-Secretary, H. J. Tennant, as an official reply to those who claimed that conscientious objectors were being roughly handled.[4] Men who as public schoolboys or officer cadets had survived the rigours of initiation saw no reason to fuss when a recruit was subjected to what they regarded as 'ragging'. But this was precisely the sort of behaviour, with its overtones of institutionalized violence, that the conscientious objectors and their supporters abominated. The facts in a particular case were not so much in dispute as open to different interpretations. It was not uncommon for a conscientious objector who refused to put on

[1] WO 32/2055/6923. [2] Ibid.

[3] Childs to Lt.-Col. Clive Wigram, 17 September 1917, RA GV5910/2.

[4] On 1 June 1916 Kitchener and Childs received a deputation of Free Church leaders who were concerned about the treatment of conscientious objectors. The official report of the meeting records that 'It was also pointed out that inevitably in the life of a soldier in barracks there was bound to be a certain amount of horseplay amongst soldiers.' Kitchener 74/WS/73.

uniform to be relieved of his civilian clothes by force or by fraud. To regular officers such treatment was unremarkable; to the nonconformist conscience it was intolerable. *The Times* thought it all rather undignified: 'they [the conscientious objectors] seem to have been handled in a singularly crude and ineffective fashion, more worthy of schoolboys than of a great state.'[1]

If the army's tolerance of horseplay encouraged Childs to dismiss some complaints as irresponsible, his own hostility to the N.C.F. tempted him to deny its members even those safeguards that were available to the ordinary soldier. Childs and his colleagues could not understand why the Cabinet allowed the N.C.F. to carry on its activities when victory might well depend on the success of conscription. The War Office from Kitchener downwards made the mistake of believing that membership of the N.C.F. was synonymous with the acceptance of subversive aims, and that members resisting military orders were part of a plot to undermine the discipline and morale of the army.[2] This interpretation was accurate for some members of the N.C.F. but not for all: there were many whose refusal to obey orders was no more than a personal witness against conscription. Childs was not at first prepared to make any distinction: he told Macready, 'as far as I am concerned, I have no intention whatever of making any investigation as to the treatment of members of this organization.'[3] If Childs had acted in accordance with this statement, he would have turned a blind eye to some of the worst cases of ill-treatment, but when it came to the point he was unable to do so. In the conflict between his sympathy for the individual and his antagonism towards the organization, his sympathy won. In time he came to rely on the officers of the N.C.F. to provide him with information, and when their allegations proved correct he did not hesitate to act. But the ambivalence remained: even while he was co-operating with the N.C.F., he was seeking ways to suppress the Fellowship for good; and he never abandoned his conviction that if the politically motivated objector was not subjected to the full rigours of military discipline, the nation's war effort would be weakened, perhaps irreparably.

It was fortunate for the War Office that the majority of commanding officers were puzzled rather than aggressive when first

[1] *The Times*, 6 July 1916. [2] Kitchener 74/WS/72.
[3] WO 32/2055/6923.

confronted with recruits who refused to obey orders. George Sutherland, a mathematical master at Harrow before he was arrested, wrote from the Happy Valley Camp at Shoreham:

The colonel resolutely refuses to punish us; to avoid friction instructions are issued that we shall be given no military orders. Some of us have started cutting turf with a view to tilling the ground and planting cabbages, which the colonel promises will go to the civil population. The RSM is greatly distressed about the whole business. He put us all into a large detention room together last night and says they will have to wire the War Office to put up a bigger one.[1]

This comic opera situation was not necessarily typical, but neither was the military brutality to conscientious objectors that was to become one of the most persistent myths of the First World War. There were a few authenticated cases of cruelty that could not possibly be dismissed as horseplay, and it is these that have been remembered, but for the most part conscientious objectors handed over to the military were treated with tolerance, even kindness, and received only those punishments that were prescribed by the Army Act. On 19 May, *The Friend* paid this tribute:

We desire at once to acknowledge the courtesy and consideration of many military officers, particularly those in high command and we make no general criticism of military authority. Over and over again military officers have shown kindness and forbearance in these awkward circumstances.[2]

Even more significant was the tribute of the N.C.F., published in *The Tribunal*:

We have to acknowledge a decided improvement in the treatment of conscientious objectors by the military authorities. With some exceptions, notably three cases of alleged brutal ill-treatment which we are investigating, our men are receiving a fair measure of consideration. In many cases we find officers and men expressing sympathy with their views and in most cases their sincerity is acknowledged.[3]

The reaction of officers and men to the conscientious objectors in their midst is the more remarkable when it is remembered that the summer of 1916, the period during which the number of conscientious objectors in military hands reached its peak, was

[1] *The Friend*, 19 May 1916. [2] Ibid. [3] 4 May 1916.

also the time when the British army first experienced casualty lists that ran into tens of thousands on a single day. The Battle of the Somme opened on 1 July and continued until October. If the mounting losses intensified feeling against conscientious objectors this was not reflected in the behaviour of the military authorities; on the contrary complaints of ill-treatment became rarer as commanding officers concentrated on accelerating the transfer of conscientious objectors to civilian control. In both wars, active hostility to conscientious objectors coincided with times of military crisis, such as April 1918 and the early summer of 1940, rather than with the news of heavy casualties.[1] In 1916 the use of physical or mental pressure to force conscientious objectors to obey orders was the exception not the rule; this was acknowledged not only by the conscientious objector 'press' but also by those M.P.s whose Quaker or socialist connections made them the recipients of allegations against the military. Arnold Rowntree and Philip Snowden agreed that instances of ill-treatment represented only a small proportion of the cases of conscientious objectors handed over to the army.[2] But the suffering could not be ignored merely because it affected only a few. 'I could give instances of extraordinary kindness . . .,' Rowntree told the Commons, 'and I do feel that these exceptional cases of bullying want meeting and meeting sternly.'[3] It was easier for the War Office to accept Rowntree's mild rebuke than to give a guarantee that bullying would never occur. Kitchener, Macready, and Childs all insisted that if horseplay became physical coercion the military personnel would be severely punished, but quite apart from the varying interpretations put on the word horseplay, hard evidence was difficult to obtain. When it was obtainable, Childs acted promptly and in accordance with his declared policy. His position was not unlike that of a headmaster: he sincerely deplored the ill-treatment of soldiers and he believed that it reflected badly both on the army and on his own department; like a headmaster he was inclined to regard a certain amount of ragging as normal, but to react strongly when a serious case of victimization was uncovered, particularly if the circumstances implied a measure of contempt for his own authority.

[1] See p. 189, below, and Rae, op. cit., p. 346.
[2] 5 HC 82, col. 2633 and 2658, 30 May 1916.
[3] 5 HC 82, col. 2633, 30 May 1916.

Childs's methods are best illustrated by two cases in the summer of 1917. Long before this the politicians and the military had decided that conscripts whose refusal to obey orders was inspired by conscientious objection should be placed under the Home Office;[1] and a letter had gone out to all District Commanders warning them that in no circumstances was physical coercion to be used to persuade these men to become soldiers. This letter—dated 19 September 1916—bore the unmistakable stamp of Childs's drafting:

I am commanded by the Army Council to inform you that it appears from reports that have been received in this Department that in certain instances attempts have been made by Commanding Officers to compel conscientious objectors to perform their military duties by ignoring acts of grave insubordination and ensuring compliance by physical means. . . . It should be clearly pointed out to all concerned that the treatment of the conscientious objector who is resisting lawful military commands should be exactly similar to that accorded to any other soldier who is guilty of acts of insubordination . . ., that any special treatment in the way of coercion other than by the methods of punishment laid down in the Army Act and King's Regulations is strictly prohibited, and that very serious notice will be taken of any irregularities in this respect which may come to light.[2]

In June 1917, nearly a year after the publication of this letter, the N.C.F. informed Childs that the authorities at Atwick Camp, near Hull, had used physical coercion to persuade a conscientious objector, Private John Gray, to accept military service.[3] Childs established a court of enquiry at once. The court found that Gray had been repeatedly pushed into a pond in the camp, that he had been frog-marched and punched on the mouth. The allegations published in *The Tribunal* some weeks later would appear to have been substantially correct: Gray had been stripped naked and a rope tied round his waist; he had then been totally immersed in the pond eight or nine times, the rope being used to pull him out after each ducking.[4] The Commanding Officer, Lt.-Col. Gresson,

[1] On 22 May 1916, see p. 159, below.

[2] The text of the letter was given by Macpherson in 5 HC 96, col. 873, 23 July 1917.

[3] The details of Private Gray's case are in WO 32/2055/1714.

[4] *The Tribunal*, 12 July 1917.

defended his treatment of Gray in terms that should have caused some heart-searching at the War Office:

In the old days, cadets at Sandhurst were ducked in the lake by other cadets. Also at Hythe, officers were ducked in the canal, and I maintain that when officers have undergone this treatment without lowering discipline and prestige of the Army, and usually with beneficial results, then a private soldier subjected to the same treatment suffers no indignity or injustice.[1]

This was the theory of horseplay come home to roost but it did not deter Childs from taking action. Gresson had clearly disobeyed the War Office letter and Childs saw to it that on this charge he was relieved of his command and placed on half pay. Gray's fate remains a mystery. Although he had accepted military service only under duress, he does not appear to have gone back on this decision. Gresson (who no doubt considered Gray's attitude as further vindication of his own behaviour) was made available for re-employment in the army in November 1917.

Three days after he had first heard of Gray's case, Childs received another letter from the N.C.F.: it contained allegations that would have seemed exaggerated or entirely false to anyone unfamiliar with the camp and the officers involved.[2] The N.C.F. claimed that at South Sea Lane Camp, Cleethorpes, a conscientious objector, Private James Brightmore, had been sentenced to solitary confinement in a pit some ten feet deep and three feet in diameter, dug within the camp area. However extraordinary these allegations, Childs must have suspected that they were true. He had already had trouble with the Camp Commandant at Cleethorpes, Brigadier-General G. S. Elliot, who earlier in the year had sent five conscientious objectors to France in defiance of War Office instructions. On the day that Childs received the N.C.F. letter, he sent a priority telegram to General Maxwell at Northern Command:[3]

Continual complaints being received that conscientious objectors of 3rd Manchesters at Cleethorpes Camp are being ill-treated and subjected to irregular and illegal procedure. . . . Send staff officer at once to investigate and personally interview every conscientious objector in this unit. . . .

[1] Gresson's statement in WO 32/2055/1714.

[2] The details of Private Brightmore's case are given in WO 32/2054/1654.

[3] Lt.-Gen. the Rt. Hon. Sir J. G. Maxwell had been in command of the troops in Dublin during the Easter Rising, 1916.

Before Childs received a report from Cleethorpes, the *Manchester Guardian* published a letter written by James Brightmore and said to have been smuggled out of the camp by a friendly soldier;[1] Brightmore's description of his own suffering suggests a degree of hysteria, but in the circumstances this is hardly surprising. The publication of the letter placed the War Office in a difficult position: without a report from General Maxwell's staff officer, Childs could neither confirm nor deny Brightmore's allegations. When the report did come, Childs told Maxwell that it was 'eminently unsatisfactory' and demanded to know the full story. It was all too obvious that the staff officer, Major Fryer, had undertaken nothing more exhaustive than a conversation with the Camp Adjutant. While Fryer was sent back to Cleethorpes, the Under-Secretary, Ian Macpherson, was obliged to stall in the Commons: in answer to a question on the case, Macpherson replied that 'the matter yet remains somewhat obscure and I am making further inquiry'.[2] Fryer's second report opened with the admission that on his previous visit he had been misinformed by the Adjutant: Brightmore had indeed been sentenced to confinement in a pit five and a half feet deep. Although there may have been disagreement on the exact dimensions of the pit, it was clear that the principal charges against the authorities at Cleethorpes were correct. The senior officers at the camp put up a hasty but ineffective smokescreen. Major Grimshaw, the Commanding Officer of the 3rd Manchesters, claimed that Brightmore had been treated with 'undue leniency', a view that was supported a little too exactly by General Elliot. 'I enquired personally into this case on the spot', Elliot explained, 'and concluded that he had been treated with undue leniency.' Both officers may have hoped that the Adjutant would be held responsible, as it was he who had ordered that Brightmore should be isolated from the other men as he was 'a danger to discipline'. If the Adjutant had acted unwisely, there were, as Elliot pointed out, extenuating circumstances: 'It should be stated that the Adjutant has lost his mental balance through worry and illness. He has been suffering for some time and is now about to undergo a serious abdominal operation.'

The Adjutant—Captain MacBean—was found to be permanently unfit for military service and Childs took no action

[1] *Manchester Guardian*, 30 June 1917. [2] 5 HC 95, col. 1305, 5 July 1917.

against him. But for Elliot and Grimshaw, Childs had no sympathy; he described their treatment of Brightmore as 'disgraceful' and 'grossly inhuman', and he argued that neither man could be permitted to retain his command. Elliot was relieved of his appointment; Grimshaw was called upon to resign, which he did with bad grace, writing an angry letter to the *Daily Mail* to complain of 'the iniquitous manner' in which he had been treated.[1] Earlier in the year this newspaper had conducted a campaign against the leniency shown to conscientious objectors, and had published pictures of conscientious objectors alongside those of wounded soldiers.[2] Of Grimshaw's letter, the paper commented that it 'would be read with general sympathy and indignation'. Four days later this comment was withdrawn; the Editor's explanation of this volte face could not have expressed the War Office point of view more accurately if Childs had dictated it himself: 'Such irregular and illegal punishments are quite rightly forbidden by the Army authorities and it was owing to such a breach of military law that the War Office took action against the responsible officers.'[3]

In private, Macready and Childs found themselves urged to show clemency, particularly in the case of Elliot. They had good reason to resist these appeals: this was not the first time that Elliot had, in Macready's words, 'played the fool with conscientious objectors'.[4] It was not until the final months of the war that Elliot and Grimshaw were re-employed. Elliot retired from the army in 1920. In the previous year he had been awarded the C.B.E., which together with the Order of the White Eagle of Serbia, 4th Class, represented the extent of official recognition of his services during the war. It was a not inconsiderable reward for a man who had defied and embarrassed his superiors. Elliot's military career, if hardly distinguished, retains some curiosity value, for apart from his clash with conscientious objectors he held a number of colourful appointments including that of British staff officer attached to the Macedonian Gendarmerie. As for James Brightmore, it was decided that the sooner he was out of military hands the better; although his application for exemption had

[1] *Daily Mail*, 14 September 1917. [2] Ibid., 23, 24, 27, and 30 April 1917.
[3] Ibid., 18 September 1917.
[4] Macready to Maj-Gen. Sir S. B. Von Donop, 23 July 1917, WO 32/2054/1654.

previously been rejected, his conscientious objections were now discovered to be sincere, and he was transferred to the civilian control of the Home Office Scheme.

The cases of John Gray and James Brightmore were exceptional but significant. A brigadier-general, a lieutenant-colonel, and a major commanding a battalion, had all been removed from their positions; technically their offence was failure to act in accordance with the War Office letter of September 1916, but the army and the public knew that the real offence was that they had countenanced the ill-treatment of conscientious objectors. In Childs's reaction to the behaviour of these officers, the conflict in his attitude was for once resolved. He condemned them not only for their ill-treatment of individual conscientious objectors, but also for making it more difficult for him to proceed against the N.C.F. He wrote to General Maxwell: 'This case and that of Private Gray and those of the five conscientious objectors sent to France have done more damage and produced more sympathy and support for the revolutionary and pacifist movements in this country than any other incident which has occurred in the past twelve months.'[1] Childs's policy was no doubt inspired by various motives; yet however complex the motivation he had been as good as his word and had successfully defended the right of the most unwilling and insubordinate soldier to be treated in accordance with the law.

The work of AG3(CO) was not confined to those cases in which attempts were made to coerce conscientious objectors by illegal methods. During April and May 1916 commanding officers were (as Macready warned the Cabinet) obliged to make soldiers of all recruits by the 'legitimate means' at their disposal; and the application of legitimate means could place conscientious objectors in situations that were potentially more dangerous than those experienced by Gray and Brightmore. A conscientious objector who persisted in disobeying orders was either dealt with summarily by his commanding officer or sent for court martial. There was no uniformity in procedure or in sentence; the latter varied from a short period of confinement to barracks to two years hard labour. Those who received light sentences proved no more amenable to orders and soon progressed to a district court martial;

[1] Childs to Lt.-Gen. Sir J. G. Maxwell, 17 August 1917, WO 32/2054/1654.

heavier sentences were, however, commuted by the Army Council, so that two years hard labour became 112 days detention. In this way the majority of conscientious objectors faced a 'net' sentence of between 28 and 112 days in a Military Detention Barracks or Military Prison. A few were transferred to the nearest civil prison, but in the early days this was exceptional.

It was one thing for a conscientious objector to disobey orders in a training battalion; it was quite another for him to do so in a Military Detention Barracks where the staff had no doubts about their aim and few qualms about their methods. The Rules for Military Detention Barracks[1] had been designed to deter the brute elements of a regular army. They prescribed a daily routine and a scale of punishments that were unpleasant enough for the prisoner who was determined to display 'industry and good conduct'; for the conscientious objector who chose to resist, they could be hard indeed. Life in a Detention Barracks was organized as a system of stages. A new prisoner began in stage one: he had no mattress, worked for nine hours a day, and was allowed no recreation apart from books of religious and secular instruction. The second stage, which allowed the prisoner a mattress, a book from the library, and a visit of twenty minutes from a friend, was reached by earning sufficient points. As these points were awarded for good conduct and attention to drill, the conscientious objectors seldom accumulated enough to leave stage one. Instead of making progress they collected punishments; they were placed in close confinement and on punishment diet. The latter, like the daily routine, was on a progressive scale: number one punishment diet consisted of one pound of bread 'per diem' and water; number two consisted of eight ounces of bread for breakfast and supper, with a pint of 'stirabout' (a distasteful mixture of oatmeal, salt, and potatoes) for lunch.

Conscientious objectors who were sentenced while in France were liable to further refinements of military discipline. For an offence committed on active service a commanding officer could award up to twenty-eight days Field Punishment Number One. This punishment, which had been introduced as a humane substitute for flogging, was popularly, but in view of pacifist sensi-

[1] Rules for Military Detention Barracks and Military Prisons, 1911 (issued January 1912 and current in 1916), H.M.S.O.

tivities unfortunately, known as crucifixion. During his punishment, the offender was kept in irons or employed on hard labour; for two hours a day he was attached to a 'fixed object', such as a wagon or gun wheel. Although the War Office insisted that the punishment should not 'cause injury or leave any permanent mark on the offender', an experienced NCO could impose the maximum discomfort without breaking the rules.[1]

The application of punishments such as this to conscientious objectors shocked liberal opinion which had little knowledge of the less publicized sides of military life. Ignorance of the Rules for Military Detention Barracks and Prisons gave rise to numerous complaints that conscientious objectors were being singled out for brutal treatment, but, as Childs pointed out to Asquith, where men were subjected to punishments authorized by the Army Act 'enquiry would be only superfluous and productive of no result'.[2] Childs suggested that the Rules should be published, but his superiors seem to have been reluctant to do this.[3] It was left to the conscientious objectors to expose not only the rigour of the authorized punishments but also the danger of unauthorized brutality in institutions whose life was screened from the public gaze and whose usual inmates knew better than to lodge a formal complaint. The conscientious objectors were less vulnerable than the other prisoners; they had their organizations to watch over their interests and M.P.s who were prepared to ask questions in the House. Commandants who imagined that they had a free hand to discipline conscientious objectors as they wished were soon disabused. Lieutenant-Colonel Reginald Brooke, who commanded the Military Detention Barracks at Wandsworth, was dismissed by Macready within an hour of the Government being informed of the treatment of conscientious objectors in his charge.[4] As in the case of other officers dismissed for permitting the ill-treatment of conscientious objectors, Brooke sought to justify his conduct in the columns of the popular press. The nature of his policy at

[1] For the Rules for Field Punishment see *Manual of Military Law*, War Office, 1914, pp. 721–2.

[2] Notes for the Prime Minister on the History of Army Order X by Brigadier-General Childs (undated but belonging to the period May–June 1916), Asquith Papers 127.

[3] The suggestion was made to Macready; see WO 32/2055/6923.

[4] Philip Snowden was instrumental in obtaining Brooke's dismissal; see Snowden, *An Autobiography*, I, pp. 411–12.

Wandsworth may be deduced from the admissions he was prepared to make in his own defence:

No doubt some of the men were treated with some roughness. There was no other way of treating them and they were not physically injured. . . . Some of the early batches when nothing could be done with them, were taken singly and run across the yard to special rooms—airy enough but from which they could see nothing. They were fed on bread and water and some of them presently came round. . . . I had them placed in special rooms, nude, but with their full army kit on the floor for them to put on as soon as they were so minded. There were no blankets or substitutes for clothing left in the rooms which were quite bare. Several of the men held out naked for several hours but they gradually accepted the inevitable. Forty of the conscientious objectors who passed through my hands are now quite willing soldiers.[1]

Those who were not prepared to become willing soldiers, whether at Wandsworth or at other Detention Barracks, still faced the sanctions authorized in the Rules. They were the victims of a harsh code of discipline rather than of deliberate persecution, and their experiences generated a widespread civilian uneasiness about the nature of military punishments. It was not long after the end of the war that the most notorious of these punishments—Field Punishment Number One—was abolished.[2]

In its most extreme form, the problem of the conscientious objector resisting military orders posed the question of whether continued disobedience would ultimately incur the death penalty. This point had been missed by Parliament, although the Commons had recognized that a conscientious objector who refused to comply with an order calling him to the colours might be sentenced to death as a deserter under orders for active service. The Government had inserted a statutory safeguard against this danger, but the wording of the amendment seemed to imply that the safeguard did not cover subsequent acts of disobedience.[3] The interpretation accepted by the Army Council was that the Military Service Act divorced the first refusal from liability to the death penalty, but that after this the conscript was in exactly the same position as

[1] *Daily Express*, 4 July 1916.

[2] By Army and Air Force (Annual) Act, 1923 (13 GEO 5, Ch. 3), 44 (5).

[3] 'A man who is deemed to have been enlisted and transferred to the reserve under this section shall not be liable to suffer death in respect of failure to obey an order calling him up from the reserve for permanent service.' Military Service (No. 2) Act, 1916, I (2)(c).

other men under military law.[1] The latter prescribed the death penalty as the maximum punishment for a variety of offences, and not only those committed on active service.[2] A soldier who disobeyed a lawful command 'in such a manner as to show wilful defiance of authority' could be sentenced to death whether he was on active service or not. Nevertheless it was on active service that the death sentence was most likely to be confirmed rather than commuted for a lesser punishment. 'On active service' was defined as being part of a force engaged in operations against the enemy or in operations in a country wholly or partly occupied by the enemy.[3] Conscientious objectors who were sent to France as members of the Non-Combatant Corps were on active service, even though they were stationed far behind the front line.

These provisions of the Army Act might have led to the widespread application of the death penalty during the First World War if it had not been for General Childs. Childs was convinced of the deterrent value of the death penalty, but initiated a reform in the sentencing procedure that enabled the Commander-in-Chief to remit this penalty in 89 per cent of the cases in which it was inflicted by courts martial. Under the new procedure, the Commander-in-Chief was provided with the fullest possible information about a soldier sentenced to death so that the decision to confirm or remit the sentence would no longer be based solely on the conduct sheet and the record of the court martial, neither of which was likely to contribute much of value about the man's character.[4] Despite this improvement, the death sentence had been confirmed in 133 cases up to September 1916,[5] and it was theoretically possible therefore for a conscientious objector to be executed. The assurances to the contrary given by David Lloyd George and Walter Long only served to underline the Cabinet's failure to think through to its logical conclusion the conflict between conscientious objection and military law.[6] Yet, despite the provisions of the Army Act, the limitations of the Cabinet's safeguard, and

[1] See ACI No. 968, 1916, and *Registration and Recruiting*, p. 14.

[2] See the Army Act, 4, 6, 7, 9(I).

[3] For the legal definition of 'on active service' see the Army Act, 189 (I).

[4] Childs, op. cit., pp. 140–42; see also Childs's Obituary in *The Times*, 30 November 1946.

[5] *Military Statistics 1914–1920*, p. 648.

[6] For the statements of these two members of the Cabinet see 5 HC 81, col. 308 and 327, 22 March 1916.

the brave obstinacy of the resisters, no conscientious objector was shot or, indeed, ever came close to being so. Conscientious objector circles believed that their men had been saved only by the vigilance of the N.C.F. and the personal intervention of the Prime Minister. This view was reinforced by John Graham, whose account suggests the existence of a military plot to outwit the Government and make an example of those conscientious objectors resisting orders in France.[1] The evidence for a military plot is unconvincing, but Graham's version has been so widely accepted that the evidence should be re-examined.

The first draft of the Non-Combatant Corps that contained men resisting orders arrived in France on 8 May 1916.[2] Depot commanders had not received instructions to exclude these men from drafts posted overseas, and there is no need to see this as the first step in a military plot. The parents of one of these conscientious objectors appealed to Gilbert Murray, who, with friends among the conscientious objectors and a brother-in-law as Liberal Chief Whip, was increasingly called upon to act as a go-between. Murray described his response to this appeal in a letter to John Graham, written after the war:

> As to the incident about which you write, I find from my diaries that it was about May 9 or 10, 1916. I had just been in France and arriving in town I found waiting for me a telegram from the parents of a CO in Cambridge (the Wyatts) and also a letter from some other source—I forget now the name of the writer—saying that some of the 34 COs in France had been sentenced to death and that the sentence was expected to be carried out in the next few days. Meantime it was being used to intimidate others. I had already reason to believe that these men had been taken to France for the express purpose of rendering them liable to the death penalty, so that this message only confirmed my fears. I went at once—in a very untidy state—to the House of Commons, where I saw Mr. Geoffrey Howard one of the Liberal Whips, and put the case to him. He advised me to see Lord Derby who was secretary for war. I managed to see him in the lobby. Lord Derby said the men were condemned to be shot and would be shot and quite right too. I was not clear from his manner whether he knew about the business already and approved, or whether he was merely bluffing. I left him and went back to Geoffrey Howard who said he would try and get me five minutes

[1] Graham, op. cit., p. 114.
[2] See Tennant's statement, 5 HC 82, col. 892, 11 May 1916.

with Asquith who was of course terribly busy. I waited and presently he took me to the Prime Minister's room where Mr. Asquith was writing. I told him briefly how the men had been taken to France and, according to my information, were now condemned to death. He listened attentively, read the telegram and muttered the one word, 'Abominable'. He asked one or two questions and then wrote a letter rapidly. He then said, 'I have written to the Commander in Chief, directing—(if my memory is correct)—that no death sentences were to be carried out on conscientious objectors without the consent of the Cabinet.' The matter was settled in five minutes: I was greatly struck by his rapidity both in decision and action. I was then taken by Geoffrey Howard to see H. J. Tennant, the Under Secretary for war and told him what had been done.[1]

John Graham was not above tampering with this evidence in order to establish the existence of a military plot. Whereas Murray had written of Lord Derby: 'I was not clear from his manner whether he knew about the business already and approved, or whether he was merely bluffing,' Graham removed the uncertainty by writing: 'He gave the impression that he knew all about the plan.'[2] Derby was not, as Murray supposed, Secretary of State for War,[3] and his comments did not represent any official view, nor were they accurate. Men who had arrived in France on 8 May could not have been court-martialled, sentenced to death, and have had that sentence confirmed all within forty-eight hours. Gilbert Murray's anxiety was unnecessary but it was not entirely without justification. For several weeks officers and NCOs had used the threat of shooting as a means of persuading conscientious objectors to obey orders, and the military had only themselves to blame if these threats were taken seriously. Suspicion of the army's methods had already been increased by the rumours reaching England since the end of April that a number of captured Irish rebels had been shot without trial during the Easter Rising; and it was on 9 and 10 May that Asquith was asked questions in the House about the arbitrary execution of the Irish pacifist, Sheey Skeffington, two weeks previously, so that at the time of

[1] Gilbert Murray to John Graham (carbon copy), 28 December 1920, Gilbert Murray Papers, 2.

[2] Graham, op. cit., p. 112.

[3] For Lord Derby's tenure of office as Under-Secretary and Secretary of State see p. xv above.

Murray's visit the Prime Minister was predisposed to doubt whether the military could be trusted.[1]

The party of seventeen conscientious objectors about whom Murray had been concerned were sentenced to twenty-eight days in the Field Detention Barracks at Boulogne.[2] Asquith's directive to General Sir Douglas Haig, the Commander in Chief of the BEF, had not been needed, but it remained in force nevertheless. On 22 May David Davies, a Liberal M.P., wrote to Gilbert Murray on McKenna's instructions: 'As you probably know, Sir D. Haig was directed some time ago not to confirm the death sentence on any CO.'[3] But the directive was not made public, so that, as further groups of conscientious objectors resisting orders were posted to France, fears for their safety increased. These men were in no danger either of being shot or of being left to languish in military prison. Before the end of May the Cabinet accepted in principle a procedure for ensuring that conscientious objectors who were court-martialled should be transferred to civilian control.[4] But this procedure—like the directive on the death penalty—was not made public. The Cabinet's reticence was a reflection of its fear that publication would encourage spurious claims to conscientious objection under the new Act; Asquith refused to make a detailed announcement of change in policy until after the closing date for applications for exemption, which was 24 June.[5] During the period between the Cabinet's decision and the public announcement, the military had to do their best to discourage a new wave of conscientious objection among the married men who now became liable for service, and to prevent the subversion of discipline at a time when the army was girding itself for a major offensive on the Western Front. Sentences of detention had not deterred conscientious objectors who were determined to resist, and the only heavier punishments available to courts martial were the death penalty and penal servitude. The former was excluded

[1] See Asquith's answer, 5 HC 82, col. 632–4, 10 May 1916. Skeffington had been shot on the morning of 26 April. See also Mrs. Skeffington's account in Julian Bell (ed.), *We Did Not Fight, 1914–1918: experiences of war-resisters*, London, 1935, pp. 339–56.

[2] See *The Friend*, 9 June 1916.

[3] David Davies to Gilbert Murray, 22 May 1916, Gilbert Murray Papers, 2. Davies was the Member for Montgomeryshire and in June 1916 became Lloyd George's Private Secretary.

[4] See p. 159, below.

[5] Military Service Act, 1916 (Session 2), I (I).

by Asquith's directive but might still be an effective deterrent if imposed and commuted to penal servitude. This was probably the reasoning behind the death sentences imposed in June. On 14 June T. E. Harvey reported to Gilbert Murray:

I heard some rather disquieting news at the War Office. Macpherson thought it doubtful if they could prevent a further batch of men who are in detention and resisting all orders at Richmond Castle from being sent off to France along with another draft of NCC men; and said serious measures are shortly to be taken to prevent organised opposition.[1]

The following day four conscientious objectors were sentenced to death at Boulogne; a further thirty were similarly sentenced during the ensuing week.[2] In every case the sentence was commuted to penal servitude.

In view of the Cabinet's decision to transfer conscientious objectors to civilian control, it is doubtful whether the military needed to go so far; if they had allowed the new procedure to take its course, the conscientious objectors would have become the responsibility of the Home Office within a few weeks. As it was, the military had played into the hands of their critics who had maintained that the army was trying to outmanoeuvre the Government and execute conscientious objectors in order to break the spirit of resistance. This theory gained wider support when it appeared that the members of the Government responsible for the War Office had been kept in the dark about the thirty-four death sentences that were imposed. Asquith was himself acting as Secretary of State for War following Kitchener's death on 29 May.[3] H. J. Tennant continued as Under-Secretary and it was he who declared confidently on 22 June (one week after the first conscientious objectors had been sentenced to death), 'I can assure my right hon. Friend who has put the question that there is no intention of dealing with them in any way harshly and that there will be no question of their being sentenced to death.'[4] Four days later, Tennant had to announce that thirty-four conscientious

[1] T. E. Harvey to Gilbert Murray, 14 June 1916, Gilbert Murray Papers 2.

[2] See Tennant's statement, 5 HC 83, col. 523, 26 June 1916.

[3] Kitchener was drowned when H.M.S. *Hampshire*, on which he was travelling to Russia, struck a mine.

[4] 5 HC 83, col. 492, 22 June 1916.

objectors had been sentenced to death and that the sentences had been commuted to penal servitude.[1] His announcement, Herbert Samuel reported to the King, 'was evidently disturbing to a large section of the House'.[2] Tennant had blundered, but the fault was not entirely his. He must have known both that such death sentences could not be confirmed and that the conscientious objectors concerned would soon be in civilian hands, but he could not reveal either of these Cabinet decisions to the Commons. At the same time he evidently did not know that the death sentences had been imposed, or he would not have given such a categorical assurance. There had been a serious failure of communication and no doubt the event was followed by angry recriminations behind the doors of the War Office.

It is not clear whether Macready and Childs played any part in this affair; most probably they were prepared to let the law take its course within the limits imposed by the Cabinet. For Childs the use of the death penalty in these cases would have presented the difficulty that some of the conscientious objectors resisting orders in France were men he regarded as genuine. If it had been possible to isolate the politically motivated and to court-martial them for wilful disobedience, it is unlikely that Childs would have had many qualms about the subsequent execution. As the war continued season by season, the spring offensive and the autumn lull, with no sign of victory, Childs's hostility to the political objector became more intense. It reached a peak in March 1918; the Germans had made a decisive break in the Allied line and, in a moment of panic, Lloyd George's Government proposed to extend conscription to Ireland. Childs warned Macready that unless measures were taken to crush political opposition to conscription in England, the Sinn Fein would be encouraged to follow the example of the N.C.F. In a Minute dated 23 April, Childs made some recommendations.

That it should immediately be made known that conscientious objectors who disobey a lawful command *in such a way as to show a wilful defiance of authority* (Section 9(I) of the Army Act) will be tried by General Court Martial and, if sentenced to death by that court, the sentence will be carried out if it appears that their objection is based on political

[1] 5 HC 83, col. 523, 26 June 1916.

[2] Home Secretary's Report to the King on the Proceedings in Parliament, 26 June 1916.

and not religious grounds. . . . If this proposal is adopted, it is no good disguising the fact that it will in certain cases mean shooting, and it should be recognised that Sinn Feiners will be shot as well as the anarchical atheists in this country who on the termination of their sentence of imprisonment again disobey the lawful commands of their superior officers.[1]

Although this Minute was written at a time of acute military crisis when extreme proposals were by no means confined to the War Office, Childs was being consistent with the views he had expressed in 1916 and that had been shared by other senior officers: objection on political grounds ought not to exempt a man from compulsory service or protect him from the punishments prescribed in the Army Act. This view would also have commanded some support among the members of Lloyd George's administration, but Lloyd George himself was too shrewd a tactician not to recognize that the political consequences of shooting a man who claimed to be a conscientious objector would far outweigh any deterrent value. As it turned out this was a decision that he did not have to make: the plan to extend the Military Service Act to Ireland was discarded, and with it Childs's justification for sentencing the 'anarchical atheists' to death.

Nearly six thousand conscientious objectors who had no intention of becoming soldiers were handed over to the military authorities. No one had worked out in advance how to cope with this unprecedented challenge to military discipline, and for several weeks the problem was left to commanding officers. The latter had no choice but to set the offenders on the road that led from summary jurisdiction to General Court Martial. In this situation, it is the absence of executions that is significant. In May 1916 it would have required neither a conscious War Office policy nor a sinister military plot to bring conscientious objectors before a firing-squad; Asquith's directive saved conscientious objectors from the letter of the law, not from the machinations of the War Office.

Five weeks before the conscientious objectors were sentenced to death at Boulogne, Macready had decided that the army did not wish to be responsible for large numbers of recruits who were a threat to discipline. The Memorandum that he wrote for

[1] WO 32/2055/6923.

Kitchener on 15 May, and that Kitchener circulated to the Cabinet, concluded with the recommendation that the Government should establish a civilian organization to employ, 'under conditions as severe as those of soldiers at the front', any conscientious objectors who were found to be useless to the army.[1] The question of extricating conscientious objectors from the army had been under discussion since the middle of April,[2] but there was not yet agreement on how and when this should be done. Although Asquith and his Liberal colleagues wanted to place all genuine conscientious objectors under civilian authority, Conservative members of the Cabinet, particularly Walter Long, were opposed to any move that might be interpreted as a concession to the militants of the N.C.F. On 3 May, Long told the Commons:

> If appeals are made on behalf of men of that kind, all I can say is that the House has given them all they are entitled to, and I go further and say that I, for one, would most strongly resist any suggestion to give them more.[3]

While Macready would have been no less reluctant to 'give them more', he could not tolerate a situation in which an increasing number of recruits were defying authority under the pretext of conscience. The problem was to find a formula for transferring the genuine conscientious objector to civilian control without providing a means of avoiding active service that would be tempting to other conscripts. The military believed that there was a large number of men prepared to evade service if given the chance. Although this fear may have been exaggerated, the scale on which evasion was occurring in 1916 and the open abuse of the conscience clause by men released from essential industries in 1918, suggest that it was not altogether unfounded.

One week after Macready's Memorandum had been circulated, Kitchener made a rare and final speech in the Lords, announcing that it was the Government's policy to place the genuine conscientious objector under the civil power.[4] Although Kitchener gave no details of how the policy would work, Liberals in the Cabinet saw to it that sufficient information was passed on to

[1] CAB 37/147/35.
[2] See Tennant's statement, 5 HC 81, col. 2259–60, 18 April 1916.
[3] 5 HC 82, col. 94–5, 3 May 1916.
[4] 5 HL 22, col. 14, 22 May 1916.

Gilbert Murray, who could be trusted to use it judiciously. On the day of Kitchener's statement David Davies wrote to Murray:

> McKenna told me this afternoon to let you know in confidence that the government have decided to settle the conscientious objector question. . . . a man who is refused exemption on conscientious grounds and handed over to the military authorities and by them sentenced for disobedience to orders, will now be handed over to the civil authorities for the carrying out of his sentence. He will thus come under the jurisdiction of the Home Secretary who will be able at his discretion and on his own conditions to release him from gaol. . . . The government do not wish their decision to be made public for the present as they fear an embarrassing increase in the number of claimants to conscientious objection.[1]

The Cabinet left the detailed planning to Childs and Herbert Samuel, the Home Secretary. Childs drafted an Army Order—known as Army Order X[2]—which directed that a conscientious objector found guilty of an offence against discipline should be sentenced to imprisonment and not detention, and that after court martial he should be committed to the nearest civil prison. The new order had its teething difficulties. When it was issued on 25 May, there were 156 conscientious objectors who had already been court-martialled, and it was not clear whether the order was retrospective in effect. Asked about this in the Commons, Tennant confessed that he did not know.[3] Commanding officers and presidents of courts martial were no better informed, and in some cases they ignored the new Army Order altogether. These operational difficulties were susceptible of direct administrative solution, though Childs chafed under the Cabinet's refusal to make a full statement of how the new policy would work. He believed that uncertainty about what would happen to conscientious objectors after they had been committed to civil prison, far from discouraging spurious claims to conscience, was likely to have the opposite effect. He urged Asquith to make a full statement in the Commons:

> We have never told the public what is to be their fate when they get to civil prisons and it is clear that the general belief is that once they have

[1] David Davies to Gilbert Murray, 22 May 1916.
[2] AO 179, 1916.
[3] 5 HC 82, col. 2659, 30 May 1916.

passed to such prisons, their military career is ended. I think that when a full disclosure of our methods is made, it will act as a great deterrent to absentees of this description. . . .[1]

Not all the methods that Childs recommended were acceptable to Liberal opinion. Asquith agreed that the cases of conscientious objectors committed to civil prison should be reviewed by the Central Tribunal and that those deemed to be genuine should do work of national importance under the Home Office. But Childs drew a sharp and characteristic distinction between the treatment of men who were inspired by 'religious sincerity' and those who in his opinion were not genuine:

Briefly I think the impression we ought to attempt to create is that the genuine conscientious objector will receive relief from military service, and that the humbug will, with equal certainty, be broken to discipline under the military machine and that there is no possibility of his escaping the searching investigation of his sincerity.[2]

The prospect of breaking men to discipline under the military machine would not have commended itself to Asquith, and yet he could not ignore the need to provide some deterrent. The deterrent that Childs wanted was the return to Military Detention Barracks of the non-genuine and those who refused to cooperate. He warned the Prime Minister that 'the critical moment when the support of the government will be most required' would be when the first alleged conscientious objector was sent back to face military discipline. Whatever Asquith's misgivings about handing back to the military men who had claimed to be conscientious objectors, he accepted the principle for the time being. He may well have considered that unless the Government promised to take a tough line with those whose sincerity was in doubt, the whole procedure would be rejected by the Conservatives and by public opinion.

Herbert Samuel welcomed[3] Childs's proposals for transferring responsibility for conscientious objectors to the Home Office, though he would have been less inclined to do so if he had known how many of these men would prove no more amenable to civil

[1] Childs's Notes for the Prime Minister on the History of Army Order X.

[2] Ibid.

[3] Memorandum on Conscientious Objectors by Herbert Samuel, 16 June 1916, Asquith Papers 127. See also Samuel's Confidential Report to the Central Tribunal, attached to the Tribunal's Minutes, 10 July 1916.

discipline than they had been to military. Samuel's procedure for dealing with the genuine conscientious objectors was dictated by two considerations: it was not possible to keep in prison men whom the Central Tribunal and the War Office had accepted as genuine, nor was it possible to release these men unconditionally without appearing to reverse by administrative action the statutory tribunal decisions. Samuel proposed, therefore, that the men should not be formally discharged from the army, but transferred to section W of the Army Reserve which was created for 'all soldiers whose service is deemed to be more valuable to the country in civil than military employment'.[1] To determine the conditions of work and to take the necessary executive action, Samuel appointed a small committee under the chairmanship of William Brace, an Under-Secretary at the Home Office and one of the three Labour M.P.s brought into the Coalition Government by Asquith.

By the third week in June the main lines of Government policy had been established, but were still largely unknown outside official circles. 24 June was the last day on which applications to the tribunals could be made under the new Military Service Act. On 29 June, Asquith at last gave a full explanation of the procedure for dealing with conscientious objectors who were resisting orders in the army. He made it sound straightforward: conscientious objectors sentenced by court martial would have their cases reviewed by the Central Tribunal; those classified by the Tribunal as genuine would be released from prison to work under the Brace Committee; those refused this classification would be returned to detention barracks to complete their sentences. He concluded:

> Perhaps I may add to that statement two general propositions which I hope may receive universal assent. The first is that all men whose objections to active military service are founded on honest conviction ought to be and will be able to avail themselves of the exemption which Parliament has provided. And, in the second place, it is necessary that men who put forward objections of this kind as a pretext and a cloak to cover their indifference in responding to the national call, and are therefore guilty of the double offence of cowardice and hypocrisy, should be treated as they ought to be treated, with the utmost rigour.[2]

[1] AO 203, 1916.

[2] Asquith's statement, 5 HC 83, col. 1014–15, 29 June 1916.

CHAPTER EIGHT

THE HOME OFFICE SCHEME

The policy worked out by Childs and Samuel represented the principal attempt by Asquith's Coalition Government to recover from the failure of its initial provisions for conscience. The failure was not admitted but the official assurances that the Central Tribunal was only reviewing and not reversing the decisions made by the tribunals in their statutory capacity could not disguise the fact that men who had been handed over to the military were now to be returned to civilian control, if not to civilian status. This administrative manoeuvre was in one sense a victory for the conscientious objectors who had stubbornly refused to be browbeaten or beguiled into becoming soldiers; in another sense it was a victory for the Government, who would now find it easier to separate the less determined resisters from the hard core of uncompromising absolutists. But in operation the Scheme devised by William Brace's Committee was a victory for no one; throughout its existence the so-called Home Office Scheme probably caused more frustration for those involved than any other aspect of conscription.

The first step in the new policy was to decide which of those conscientious objectors who had been court-martialled and transferred to civil prison should be released to work under the Brace Committee. It had been Childs's suggestion that the Central Tribunal should be asked to review these cases and to make recommendations to the Army Council.[1] In this way the Tribunal would be acting as an advisory body to the Council, and the military would retain ultimate control over the men, who were still soldiers in law. In Childs's approach to the exercise of this control, however, there was a fundamental contradiction: he had told Asquith that it was essential for the 'humbug' to realize 'that there

[1] Childs's Notes for the Prime Minister on the History of Army Order X.

is no possibility of his escaping the searching investigation of his sincerity';[1] but Childs knew that if the investigation were too searching, a large number of men might be returned to the army, where they would once again interfere with discipline and with the training of recruits. In theory Childs wanted the new procedure to act as a deterrent to those who saw conscientious objection as a safe alternative to active service, and at the same time to relieve the army of the thankless task of trying to make soldiers of men who were prepared to guard their civilian purity with the tenacity of nuns defending their virtue. In practice Childs could not have it both ways; he had to be prepared to weaken the deterrent in order to ensure that it was the Home Office and not his own department that would have the problem of employing and controlling thousands of men who had already demonstrated their disinclination to accept authority.

The deterrent was weakened in two ways. In the first place, the Central Tribunal was advised not to adopt the same standard that it applied to the statutory appeals for exemption,[2] with the result that a very high proportion of those whose cases were reviewed were recommended for release from prison. This was a policy of expediency, and although the Brace Committee complained that it was having to deal with many men who showed no signs of being actuated by conscience,[3] the Central Tribunal continued to recommend release on a scale that suited General Childs rather than the Home Office. And in their final report the Tribunal members justified this policy by pointing out that 'many of the men were of no use to the Army; their presence in military units was a hindrance to the performance of military duties at a time when all officers were fully employed in training new levies.'[4] Childs was prepared to go further to protect the army from a repetition of the difficulties experienced during the first influx of resisters. He appears to have agreed that the non-genuine and those who refused to cooperate with the Central Tribunal should not after all be returned to detention barracks 'to be broken to discipline under the military machine'. Instead these men would be allowed to finish their sentences in civil prison before returning to the army,

[1] Ibid. [2] Report of the Central Tribunal, p. 23.

[3] The Home Office and Conscientious Objectors, A Report prepared for the Committee of Imperial Defence, 1919, Part I, The Brace Committee (hereafter The Brace Committee), p. 5.

[4] Report of the Central Tribunal, p. 23.

where the operation of Army Order X would ensure that their second stay in military custody was brief. This change may have been insisted upon by the Liberals in the Cabinet to whom the military machine was unpalatable at the best of times, or it may have been made in response to protests that a return to detention barracks would provoke the very conflict that the new procedure was designed to avoid. Whoever initiated the change—the official report says only that 'objections were raised to this course'[1]—Childs must have reckoned that it was not altogether contrary to the army's interests if the breaking to discipline was left to the Home Office.

The Central Tribunal began interviewing in Wormwood Scrubs Prison on 27 July. As many as possible of the conscientious objectors who had been court-martialled were sent to the Scrubs or to the Barlinnie Prison in Glasgow so that the Tribunal members did not have to visit the numerous prisons in which the men were being held, a procedure that would have resulted in long delays. The last interview was given on 16 May 1919. In almost three years, the Tribunal reviewed the cases of 5,944 men.[2] In each case the interviewing committee of the Tribunal studied the papers of the man's tribunal hearings and of his court martial. At the interview the pattern of questioning was based on the questionnaire that the Tribunal used in its statutory capacity; if the man's answers were considered unsatisfactory he was required to furnish the names of two 'referees' who could testify to the sincerity of his convictions.[3]

When all the evidence had been obtained the Tribunal placed the man in one of the following categories:

Class A: Men who should undoubtedly be treated as having a conscientious objection to all military service.

Class B: Men who allege conscientious objection, but whose convictions appear to be so uncertain as not to warrant a distinct finding as above.

Class C: Men who have a strong objection to war in general, but who, it seems, would fight in a war for a purpose of which they approved.

[1] The Home Office and Conscientious Objectors, Part II, Conscientious Objectors in Prison (hereafter Conscientious Objectors in Prison), p. 1.

[2] The figure given in the Supplementary Report of the Central Tribunal.

[3] The procedure is described in the Report of the Central Tribunal, pp. 21–2.

Class D: Men who cannot be said to have any real conscientious objection to military service.

Class E: Men who refused to plead before the Tribunal or who refused the conditions of the Tribunal's enquiry.

The numbers of men placed in each category to 31 December 1918 are given in Appendix G below. In 141 cases, the man was not classified because he withdrew his objection to combatant or non-combatant service, or because he was released unconditionally on the grounds of health.[1]

For several months the Tribunal recommended to the Army Council that men classified A and B should be released for work under the Brace Committee. Consistent with the wishes of the military authorities, the proportion of men placed in these classes in 1916 was 89·1 per cent.[2] The N.C.F. had claimed that the new investigation would be characterized by the same inequalities and injustices as the old,[3] but it was the members of the Brace Committee not the conscientious objectors who had cause to feel aggrieved by the Tribunal's indulgent policy. After a few months the Committee refused to offer work to men classified B, but it could not persuade the Central Tribunal to make a significant reduction in the proportion of men classified A. In 1917 and 1918, however, the proportion in category A fell for other reasons, notably the increasing number of prisoners whose claims to conscientious objection could not meet even the unexacting standard required by the Tribunal; even Childs could not expect the Tribunal to recommend release for men who had voluntarily left their ordinary work to join munitions factories only to embrace conscientious objection when they became liable for military service.[4] Despite the gradual decline in the proportion of credible candidates, the Central Tribunal recommended to the Army Council that a total of 4,522 men should be released for work under the Brace Committee.[5] There is no evidence that the Army Council showed the slightest hesitation in accepting any of these recommendations for release.

Men classified C and D (and later those classified B) remained

[1] See Appendix E 'Other Recommendations'.

[2] See Appendix G. [3] *The Tribunal*, 10 August 1916.

[4] The Central Tribunal claimed that the evidence 'proved beyond doubt' that some conscientious objectors had done this. See Report of the Central Tribunal, p. 22.

[5] *Military Statistics, 1914–1920*, p. 673.

in prison to complete their sentences. When, after a second court martial, they returned to prison, the Central Tribunal was prepared to reconsider their cases if new evidence was submitted. Although it is not clear what new evidence could be available (other than the man's willingness to undergo a second court martial and sentence) the Tribunal reported that 'in many cases as a result of the submission of fresh evidence the men have been placed in category A'.[1] The Tribunal's Minutes suggest that there were occasions when the reclassification was based less on fresh evidence than on the need to prevent the return to the army of a man who had already been a considerable embarrassment to the military authorities. The reclassification may have been at Childs's request, but there is nothing in the records of the Tribunal or of Childs's department to substantiate this.

The men in categories C and D were not absolutists. They had been prepared to compromise with the Government but had failed to establish their bona fides. The 46 classified C were political objectors; there were certainly other men whose objection had a political base but these must either have been among the absolutists or have played down their political convictions in order to obtain release from prison. The unqualified rejects in category D numbered 267: that they were unable to convince men who were bending over backwards to recommend release is some indication of the calibre of their 'conscientious objections'. Whether they were subjected to repeated prison sentences or were subsequently reclassified and released to work under the Brace Committee, the 313 men who were, in effect, declared not genuine remained the group that created the most acute disciplinary problems for the Home Office. They had everything to gain by bad behaviour and little to lose; they wanted to smash the system because the system had rejected them, or perhaps only because it had found them out.

The men classified E were absolutists. They either refused absolutely to appear before the Central Tribunal or refused to accept the conditions of the Tribunal's inquiry. In the summer of 1916 the Tribunal informed all men whose cases were to be investigated of the conditions under which they would be released from prison if found genuine. In some cases, however, men classified A or B only refused the conditions of work *after* they had

[1] Report of the Central Tribunal, p. 23.

been released from prison and had to be returned to custody. The number of these men was 293.[1] As a result of these cases, the Tribunal subsequently refused to interview a man unless he was willing to give an undertaking to accept the conditions of work of the Brace Committee. 692 men would not give this undertaking or made it clear in other ways that they would have nothing to do with the Tribunal's investigation on behalf of the Army Council.[2] The total number of absolutists (excluding those granted absolute exemption by the statutory tribunals) was therefore 985. On 25 May 1916 Clifford Allen, speaking for the N.C.F., had warned that there were 20,000 men who would bend to none of the Government's attempts to get round the militarism of the Military Service Act.[3] This tactical exaggeration, which bore no relation whatsoever to the truth, reflected the N.C.F.'s despairing attempts to disguise the collapse of its policy. The Fellowship's leaders had hoped to bring about the repeal of the Act by a wholesale refusal to compromise with its provisions. On 6 April Allen had written: 'If ever we might expect an inclination to compromise it should be evident now that persecution has commenced, but it is already clear that opposition to militarism is an issue about which men cannot and will not compromise.'[4] Six months later, Allen and his colleagues had to recognize that the majority of conscientious objectors were more concerned to obtain individual relief than to achieve the breakdown of the law; in increasing numbers men were accepting non-combatant military duties or civilian work of national importance at the tribunals, and now the procedure instituted by Childs and Samuel was reducing the absolutists among those who had been resisting in the army to under one thousand.

The absolutists were treated no differently from the men classified as not genuine; they were returned to their army units on the completion of their prison sentences. But unlike the 'not genuine', the absolutists did not avail themselves of a second chance to appear before the Tribunal and obtain a classification that would lead to release.

The Cabinet and the War Office had originally intended that the Central Tribunal's investigation should separate once and for all the sincere objectors from the humbugs, enabling the former to be

[1] *Military Statistics, 1914–1920*, p. 673.

[2] See Appendix G.

[3] *The Tribunal*, 25 May 1916.

[4] Ibid., 6 April 1916.

released while the latter were, in Asquith's own words, 'treated as they ought to be treated, with the utmost rigour'. It soon became clear, however, that the principal separation being achieved by the Tribunal was between those who were prepared to accept the conditions of work on the Home Office Scheme and those who refused to make any compromise with the machinery of conscription; and this was in no sense a separation of the sincere from the insincere, as release from prison was often a gesture of expediency, while an absolute refusal to compromise was at least an indication of depth of conviction. The fact that the 313 men classified as not genuine were left in prison with the absolutists only served to confuse the public, because it appeared that the extremes of shallow and deep conviction were being treated in exactly the same manner.[1]

When the Brace Committee (or Committee on Employment of Conscientious Objectors) was appointed by Herbert Samuel on 21 June, it was assumed that the Central Tribunal's investigation would fulfil its intended aim. The Committee understood that what was going to happen was that the

> Central Tribunal or a Committee thereof, sitting as an advisory body, was to sift out the genuinely conscientious who were to be offered work under the Home Office and, if they accepted it, were to be released under conditional pardon, transferred to Army Reserve W, and not returned to prison or recalled to the Army, so long as they continued to work.[2]

The members of the Brace Committee believed that they would be dealing only with genuine conscientious objectors who were prepared—indeed anxious—to do work of national importance; they were not told at the outset that the Central Tribunal had been advised to lower its standards and that this would mean the release of men who were not especially conscientious either in their objection to military service or in their approach to civilian work. When Brace and his colleagues appreciated that they had been misled they were not unnaturally resentful; the Home Office Scheme presented difficulties enough without the introduction of men whose motivation was suspect. Within a year the Committee

[1] For the treatment of the conscientious objectors in prison see Chapter 10 below.

[2] The Brace Committee, p. 1.

had to be reconstituted, but even before then the original members would have been glad to resign. The nature of their feelings may be judged from William Brace's own comment in the Commons in April 1917:

I accepted a responsibility very distasteful to me and it has been one of the most critical problems which I have ever been called on to face since I entered public life.[1]

The Brace Committee's difficulties sprang from the dilemma of being required to satisfy too many different interests. The military, the Central Tribunal, the Treasury, public opinion, and the conscientious objectors themselves all made demands on the Committee that were seldom complementary and often in direct conflict. Some of these conflicting interests were revealed long before the first conscientious objectors were released. Between 21 June (when the Committee was appointed) and 27 July (when the Central Tribunal began interviewing the conscientious objectors in Wormwood Scrubs) the Committee held a number of planning meetings. At these meetings the Committee sought the advice of various 'witnesses' including General Childs, Captain Stevenson, who was Deputy Governor of Wormwood Scrubs, and representatives of the Board of Agriculture, the Labour Exchange Department of the Board of Trade, the Railway Executive Committee, the Road Board, and the Post Office.[2] Inevitably much of the discussion centred round the problem of finding suitable employment, a problem that had been made more difficult to solve by Samuel's firm belief that the men should work in large groups. The Home Secretary had written:

Unless no other course is possible, I am averse from sending men as individuals or in small groups into private employment, and certainly not in the districts from which they came, as I believe such a course would be disapproved by public opinion.[3]

The argument was that public opinion demanded of conscientious objectors in general and of these conscientious objectors in particular, a sacrifice that was comparable if not identical to that made

[1] 5 HC 93, col. 186, 30 April 1917.

[2] Interim Report of the Brace Committee, 28 June 1916, attached to the Minutes of the Central Tribunal, 10 July 1916.

[3] The Brace Committee, p. 2.

by the soldiers. It was hoped that the principle of equality of sacrifice would convince those whose relatives were serving in the armed forces that conscientious objection was not being used as a soft option. *The Times* was expressing a widely held view when it recommended that the men released from prison should be employed on 'a form of arduous and unremunerative public service'.[1] This newspaper also suggested that the men should be denied the right to vote, since the privileges of citizenship should be reserved for those who were prepared to shoulder its responsibilities.[2] The disfranchisement of conscientious objectors, which appeared to be both just and logical to some sections of public opinion, found no official support at this stage in the war, but the need for equality of sacrifice was accepted by the Cabinet and by Parliament with few dissentient voices. M.P.s who were not unsympathetic nevertheless argued that willingness to embrace unattractive conditions was a mark of sincerity. 'There must be some sign', said Commander Wedgewood, 'that a man who pleads conscience suffers for that conscience.'[3] To achieve something approaching equality of sacrifice, the Brace Committee agreed not only that the men should be employed in large groups but also that the conditions of employment 'should not be appreciably better than those applying to Non-Combatants on Home Service. . . .'[4] This did not satisfy those Conservative M.P.s who, like Major Hunt, would have preferred to pack the conscientious objectors off to Germany with Lord Haldane[5] and remained highly critical of the concessions that they considered the Brace Committee to be making.

Major Hunt's was not the only or the most serious form of hostility with which the Committee had to deal. All the private firms approached refused to employ conscientious objectors 'either because of their prejudice against them or because of the risk of trouble with ordinary workmen'.[6] Similar objections were put forward by those responsible for labour in the docks, on the railways, and on the land. Though the Government talked in terms of civilian work of national importance, the truth was that the men

[1] *The Times*, 6 July 1916.

[2] Ibid.

[3] 5 HC 86, col. 873, 19 October 1916.

[4] The Brace Committee, p. 3.

[5] 5 HC 84, col. 1479, 25 July 1916. Haldane had been Lord Chancellor in the Liberal Government but had been dropped by Asquith when the Coalition was formed. He was regarded as pro-German by the Tories.

[6] The Brace Committee, p. 2.

and women engaged on such work were seldom prepared to have conscientious objectors working alongside them. To make matters worse, the men who were to be released from prison would themselves object to any work that was associated, however indirectly, with the war effort.

In these circumstances, the Committee could not have been blamed if it had failed to find enough jobs, but by the middle of July the Road Board had been persuaded to employ up to one thousand conscientious objectors on roadmaking and quarrying, and the government-sponsored Home Grown Timber Committee had agreed to occupy gangs of thirty to forty men on felling small stuff. In addition, the Board of Inland Revenue and the Llanelly Rural District Council offered to take some men, the former for clerical work and the latter for the repair and maintenance of its waterworks. As work of national importance, these jobs would no doubt fall short of some conscientious objectors' expectations, but the uninspiring nature of the tasks would be a source of satisfaction to those who wished to ensure that conscientious objectors were not enjoying themselves.

The policy of the Treasury and the belief in the need for equality of sacrifice meant that the Scheme would have to be run on a shoestring. Samuel insisted that the conscientious objectors employed should receive no more than an ordinary soldier's pay,[1] but he need not have worried: as a result of the financial limitations imposed by the Treasury, the Committee was unable to give the men more than 8*d.* a day, which was two-thirds of the minimum pay of a private. The Committee was credited with the value of the work done at the rates obtaining in local industry, but this income had to cover not only the men's wages but also their board and lodging, medical attention, clothing, railway fares, and Separation Allowances. The very low level of earnings, which averaged less than 10*s.* per man per week, gave substance to the N.C.F.'s claim that the Scheme was being used by the Government to depress workers' wages generally and to undermine the position of the trade unions; low earnings also furnished an excuse for those conscientious objectors who shrank from the long working day prescribed by the Committee.

Although the Scheme had to be self-sufficient as far as its

[1] Ibid.

running costs were concerned, the Treasury allowed £10 per man for capital expenditure; this was supposed to meet the cost of building and equipping the camps that would be needed for those projects—such as quarrying and road-building—on which large numbers of men would be employed. But the per capita grant proved hopelessly inadequate and the Committee soon abandoned its plans to accommodate the men in huts: tents, old cottages, and disused barns were the best that the Committee could afford.

The dull, back-breaking irrelevance of much of the work, the low pay and rough living, above all the employment in large groups, were not the conditions to inspire good discipline and active cooperation. Yet the Committee continued to plan on the optimistic assumption that the men released from prison would be ready to cooperate. This view seemed to be confirmed by the Deputy Governor of Wormwood Scrubs, who told the Committee that from his conversations with the conscientious objectors in the prison he was satisfied that they were willing to work under supervision.[1] The Committee was encouraged to think that there was no need to draw up an elaborate code of rules and that the supervision of the camps could safely be left to the Committee's agent on the spot, who would have the power to impose stoppages of pay. Even more optimistic was the decision to allow the conscientious objectors in each camp to elect their own committee so that much of the internal government would be in the hands of the men themselves. Participation in the running of their own affairs was welcomed by some conscientious objectors and abused by others; no doubt it was intended as a practical and enlightened measure, but it was to prove a source of indiscipline and confusion rather than the reverse. A more realistic approach to the problem of discipline had already been adopted by Samuel and Childs, who had agreed that the men who did not work or whose conduct was unsatisfactory should be returned to the prison and thence to the army.[2] Both Samuel and Childs believed that this deterrent would enable the Brace Committee to 'maintain a sufficient hold

[1] The Brace Committee, p. 2.

[2] Minutes of the Central Tribunal, 10 July 1916. Samuel also suggested that the men's release from prison should become unconditional when their term of imprisonment expired, but Childs did not agree; the military were not prepared to lose their hold over the men altogether.

upon the men', but they seem to have overlooked the fact that the threat of return to the army would have little force if it was known that the military had no intention of subjecting conscientious objectors to normal discipline.

With this structure of employment, finance, and control, the Home Office Scheme was ready to receive the first conscientious objectors released from prison. The N.C.F. was highly critical of the Committee's plans and forecast that the Scheme would be a disaster. Clifford Allen had earlier poured scorn on the whole concept:

> We know that some of our friends (who seem determined to 'meet' the Government as we are to refuse any compromise) are leading the Government to imagine that the way out is to be found in the organisation of Labour Battalions at sweated rates of pay. What hypocrisy it all is! We are not willing to be used to exploit trade unionism and so lower the standard of wages.[1]

Allen claimed that the new scheme resulted from 'an entire misconception of our views and the character of our protest'.[2] The young Quakers and the Fellowship of Reconciliation joined the N.C.F. in attacking the scheme, but the Government had no intention of being diverted from a policy that, it was hoped, would settle the conscientious objector question for the remainder of the war. As had been the case with the drafting of the Military Service Bill in December 1915, Asquith and his colleagues seem to have thought that, a concession to conscience having been made, no further problems would arise, as though their generosity would itself be sufficient to iron out difficulties; mistaking concessions for solutions, they were disappointed and angry when the problem refused to lie down.

The first conscientious objectors started work under the Brace Committee on 12 August; they were quickly followed by others as the Central Tribunal worked its way through the large number of men awaiting interview in Wormwood Scrubs. By mid-October the Committee had had to find jobs for one thousand, and fourteen months later—in December 1917—the total in employment reached a peak of three thousand.[3] In all, 4,126 conscientious

[1] *The Tribunal*, 22 June 1916. [2] Ibid., 6 July 1916.
[3] The Brace Committee, p. 7.

objectors were employed at one time or another during the lifetime of the Scheme.[1]

The early groups to be released from prison were divided between the three principal employers: the Road Board, the Home Grown Timber Committee, and the Llanelly Rural District Council. But the Central Tribunal was soon releasing more men than could be absorbed in these projects. The Committee could not refuse to accept them and yet had no work to offer. To the Home Office officials there appeared to be no alternative to adapting two disused prisons, at Wakefield and Warwick, as 'work centres', initially for those conscientious objectors who were unfit for manual labour but subsequently for anyone who could not be placed elsewhere. That the Committee had so soon to take over prison buildings where the men would be employed on what were somewhat grandly described as prison industries, was a bad omen for the success of a scheme that had been designed to allow the genuine conscientious objector to do work of national importance out of custody.

Another flaw in the Scheme's conception was exposed. With unconscious naivety, the Committee reported:

> A few weeks' experience suggested that the Conscientious Objectors were not all of one type, and that there were large sections who either could not or would not work, but who could and would cause trouble.[2]

The Committee's earlier optimism had been partly based on the conviction that conscientious objectors were a homogeneous group whose members, however intractable, were motivated by high principles and wedded to unselfish goals. The Committee was not alone in holding this simple belief: the conscientious objectors not infrequently thought of themselves in the same way, and Herbert Samuel had earlier expressed a widely accepted view when he had referred to conscientious objectors as 'men who unquestionably, by common consent, are men of the highest character, and in other

[1] *Military Statistics 1914–1920*, p. 673. Of the 4,522 men recommended to the Brace Committee, 293 refused to work under the Committee, 82 were unconditionally released by the military authorities (presumably on the grounds of health), 10 agreed to return to the army, 10 were unfit to leave prison, and 1 was recommended too late in April 1919 to be employed.

[2] The Brace Committee, p. 3.

matters good citizens'.[1] But the experience of the Home Office Scheme tarnished the image. In 1919 the Committee concluded:

Many of the men were feeble in physique, weak of will or unstable of character. Nearly all were cranks, incapable of sustained collective effort, and cohering only to air their grievances or to promote queer and unusual ends.[2]

It was as inaccurate to dismiss the majority of conscientious objectors as cranks as it was to claim for them superior qualities of character. Indeed one of the Brace Committee's difficulties was that it could not generalize about the men working on the Scheme. The policy urged on the Central Tribunal by General Childs ensured the release of some men for whom the popular taunt of slackers was not altogether inappropriate. Yet the majority of conscientious objectors on the Scheme, though not as devoted to the principles of 'diligence and fidelity' as the Committee would have wished, determined their attitude to work and authority by something more inspiring than self-interest. There were those who left prison prepared to honour the undertaking that they had given to the Central Tribunal and willing to participate in the running of their own affairs. This group included the Christian pacifists and many of the socialists who had obtained release, particularly those whose objections, as many-sided as the Players' repertoire, should probably be described as intellectual-political-ethical-historical. Regardless of whether or not they were members of the N.C.F. (which was divided against itself on the issue of cooperation[3]), all these men tried at first to make the Scheme work. They accepted the rough living conditions and the low pay, though they found it difficult to acquiesce in the waste of their skills and experience that equality of sacrifice demanded. In time, however, they became disenchanted; the lack of purpose and the sense of frustration it engendered encouraged some to return voluntarily to prison and drove others to sympathize with the

[1] 5 HC 78, col. 451, 19 January 1916. Cf. Mr. Rhys J. Davies, a pacifist M.P., writing in the October 1942 issue of the *Central Board for Conscientious Objectors Bulletin:* 'It is seldom that we find a drunkard or wastrel among COs; they are for the most part men and women of excellent personal character, and they are generally reliable and honest in business.'

[2] The Brace Committee, p. 9.

[3] For the arguments for and against cooperation see *The Tribunal*, 27 July 1916.

methods of the militant marxists and anarchists who had never had any intention of cooperating with the Committee, and whose release from prison had been a triumph for expediency. The militants used the jargon and essayed the tactics of the revolution, though they proved to be amateur revolutionaries. They gave effective leadership to the miscellaneous anti-authoritarian elements and to the increasing number of men alienated by what appeared to be the inept and insensitive management of the Scheme. The task of the militants was made easier by the juxtaposition of the Committee's optimistic plans for self-government with the extreme sanction of return to prison (as though a school should try to maintain good order with no rules but an ever-present threat of expulsion), which provided the minimum of stability with the maximum of ill-feeling. For men who wanted to stir up trouble, embarrass the Government, and provoke public hostility, the Home Office Scheme gave ample opportunity.

A third group, though prepared to work diligently enough, stood aside from both participation and revolution. These were the apocalyptic sectarians, mostly Jehovah's Witnesses and Plymouth Brethren, who had no interest in the running of the camp or in the improvement of society. With their eyes on the Second Coming and their faith firmly embedded in the Word of God, they regarded the aims of the revolutionaries as irrelevant, an attitude that the young marxists must have found peculiarly irritating.

The first large camp was established at Dyce, a village five miles north-west of Aberdeen. Here it was planned that several hundred conscientious objectors should be employed on the repair and construction of roads in the area. The men travelled north without escort. Many were thankful that at last they would be able to undertake a form of alternative service that did not conflict with their conscientious objections; all were glad to be putting behind them the restrictions of prison life, anticipating with pleasure the chance to breathe clear air and to exercise in the open country, on grass and heather, instead of on the rigid patterns of the prison yard. It was high summer and a time, if not of high hopes, then at least of modest expectation and lifting morale. Yet within three months the camp at Dyce had been shut down and the work abandoned, because in the Committee's view 'the results as regards discipline and return for labour had been so bad. . . .'[1]

[1] The Brace Committee, p. 5.

The failure of Dyce was symptomatic of the weakness of the whole Scheme. When the men arrived at the camp, they found that their work would consist of shifting stones in barrows from the quarries to the crushing-machines, and thence in trucks to the site of the road-works. The long day's slog in the stone quarries inevitably suggested comparisons with a penal settlement. No doubt the work was of national importance, but the men could hardly be blamed for thinking that its value to the government lay less in the improvement to communications in Scotland than in the provision of that 'arduous and unremunerative public service' for which *The Times* had called. The Committee expected the men to work the same ten-hour day as the other employees of the Road Board, a logical decision but one that did not take into account that the conscientious objectors were school-teachers, clerks, skilled artisans, and traders in a small way of business, who were not accustomed to heavy physical work and had just spent several weeks in the confinement of a closed prison. The men at Dyce ignored the Committee's requirement and negotiated their own agreement with the local officials of the Road Board; faced with the prospect of a type of labour trouble of which they had had no experience, the officials accepted the men's offer to work in shifts. The hours were cut from ten to five, and although the Brace Committee disapproved of what it regarded as 'concerted idleness',[1] it was forced to recognize that, in the face of collective disobedience, stoppages of pay were ineffective and the threat of a mass return to prison lacking in credibility. 'Concerted idleness' could have been avoided if the character and conditions of employment had been acceptable to those conscientious objectors who were prepared to do work of national importance, but the Committee was never in a position to satisfy even the minimum expectations of these men; instead of being able to encourage cooperation by offering worthwhile employment, the Committee was forced to rely increasingly on a system of rules and penalties.

At Dyce, the deterioration of work and morale was accelerated by the poor living conditions. The men had been issued with old army tents (which their consciences had not prevented them using) and the same blankets, palliasses, and waterproof sheets provided for soldiers in the field. This equipment was adequate while the summer lasted, but the autumn rains soon soaked through the

[1] Ibid., p. 3.

rotting canvas onto clothes, bedding, and personal possessions; and by the beginning of October the sodden turf of the camp site had been trodden into a quagmire of mud and standing water. Life in the camp, like the work in the quarries, was both demoralizing and degrading. Those men who were still prepared to work the shifts found the prevailing mood against them and lost heart. Discontent was expressed either in writing direct to the Home Office or by organized protest through the men's elected committee. Brace had never defined the role that the elected committees would play, beyond expressing the hope that the camps would be in part self-governing; he now found that the committee at Dyce, instead of acting as an organ of self-government, was being used as a vehicle for complaint. In due course, the men's complaints were raised in the Commons by Ramsay MacDonald. MacDonald had visited Dyce and knew the conditions there, and he pleaded for the more intelligent use of the men's talents:

> Here is this country at death grips with an enemy fighting for its existence in a way it has never had to do before, and it ought to make every one of us bend our backs to do the work we can do. . . . These men do not want comfortable beds; they do not want better food; they do not want shorter hours; they do not want easier work. They want to be put to something in which they feel they can put their heart and in regard to which they can feel that it is work that is really useful to the State.[1]

While MacDonald's estimate of the conscientious objectors' willingness to suffer discomfort in the service of the state may have been pitched rather high, he was unquestionably correct in arguing that there would be fewer difficulties and greater benefits to the country if the men were allowed to do work for which they were equipped. But the rational use of manpower was a concept that, even in the third autumn of the war, had not been fully grasped and stood no chance of outweighing the popular demand for equality of sacrifice. It did not matter that the men's skills were being wasted; it did not matter that other conscientious objectors who were more fortunate or more convincing before the tribunals were allowed to do work of their own choice on an individual basis: these were, as Lord David Cecil pointed out, 'the incongruities and inconveniences' of the Military Service Act. The overwhelming feeling in Parliament was that the men on the Home Office Scheme

[1] MacDonald's speech, 5 HC 86, col. 802–15, 19 October 1916.

should be grateful for release from prison and that they should show their gratitude (and incidentally confirm their sincerity) by accepting whatever work and conditions were prescribed by the Brace Committee.[1]

The Commons was no more sympathetic to complaints of mud and leaky tents. In September one of the conscientious objectors at Dyce, Walter Roberts, died after a short illness. To some of the men Roberts's death was a direct result of the damp and unhygienic conditions in which he had been forced to live, but when Ramsay MacDonald referred to the severity of these conditions, he provoked an impatient response from Mr. C. B. Stanton:

What about our sons and brothers and others who are at the front? Do they cry about a little mud in their camps? What about the boys whom I saw out at the front, my own son among them, up to their eyebrows in mud—boys who are risking everything? Yet we can find time here to cry out about the woes of the poor creature who is a conscientious objector in his own country's greatest hour of trouble. . . . We can ill afford in this country to coddle and canoodle around these people.[2]

To the conscientious objectors the death of Walter Roberts had a symbolic significance that would certainly have been lost on Mr. Stanton. Although Roberts had died of natural causes he was regarded as the first victim of official persecution and elevated to the rank of martyr. It was an understandable but inaccurate interpretation of the facts: Roberts no more died of persecution than a soldier succumbing to the influenza epidemic could be said to have died of conscription. When Roberts was buried near his home in Cheshire, Fenner Brockway wrote a heroic valediction in *The Tribunal* that skilfully reconciled the ideals of international socialism with the claims of the Christian faith:

And now the struggle of this brave bearer of the banner of Peace is over. His body rests beside those of many noble men at Hawarden; his spirit is free and united with the Life Universal in which Englishman and German, Austrian and Russian are one. He has followed faithfully the vision of Universal Peace; he has won the Peace that is Eternal. To all of us his life and death must be an inspiration. . . . He was worthy to be the first to die in our struggle.[3]

[1] The whole debate is interesting as an indication of the growing parliamentary impatience with the problem of the conscientious objector: see 5 HC 86, col. 802–39, 19 October 1916.

[2] 5 HC 86, col. 835, 19 October 1916.

[3] 14 September 1916.

The outcry in conscientious objector circles over Roberts's death, the talk of martyrdom, and the demand for better conditions, suggested to some people that the conscientious objectors were indifferent to the wider suffering of the war. Mr. Stanton was only one of many M.P.s, including members of the Cabinet, whose sons were on active service and for whom the lengthening lists of casualties intensified personal anxiety. Walter Long, whose elder son was commanding the 56th Brigade in France, told the Commons:

> Many of us who have our dearest in the war know that if we lose them we lose that for which we care most of anything in the world.[1]

The British casualty figures for the Western Front for July 1916—the first month of the Somme offensive—were 196,081, three times the previous highest monthly total.[2] In the three months, July, August, September, while the Home Office Scheme was being planned and launched, the casualties totalled nearly 400,000.[3] Among the dead was Asquith's eldest son, Raymond; Walter Long was spared for a few more months until his elder son was killed in January 1917.[4] The deepening tragedy of the war helped to harden both the official and the public attitude to the men on the Scheme; by the winter of 1916 any chance there may have been of rethinking the principles on which the Scheme was based seemed to have disappeared. If there was to be adjustment, it would be in the direction of firmer control.

The authority of the Brace Committee was already being undermined by the spread of unrest and disobedience: several conscientious objectors at Warwick refused to go out to work; at Llanelly the men were accused of 'slacking and malingering' and promptly went on strike; and at Wakefield the singing of 'The Red Flag', a harmless enough gesture, provoked a general ban on all forms of propaganda.[5] In an attempt to establish control, the Committee exercised its power to recommend a return to prison: by the end of 1916 ninety-two of the worst offenders had been

[1] 5 HC 82, col. 95–6, 3 May 1916.

[2] *Military Statistics 1914–1920*, p. 253.

[3] Ibid.

[4] The extent to which a single family was affected by the fighting is illustrated by Sir George Cave, the Solicitor-General. Cave had no son, but eight nephews were in the services: two were killed, three others won the M.C., and the remaining three were serving in France, Mesopotamia, and the Royal Flying Corps.

[5] The Brace Committee, p. 4.

dealt with in this way.[1] But the disregard for the Committee's authority continued, and this was at least partly because return to prison and thence to the army proved to be an ineffective deterrent. The Brace Committee put the blame on the War Office, but Childs—as the Committee recorded—was much too astute to expose the army once again to the dangers and frustrations of trying to impose military law on conscientious objectors:

> The Army Council, however, could never see its way to adopt the only course that might have deterred effectively, namely, the application of ordinary Army discipline to men recalled for breach of the Committee's rules.[2]

To make matters worse, the Chairman of the Central Tribunal, Lord Salisbury, complained that the Committee was not being strict enough and that the treatment of the men released from prison should be 'comparable in hardship' to that of soldiers fighting in France.[3] With considerable restraint, the Committee replied that 'the presence, among the men employed, of a large number of indifferent characters might well be due to the laxity of the Tribunal in accepting claims to conscientious objections'.[4]

However unjust Lord Salisbury's criticism, the Committee had to recognize that without a code of discipline the Scheme was in danger of degenerating into a farce. While a code was being prepared, the Coalition that Asquith had been forced to accept in May 1915 and that had governed the country for eighteen months, disintegrated.[5] On 7 December, Lloyd George became Prime Minister and surrounded himself with men who had publicly committed themselves to the efficient and dynamic conduct of the war; the 'Squiffites' would not serve under him even if he would have them. Effective power was placed in the hands of a small War Cabinet containing, in addition to the Prime Minister, the Conservative and Labour leaders, Bonar Law and Henderson, as well as the two former proconsuls who had been the most consistent advocates of compulsory military service, Lord Milner and Lord Curzon. Another ardent but less intelligent conscriptionist, Lord

[1] Loc. cit. [2] Ibid., p. 5.

[3] Loc. cit. [4] Ibid., p. 4.

[5] There are various versions of Asquith's fall, though it is possible that the full story has not yet been told. The different strands are brought together in A. J. P. Taylor's short summary of the events in *English History 1914–1945*, pp. 66–70. The mounting campaign to get rid of Asquith is described in Gollin, *Proconsul in Politics*, Ch. XIII.

Derby, became Secretary of State for War. Walter Long moved—no doubt with relief—to the Colonial Office; William Brace remained—no doubt with reluctance—as Under-Secretary for Home Affairs. Brace's new chief was Sir George Cave, an orthodox Tory, who had been Solicitor-General in the Coalition and counted Sir Roger Casement among his successful prosecutions. To the problem of the conscientious objector, Cave brought qualities similar to those of General Childs: he was patient and courteous with the numerous parliamentary criticisms of his department's treatment of conscientious objectors but he was not easily swayed; it was said of him, as of Childs, that the velvet glove covered an iron hand.[1]

There was little for conscientious objectors to celebrate in these changes. The character of the new administration pointed to a reaction against the 'privileges' allowed to the men who had been released from prison, rather than to any attempt to rationalize the use of skills and experience. When Sir George Cave approved a comprehensive Code of Rules[2] for the Home Office Scheme, his action was thought to mark the introduction of a hard line, although the need for such a code had been accepted some weeks previously by Herbert Samuel. Most of the thirty-three rules confirmed existing arrangements for work, pay, leave, and discipline. The Committee's experience had not altogether dispelled its earlier optimism: the rules allowed the men to 'elect representatives for such purposes relating to their communal life as may seem to them proper', and made generous provision for leave and free railway travel. The events of the autumn had, however, identified some unforeseen problems: the new code established 'insolence to the Agent' as an offence, forbade the introduction of alcoholic liquor into the men's quarters, and reiterated the ban on public propaganda 'whether by making speeches, taking part in processions or demonstrations, or otherwise'.

[1] A press comment quoted in Sir Charles Mallet, *Lord Cave: a Memoir*, London, 1931, p. 197. Cave's widow, in an introductory chapter to this Memoir, claims that Cave was also blessed with a 'God-given gift of humour' and offered the following evidence: In an election campaign, the opposition spread the rumour that Cave's mother was Jewish. In Kingston Town Hall Cave said to the audience: 'I hear it has been said that my dear mother is a Jewess,' and turning his profile to the audience, he asked, 'Do I look like a Jew?' There was a roar of 'No you don't.' Cave commented: 'No, I do not, neither is my mother a Jewess.' Mallet, op. cit., p. 12.

[2] Published as Cd. 8550.

The Rules came into force on 1 January 1917. They did not ensure harder work or better discipline; during the first half of the year the difficulties of controlling the men on the Scheme became more acute as the Committee was obliged to accommodate an increasing number of men in work centres. The Road Board camps at Dyce, Longside, and Haverhill had been closed in the previous autumn; it had been a pious hope that conscientious objectors would eagerly embrace the opportunity to cart and quarry stones for the remainder of the war. During the winter months the work under the Home Grown Timber Committee had also been abandoned; in an administrative reshuffle, this Committee had become the responsibility of the War Office, and trees that had been felled freely enough in 1916, were now regarded by conscientious objectors as having military significance. The same uncompromising logic put an end to other projects. 'On the slightest pretext', the Brace Committee complained, 'work was objected to as having some remote connexion with the war.'[1] Meanwhile, attempts to persuade local War Agricultural Committees to employ conscientious objectors on land drainage schemes or on individual farms were unsuccessful, the Committees preferring to use German soldiers: 'while prisoners of war rapidly established themselves in favour, it was impossible to make much use of conscientious objectors; the feeling against them in country districts was strong and efforts to place them on farms met with small success.'[2]

By February 1917 the lack of suitable employment had become critical; the number of men referred to the Brace Committee was approaching 2,500,[3] but apart from a handful of surviving projects[4] there were only the work centres at Wakefield and Warwick to take all the men released from prison. A new work centre was needed urgently. The Committee appealed to the Prison Commissioners and were offered Dartmoor Prison together with the

[1] The Brace Committee, p. 3.

[2] T. H. Middleton, *Food Production in War*, Oxford, 1923, p. 222.

[3] See the statistics given to Parliament by Cave, 5 HC 90, col. 814, 15 February 1917.

[4] Including the laying out of a land colony for discharged soldiers and sailors at Patrington, near Hull; clerical work for the National Health Insurance Commissioners; and manual labour on building schemes and waterworks. The Committee admitted that some good projects broke down because of 'the unreasonableness of the employer'. The Brace Committee, p. 6.

services of part of the prison staff.[1] While William Brace might once have hesitated to use this grim outcrop on the moor, he now had little choice; unless Samuel's initial ban on individual employment was lifted, there was no practicable alternative to the accommodation of large numbers of conscientious objectors in prison buildings. This arrangement suited the Home Office well, as the prison population had been falling since the turn of the century, a trend accentuated by the war. Receptions on conviction fell from 136,424 in 1913–14 to 43,678 in 1916–17, a fall of 68 per cent.[2] The decline covered the whole range of indictable offences, one of the very few exceptions being bigamy, where the sharp rise in the number of convictions underlined the family dislocation of the times.[3]

The Brace Committee endeavoured to give its new acquisition a better image: Dartmoor Prison became the Princetown Work Centre, and elaborate measures were taken to eliminate those items—the locks on cell doors, the official prison notepaper—that would be reminders of the building's former role. But the process of 'deprisoning', however well meant, could not remove the flavour of the penal institution, particularly when the only work available was quarrying, reclaiming land for the Prison Commissioners and the Duchy of Cornwall, and 'ordinary prison industries'.[4] The inescapable overtones of punishment, which robbed the work of any claim it might have had to be regarded as work of national importance, did not discourage the Home Secretary from taking an optimistic view of the Work Centre's future. And when Cave explained the new project to Lord Stamfordham, King George V's Private Secretary, he received an enthusiastic reply:

> It seems to His Majesty an excellent one both as regards the conscientious objectors and the reclamation work at Dartmoor.[5]

[1] The Brace Committee, p. 5. See also Report of the Commissioners of Prisons and Directors of Convict Prisons (hereafter Prison Report), 1917 (Cd. 8674), p. 22.

[2] Prison Report, 1917, pp. 4–5.

[3] Prison Report, 1918 (Cd. 9174), p. 6.

[4] The Brace Committee, p. 5.

[5] Lord Stamfordham to Cave, 21 February 1917, RA GV5125/2. Lord Stamfordham was Private Secretary from 1901 to 1931. His only son was killed in the war.

On this hopeful note the Princetown Work Centre was opened in March and soon became the largest institution run by the Committee; there were 856 conscientious objectors in residence at the end of April and the total reached a peak of 1,200 in the autumn.[1]

The concentration of men at Princetown provided fertile ground for the seeds of unrest. An anarchic minority found it easy to unsettle their comrades, provoke the authorities into tactical errors, and antagonize a public opinion that, since the previous autumn, had been inclined to regard the conscientious objector as a family disgrace, unmentionable and best forgotten. The Committee faced a classic dilemma: it had good reason to believe that some of the disruptive elements should never have been classified as genuine by the Central Tribunal, yet it could not move against them without alienating the majority who, though not militant, had real grievances about work and conditions. On the other hand, if the Committee failed to control the 'revolutionaries', it would be attacked by those sections of public opinion that saw in the tactics of the militants a rehearsal for the Bolshevik revolution in Britain. As the university authorities half a century later, the members of the Committee were caught in the crossfire between the two extremes:

> The men and their friends argued that they were genuine and therefore entitled to exemption and justified in not working enthusiastically and not behaving quietly under duress: the critics of the Conscientious Objectors argued that they were men who ought to be performing military service, instead of which they were being dealt with lightly by the Committee. . . . These two arguments resulted in constant pressure on the Committee either to increase or to relax its disciplinary methods; and neither argument could be accepted as applying to the whole body of men.[2]

The militants at Dartmoor caused a degree of public hysteria that was out of all proportion to their importance. After visiting the new Work Centre, the Bishop of Exeter, Lord Rupert William Gascoyne Cecil, reported to *The Times* that 'sacks of letters come and go, no doubt carrying instructions for those plans of bloodshed which may at some future time bring, according to their view, liberty, and according to our view, ruin, to England'.[3] The Princetown revolutionaries had a more modest programme: they

[1] Brace's statement, 5 HC 98, col. 1957, 6 November 1917.

[2] The Brace Committee, p. 9.

[3] 8 October 1917.

sang 'The Red Flag', walked out of church while the national anthem was being played, and distributed subversive leaflets to the uncomprehending locals. They were flattered by their notoriety and showed no hesitation in posing for the press photographers, a vanity that the *Daily Mail* was quick to exploit. At the end of April the newspaper published a number of pictures of these men with suitable captions: 'Dartmoor Do-nothings', 'You can't catch me', and 'More pictures of the COs whose obtrusive manners and slack life are causing strong protests in Devon'.[1] The protests were echoed in Parliament by the Member for Devonport, Sir C. Kinloch-Cooke, whose daily nagging of William Brace was one of the features of question time in the Commons. In Plymouth a public meeting was addressed by a local winner of the Victoria Cross and voted unanimously in favour of confining the 'bastard, political agitators' to the prison grounds,[2] a policy that the Brace Committee accepted after parties of conscientious objectors had been attacked in the village of Princetown.[3] The imposition of bounds annoyed the mass of conscientious objectors without satisfying hostile public opinion. The harassed members of the Committee complained both that most of the men 'intended to give all the trouble they could and to work as little as possible' and that the press reports of the men's behaviour were 'highly coloured'.[4] It must have seemed to Sir George Cave that the Committee was no longer competent to deal with the repeated challenges to its authority. In July the Committee was reconstituted; although the official explanation was that members were needed who would be able to give daily attendance, the character and policy of the new men suggested a different motive.[5] Brace continued as Chairman (the only survivor of the original Committee) with Major Terrell, K.C., M.P., and Major Briscoe, a Prison Commissioner, as his colleagues. Henry Terrell, the Tory Member for Gloucester City, had commanded one of the county battalions until 1915; E. W. Briscoe had retired from the army in 1895 and had subsequently served as a prison governor. The penal-cum-military flavour was strengthened by the appointment of Captain Stevenson, the Deputy Governor of Wormwood Scrubs, as the full-time Inspector

[1] See the editions published on 23, 24, 27, and 30 April 1917.
[2] The meeting is reported in the *Daily Mail*, 26 April 1917.
[3] The Brace Committee, p. 6.
[4] Loc. cit.
[5] Loc. cit.

of all the Committee's camps and work centres. At the same time as the Committee was reconstituted, a more stringent Code of Rules was introduced.[1] There was now an explicit prohibition of insolence to the Committee's Agent and of attempting to persuade other men to disobey orders or refuse work; attendance at meetings outside the centre was also prohibited, and the fines for minor offences increased. There was no mention in the new Code of the men's right to elect their own committees.

The principal concern of the men now responsible for the Home Office Scheme was the enforcement of discipline. There was a sharp increase in the number of men sent back to prison for breaking the rules, while on a more trivial (and probably more irritating) level, the Committee introduced a system of pocket money graded according to behaviour. These measures checked for a time the activities of the militants, but did nothing to win the cooperation of the majority of conscientious objectors. If the intention was to make the Scheme less attractive, then the new policy could be counted a success: the proportion of men in prison who declined to accept work on the Scheme rose from 7·2 per cent in 1916 to 19·5 per cent in 1917.[2]

The tightening of discipline at first met with public approval, yet within four months (by November 1917) both the public and the official attitude to conscientious objectors had undergone a significant change. The bullying of John Gray and James Brightmore, though promptly dealt with by Childs, caused some uneasiness, but it was the treatment of the absolutists, whose sincerity was widely recognized, that raised serious doubts about the wisdom of the Government's policy.[3] The open discussion of these doubts revived the suggestion that official policy should differentiate between the religious and the political objector. It was the Bishop of Exeter who recommended that the political objector should be placed 'in that portion of England that is frequently visited by the enemy aeroplane', while the 'religious conchie' was released,[4] a proposal in which the King thought there was 'much common sense'.[5] But the distinction between the religious and the political

[1] Published as Cd. 8627.

[2] Report of the Central Tribunal, p. 24.

[3] For the growing concern in influential circles over the treatment of the absolutists see Chapter 10, below.

[4] In his letter to *The Times*, 8 October 1917. The Bishop lost three sons in the war.

[5] Wigram to Childs, 9 October 1917, RA GV5910/4.

objector was no easier to draw now than it had been before the tribunals; and could not be applied to the Home Office Scheme, where all the men had been classified as genuine conscientious objectors by the Central Tribunal. The men on the Scheme benefited from the shift in public opinion nevertheless. In November a Cabinet committee approved rules for what was called Exceptional Employment, which at last broke with Samuel's dictum that individual employment under a private employer was unacceptable.[1] Between July and November the Committee had swung from a repressive, even punitive policy to the introduction of the one principle of employment that could have made sense of the Scheme from the start. There was no mention of equality of sacrifice; and Samuel's fears appeared to have been unfounded. The men behaved well, disposed of their own wages as they wished, and provoked very few complaints from the public.[2] But the new rules only applied to those men who had shown industry and good conduct for twelve months, so that it was not until the Armistice in November 1918 that the majority were doing exceptional employment.[3]

The twelve-month requirement meant that for the last year of the war the work centres still held many men who were neither industrious nor well-behaved. Not surprisingly there was constant unrest. In February 1918 Harry Firth, one of the men at Princetown, died of diabetes. His friends claimed that the prison doctor had been negligent (a claim that was not upheld by the inquest) and promoted a strike on the day of the funeral. There was an inquiry, conducted by Major Terrell himself, as a result of which the strikers were confined to their quarters after work for fourteen days, and the two 'ringleaders' returned to prison. Terrell dismissed the men's complaints against the doctor as trivial: 'on the very smallest foundation they build a superstructure of oppression and improper conduct on the part of the officials.'[4] There had been complaints, Terrell told the Commons, that the doctor had failed to diagnose a case of venereal disease, a curious comment in the

[1] Published as Cd. 8884. The only condition imposed on the men doing exceptional employment was that they should refrain from propaganda and serious misconduct.

[2] The Brace Committee, p. 7.

[3] In November 1918 1,300 men remained under the direct control of the Committee. See The Brace Committee, p. 7.

[4] Terrell's statement, 5 HC 103, col. 1628–31, 28 February 1918.

circumstances, but perhaps intended to show that conscientious objectors were, after all, as fallible as other men.

The publicity given to the Dartmoor strike, followed by the military reverses of the spring, rekindled public hostility. In May conscientious objectors at the Knutsford Work Centre (that had been opened in the previous autumn) were attacked by local youths.[1] The Committee transferred some of the men to Wakefield but this only inspired further violence. The *Wakefield Express* was blatantly provocative:

> With the Funk-Hole in Love Lane already almost filled to overflowing with these 'objects' it adds to our nausea to learn that, after the mobbing the white-feathered crew received at Knutsford last Sunday, the authorities on Thursday sent a batch of fifty to Wakefield.[2]

This issue was published on Whit Saturday; on the Sunday and Monday conscientious objectors returning to the Work Centre were attacked by holiday crowds whose aggressive mood reflected the acute tension of the military crisis. The intense hostility felt for conscientious objectors in the spring of 1918 was recalled by Caroline Playne:

> In general society you could scarcely mention their existence, much less claim acquaintance with individual COs, so great was the disgust and abhorrence called forth. . . . Some families expelled the Conscientious Objector member from their midst, so keenly did they feel the disgrace of the connection.[3]

The Armistice gave the Brace Committee no relief. Many of the men still working directly under its control considered that their obligations were now fulfilled and left for home. There was a further exodus at Christmas. Those who were caught were recalled to the army, a procedure that was endorsed by the War Cabinet but that can hardly have been worth the trouble.[4] Neither the Army Council nor the Cabinet was prepared to consider the discharge of the men until the demobilization of ordinary soldiers was sufficiently advanced. Wearily, the work dragged on into the new year. The Central Tribunal solemnly continued its interviewing of the conscientious objectors in prison until, at last, on 10 April

[1] The Brace Committee, p. 7. [2] 18 May 1918.
[3] Caroline E. Playne, *Britain Holds On, 1917–1918*, London, 1933, p. 303.
[4] CAB 23/8/504(7).

1919 the Government authorized the discharge of all conscientious objectors on the Home Office Scheme. Nine days later the last man in employment was released and the Scheme ceased to exist.[1] Of the 4,126 conscientious objectors who had been employed at one time or another during the two and three-quarter years, twenty-seven had died and three had been certified insane and handed over to the Lunacy Commissioners.[2]

The Home Office Scheme was based on a fundamental contradiction. In law the court-martialled men were soldiers for the period of the war; on the Scheme they had been classified as conscientious objectors to all military service. The men released from prison were, therefore, consigned to a limbo between the military and the civilian life: free from military control, yet liable to be returned to the army; out of prison, yet increasingly under penal discipline. The difficulties and contradictions of the Scheme were aggravated by the Central Tribunal's policy of releasing as many men as possible, and by Samuel's insistence on group employment. The latter precluded for over a year the rational use of skills and experience; the former ensured the presence, in all the larger camps and work centres, of militants whose revolutionary tactics would not have impressed Lenin, but helped to undermine discipline and provoke public hostility. To successive Governments, however, the Scheme had one advantage that outweighed its many defects: it reduced the number of absolutists to under one thousand, and in doing so relieved the military and the prison authorities of the problem of imposing discipline on a very large number of conscientious objectors.

[1] *Military Statistics 1914–1920*, p. 673.

[2] For the number of deaths see *Military Statistics 1914–1920*, p. 673; for the number certified insane see Cave's statement, 5 HC 104, col. 1462, 10 April 1918. There may have been further cases in the Scheme's final year. Both Graham and Bolton imply that the deaths were the result of the treatment the men received, but apart from those who died of unnatural causes (accident or suicide), the deaths were caused by illnesses contracted before conscription (but not always diagnosed) or by illnesses, such as influenza, contracted while working on the Scheme. No doubt in some cases the conditions aggravated existing illnesses or increased vulnerability to new ones, but this does not provide a justification for Bolton's statement that the men died 'as a direct result of the treatment they received'. See Bolton, op. cit., p. 266.

CHAPTER NINE

CONSCIENTIOUS OBJECTORS WHO ACCEPTED THE TRIBUNAL'S DECISION

Public hostility to the Home Office Scheme and concern in governmental circles at the repeated sentencing of the absolutists, tended to obscure the fact that the majority of conscientious objectors had accepted the tribunal's decision and were engaged in some form of alternative service.[1] Over nine thousand conscientious objectors had either joined the Non-Combatant Corps or taken up civilian work that the tribunal regarded as of national importance. These men had little news value, but their work, if not always a best use of their talents, demonstrated that there was a role for conscientious objectors to play in a society at war.

It had been assumed from the start that the normal alternative to combatant service would be non-combatant work in the army, but there had been a characteristic absence of preparation for the moment when the first conscientious objectors reported for duty. It was not clear whether they would be attached to infantry battalions as stretcher-bearers and pioneers, posted to existing non-combatant units such as the RAMC, or organized as a separate corps. The decision lay with Macready's department.[2] On 4 March 1916 an Army Council Instruction directed that recruits holding certificates of exemption from combatant service should be attached temporarily to an infantry depot or reserve battalion pending the establishment of a Non-Combatant Corps.[3] Although General Childs wanted all non-combatants to be treated as ordinary

[1] For the figures see pp. 131–2, above.

[2] The responsibility for the running of the Non-Combatant Corps belonged to the Directorate of Organisation, a sub-division of the Adjutant-General's Department.

[3] ACI No. 456, 1916. The Corps was established on 10 March by Army Order 112, 1916.

soldiers, to have placed large numbers of conscientious objectors in existing units would have provoked friction and increased the risk of complicated demarcation disputes over marginal duties. With the Non-Combatant Corps, training was carefully prescribed:

Companies of the NCC will be trained in squad drill without arms and in the use of various forms of tools used in field engineering. The privates will be equipped as infantry except that they will not be armed or trained with arms of any description.[1]

Once trained, the companies were posted to camps in England and France; they could not be employed in the firing line, a restriction that excluded such tasks as erecting barbed wire and burying the dead, and that denied to conscientious objectors the opportunity to share the dangers and deprivations of the trenches. In the Second World War, Parachute Field Ambulances and Bomb Disposal Units gave conscientious objectors a chance to show that they did not lack physical courage, a chance that was seized by some but characteristically scorned by others.[2] In the First World War, non-combatant duties were for the most part those army chores normally undertaken by pioneer or labour battalions, or even by defaulters. NCC companies built roads, erected hutted camps, loaded and unloaded ships and railway wagons, and burned excreta, an unpleasant task euphemistically defined as 'sanitary work'. The non-combatants were prepared to undertake the most distasteful jobs, but objected when they were ordered to manhandle munitions of war. The War Office insisted that no promise had been given on this point and made its customary assumption that disobedience had been provoked by political agitators. Macready believed that the refusal to load shells had been inspired by socialists,[3] and the official military view was that 'if an impression has gained ground that men of the Non-Combatant Corps are exempt from handling or loading munitions of war, it is solely due to mischievous propaganda. . . .'[4] It should have been obvious that, whether or not they were encouraged by agitators, men who objected to the use of guns might well refuse

[1] ACI No. 551, 1916.

[2] One argument against engaging in activities that involved danger was that by doing so one was not so much rebutting the charge of cowardice as admitting that the charge had some substance.

[3] Macready, op. cit., I, p. 250.

[4] WO 32/2051/3319.

to handle the ammunition. But the War Office was adamant: those who refused were court-martialled or, at Macready's suggestion, packed off to Mesopotamia where they would be far away from propaganda and publicity.[1] There can have been little advantage to the military in pursuing this policy, which did nothing to improve the efficiency of the Corps and added to the already large number of court-martial proceedings on conscientious objectors that had to be mounted every week.[2] On their part the non-combatants could be equally perverse, such as the man who refused to sweep out a horse's stall because he said that the task 'had a distinct bearing on the prosecution of the war'.[3] A more serious difficulty confronted the Seventh Day Adventists who had willingly joined the Corps only to find that the army was not prepared to recognize their sabbatarian beliefs. When the Adventists declined to work on a Saturday, the local military authorities showed little imagination or flexibility in dealing with them; the offenders were charged and sentenced to imprisonment with hard labour.[4]

Disputes over the nature and conditions of work were sporadic and confined to a few; the majority of men in the Corps performed useful, if not very interesting, tasks without protest and in comparative obscurity.[5] As a Quaker and an advocate of civilian alternative service, T. E. Harvey considered that 'the whole institution of the Non-Combatant Corps has been a most regrettable mistake',[6] but for some three thousand conscientious objec-

[1] Macready, loc. cit.

[2] There were 8,806 court-martial proceedings on conscientious objectors between 31 March 1916 and 31 May 1919, an average of over fifty a week. The courts martial were not of course spread out evenly: during the peak period of May to September 1916, there were probably several hundred every week. The total is given in *Military Statistics 1914–1920*, p. 673.

[3] A Private Mawdsley; see Macpherson's statement, 5 HC 93, col. 1279, 11 May 1917.

[4] Wilcox, op. cit., pp. 290–91. Wilcox cites an incident during the Adventists' journey to Wormwood Scrubs. The prisoners were kept overnight in an underground military cell and were brought tea and biscuits by a man in khaki. When in the morning they inquired after the man to thank him, no one knew of his existence. 'We all feel confident', the account concludes, 'that an angel donned khaki on this occasion and was sent of God to minister to His hungry children.' The story should have appealed to the Bishop of London who had declared that 'khaki is the garment of the faithful'.

[5] *The Times*, 19 May 1916, recommended, 'The best service that can be rendered them is to forget them. . . .'

[6] 5 HC 82, col. 1019, 11 May 1916.

tors the Corps provided the right degree of exemption from combatant duties. The numbers in the NCC rose sharply from 700 in May 1916 to 3,181 by the end of the year.[1] Officers and NCOs were selected from regular infantry personnel unfit for general service but fit for service abroad on lines of communication.[2] Discipline appears to have been informal: *The Times* reported that the men were 'treated just like infantry but no arms or belts on uniforms, and have no military titles but refer to each other as Mr. or by nicknames'.[3] The same report stated that 'soldiers treat them with indifference or good nature', but Macready recalled how much ridicule the non-combatants had to suffer at the hands of the rank and file in the army.[4] Particular objects of ridicule were the cap badges and shoulder titles bearing the initials NCC for which the popular misinterpretation was 'No Courage Corps'.

All the conscientious objectors in the Non-Combatant Corps had exercised their legal right in seeking exemption from combatant service and were fulfilling their obligations under the Military Service Acts no less faithfully than soldiers in the front line, yet they were not accorded the same treatment when it came to pay and demobilization. Initially it was agreed that non-combatants should receive the same pay as infantry of the line,[5] but when the War Cabinet approved increases in forces' pay in January 1919, the conscientious objectors in the army were specifically excluded.[6] The justification could not have been that the Non-Combatant Corps was soon to be disbanded, because the members of the Corps were also discriminated against on the question of demobilization. About one-third of the men had still not been demobilized twelve months after the Armistice, and all were denied the gratuity that was paid to soldiers retained in the army in 1919. Childs, who had all along argued that the non-combatants were soldiers, protested strongly against what he regarded as the unfair and illogical withholding of this gratuity, but he was overruled.[7]

[1] Monthly strengths of the Corps are given in *Military Statistics 1914–1920*, p. 226.

[2] ACI No. 551, 1916.

[3] *The Times*, 19 May 1916.

[4] Macready, op. cit., p. 250.

[5] AO 112, 1916.

[6] CAB 23/9/520(I).

[7] WO 32/2055/3424 and 3633. Childs was not overruled by Macready, who had become Commissioner of Metropolitan Police in September 1918.

The problem of how to reconcile the principle of equal sacrifice with the rational use of manpower did not arise with non-combatants: in their loss of home comforts and civilian wages the element of sacrifice was clear, and there was never any pretence that the Non-Combatant Corps was attempting to utilize the skills and experience of its members. But with conscientious objectors who had been conditionally exempt from all military service, the concept of sacrifice and the logical choice of employment were often in direct conflict. For these men the condition of exemption was that they should be engaged in work that, in the opinion of the tribunal, was of national importance. It rested with the tribunal therefore to weigh sacrifice against common sense in a particular case.

For the first two months of conscription—that is for March and April 1916—tribunals were most reluctant to grant conscientious objectors a conditional exemption or to make use of the Pelham Committee on Work of National Importance,[1] but from May onwards, and particularly from the end of June when the married men began to come before the tribunals, an increasing number of conscientious objectors were allowed to do civilian work rather than non-combatant duties. Four thousand (or rather more than half) of these men were referred to the Pelham Committee; the remainder worked directly under the tribunals.[2] The Pelham Committee operated as an employment exchange, bringing together men referred by the tribunals and employers who needed labour. In some industries, notably agriculture, there was an acute shortage of manpower, and farmers who had refused to have anything to do with the Home Office Scheme, gladly accepted conscientious objectors through the Pelham Committee. As a result, over a quarter of the men referred to the Committee were found jobs on the land. Pelham had the essential advantage over Brace of being able to deal with conscientious objectors as individuals. A man referred to the Committee was required to provide particulars of age, dependants, education, health, employment,

[1] See pp. 125–6 above. Pelham died on 23 December 1916 and was succeeded by Colonel Sir Hildred Carlisle, the Conservative M.P. for St. Albans. The Committee's Report said of the departure of its first chairman: 'The strain upon his health consequent upon his devotion to his duties contributed largely, it is feared, to his death.'

[2] The actual total was 3,964. See Report of the Pelham Committee, Schedule I.

and earnings;[1] whenever possible he was interviewed by the Committee. With this information, the Committee recommended some work of national importance, bearing in mind that the work would have to be both approved by the tribunal and as far as possible consistent with the Committee's own policy:

> The principles generally governing the Committee's action were that young men who were physically sound should be placed on the land, that sound men of more mature age and with domestic responsibilities should do manual work assisting the most urgent national requirements so far as their consciences would permit, whilst men of poor physique were assigned work suitable to their powers. In the case of men physically unfit for hard manual work clerical employment or light manual labour was provided.[2]

Employers were asked to provide regular reports on the man's work but apart from this there was a minimum of checks and restrictions; the Committee's view was that 'the best results were obtained by according the men as much personal freedom as was consistent with efficient work'.[3] The freedom was seldom abused. Militant opponents of conscription did not find their way to the Pelham Committee, and those political objectors, such as Herbert Morrison, who were allowed to do work of national importance, seemed to be more concerned with protecting their good fortune than with promoting unrest.[4] There were other reasons why the Pelham Committee had little trouble. The majority referred to the Committee were married, and half were over the age of thirty;[5] such men had more to lose than the young idealists and political tearaways. The four thousand also included a large group of fourteen hundred Christadelphians who had agreed to undertake work useful for the prosecution of the war, and whose active cooperation was never in doubt.[6] Some eight hundred of these

[1] This information is contained in the Schedules of the Report of the Pelham Committee and represents the only analysis of a significant number of conscientious objectors made in either World War.

[2] Report of the Pelham Committee, p. 4.

[3] Ibid.

[4] Herbert Morrison was one of the very few I.L.P. members who was prepared to compromise with the law, even though he was Chairman of one of the Party's Divisional Councils. Many members of his Division, including Clifford Allen, spent much of the remainder of the war in prison; Morrison spent the time working as a market gardener in Letchworth Garden City. See Herbert Morrison, *An Autobiography*, London, 1960, p. 65.

[5] Report of the Pelham Committee, Schedules 6 and 8.

[6] See pp. 114–15, above.

Christadelphians spent the remainder of the war working in Controlled Establishments or for government contractors.

The conscientious objectors directed to civilian occupations were further encouraged to cooperate by the obvious value of the work that they were doing. In addition to the large groups in agriculture and the Controlled Establishments, men were assigned to welfare work with the Y.M.C.A., the Red Cross, and the General Service Section of the Friends Ambulance Unit (whose duties included the care of disabled soldiers),[1] to hospitals and asylums, to the railways and the docks (two industries that had rejected the advances of the Brace Committee), to the mines, and to the manufacture and distribution of food.[2] But national importance was not narrowly interpreted: one conscientious objector was assigned to the job of undertaker.

While the Pelham Committee and most tribunals came to accept a broad definition of work of national importance, they could not, in a society still wedded to the belief that patriotism was synonymous with service in the armed forces, ignore the principle of equal sacrifice. Yet the principle, though vigorously acclaimed, was unevenly applied. General Service work in the Friends Ambulance Unit was supposed to 'entail hardship and sacrifice comparable to that to which the soldier is subject',[3] but it was totally unrealistic to expect this condition to be fulfilled when members of the Unit were assigned to clerical or teaching posts. Pelham himself told the Central Tribunal that his Committee was 'in agreement with the view that men should be placed in situations that demand some definite sacrifice from them and it is their practice to place men at some distance from their homes'.[4] The Central Tribunal endorsed this policy (though disagreeing with the Committee on the definition of 'some distance'), but some local and appeal tribunals insisted that 'their' conscientious objectors should be found work in the immediate vicinity, presumably so that it would be easy to keep an eye on them. And despite Pelham's declaration of intent his Committee allowed 1,046 conscientious objectors to remain in their present occupations.[5] Many of these

[1] The Minutes of the Central Tribunal, 14 April 1916, contain a Memorandum on the General Service Work of the F.A.U.

[2] See Appendix H.

[3] Minutes of the Central Tribunal, 14 April 1916.

[4] Minutes of the Central Tribunal, 11 May 1916.

[5] See Appendix I.

were Christadelphians working in munition factories, but the list also included chauffeur, steeplejack, and tobacco drier, occupations whose national importance was somewhat obscure.

A similarly uneven application of sacrifice characterized the Committee's policy on wages. The average reduction in wages for all conscientious objectors referred to the Committee was 37·5 per cent,[1] but men who retained their ordinary jobs continued to draw the same rates of pay, so that the sacrifice made by those who were assigned to new occupations was disproportionately high. Neither the Committee nor the tribunals had the power to enforce a reduction in wages except by moving the man to a different job, although the London Appeal Tribunal overcame this problem by deciding that the difference between a conscientious objector's pay and that of a private soldier (with some allowance for rations and billet) should be given to a recognized charity.[2]

When sacrifice meant moving to a new job there was little chance of utilizing special skills or experience, but the waste was not on the scale of the Home Office Scheme, nor was the work to which men were assigned as patently irrelevant as prison industries and breaking stones. The conscientious objector who was obliged to give up his market garden to work on a farm may have regarded the move as illogical but he could not claim that his new job was unimportant. There were anomalies, particularly when a Box and Cox system operated whereby the job vacated by one conscientious objector was occupied by another, and there were occasions when the decision to move a conscientious objector was inspired by prejudice rather than by the need for sacrifice. In both World Wars there were public protests against the employment of conscientious objectors as teachers in schools.[3] In 1916 the Pelham Committee recommended that education should be regarded as

[1] Report of the Pelham Committee, Schedule 17.

[2] Minutes of the County of London Appeal Tribunal, 22 January 1916. According to Fenner Brockway, Ernest Bevin, as Minister of Labour in 1940, offered to exempt conscientious objectors who would contribute the difference between their incomes and the pay of a private soldier to a socially useful organization. The offer was refused. See Fenner Brockway, *Outside the Right*, London, 1963, pp. 26–7.

[3] In the Second World War the protests were local and, with few exceptions, confined to the crisis of 1940. A typical case is recorded in the *Birmingham Gazette*, 27 September 1940: a Council had decided not to appoint any new teachers who were conscientious objectors, after strong protests from the Women's Branch of the British Legion.

work of national importance, yet while 204 men were engaged in education when referred to the Committee, only 35 were allowed to remain in their posts or were assigned to educational posts away from home.[1] Behind this inconsistency lay the fear that in some way that was never clearly defined conscientious objectors would be a bad influence or, in the emotive language of Mr. Stanton, that they would 'prejudice and poison the minds of our children in the schools'.[2] It was Mr. Stanton too who voiced the Tory backbenchers' suspicion of the 'clever' conscientious objector. 'A crowd of them happen to be intellectuals of course,' he told the House.[3]

The position of those conscientious objectors who were allowed to remain in teaching posts cannot have been easy; quite apart from local hostility, they were threatened by proposals that conscientious objectors should be banned from teaching altogether. These proposals seldom advanced beyond the pages of the jingo press, but one was put down as a motion in the House of Lords, by Lord Charnwood in November 1917. The wording of Charnwood's motion was:

> That no person who has applied for exemption (conditional or total) from military service on the ground of conscientious objection ought thereafter to be permitted to teach in any school or college supported or assisted by public funds.[4]

Fortunately for the conscientious objectors, Lloyd George had appointed a Liberal academic, Herbert Fisher, as President of the Board of Education.[5] A close friend of Gilbert Murray and a former Vice-Chancellor of Sheffield University, Herbert Fisher was no politician, but he recognized both the injustice and the unwisdom of allowing Parliament to discriminate against teachers whose views were unpopular. He wrote to Gilbert Murray:

[1] Report of the Pelham Committee, Schedules 10, 13, and 15.

[2] 5 HC 86, col. 835–7, 19 October 1916.

[3] Ibid.

[4] The debate on Charnwood's motion is in 5 HL 27, col. 23–50, 28 November 1917. Lord Charnwood was a former Liberal M.P. and Lecturer in Philosophy at Balliol, an unexpected background for a man intent on discriminating against conscientious objectors. In the same debate he proposed that conscientious objectors should be deported rather than that they should be shown any further indulgence.

[5] No relation of W. Hayes Fisher, Long's successor as President of the Local Government Board.

I have not the slightest intention of acquiescing in Charnwood's odious proposal and have instructed Ld. Sandhurst, who represents us in the Lords, to resist it. Unfortunately S. is a very feeble fellow and won't make a good job of it.[1]

Fisher need not have worried. Charnwood introduced his motion by disclaiming any unworthy motive:

I do not put it forward in any spirit of vindictiveness or as a penalty upon these men, but as a measure of justice and of protection due to the children of the country.[2]

But his proposal was so effectively attacked that Sandhurst had little to do but state the Government's opposition. Fisher wrote to his wife: 'That ass Charnwood was very properly snuffed out in the House to my great relief.'[3]

In the First World War, despite belated attempts to organize national service in 1917, civilian employment was always a poor relation of military service. In this context the need to protect recruiting for the army was never far from the minds of the tribunal members. While they may have tried to place conscientious objectors in occupations that were of value to the community, they remained convinced that those who were exempt from military service should be seen to make some sacrifice. Even the Pelham Committee, though by no means blind to the importance of utilizing special skills, considered that one of its chief tasks was that of 'preventing as far as possible any harm to recruiting or to the efficient prosecution of the war'.[4] This negative approach could only have been dispensed with if the Government had mobilized civilian as well as military manpower. With these limitations, the conditional exemption worked well and was easily the most successful of the Government's attempts to meet the position of the conscientious objector to military service.

[1] H. A. L. Fisher to Gilbert Murray, 27 November 1917, Fisher Papers 7.
[2] 5 HL 27, col. 32, 28 November 1917.
[3] H. A. L. Fisher to his wife, 29 November 1917, Fisher Papers 5.
[4] Report of the Pelham Committee, p. 7.

CHAPTER TEN

THE ABSOLUTISTS

By accepting alternative service, whether within the framework of the Home Office Scheme or the Non-Combatant Corps, or in the comparative freedom of civilian work of national importance, the conscientious objector was coming to terms with the Military Service Act. Those who refused to compromise in this way numbered 985;[1] they did not all adopt precisely the same position (they disagreed, for example, on the extent to which they should obey prison rules) but their rejection of any form of alternative service was absolute. From the summer of 1916 until their final release, these absolutists endured repeated terms of imprisonment. Because they were still soldiers, on the completion of their sentence they rejoined their units, only to be court-martialled once again and returned to prison. This cycle of court martial and imprisonment was a test of physical and mental stamina, but above all it was a test of firmness of conviction because at any time the absolutist could have secured his release by asking for a review of his case by the Central Tribunal.

The absolutists regarded themselves with justification as the final unyielding core of opposition to compulsory military service; as such they included in their number the leading lights of the N.C.F., the Chairman, Clifford Allen, and the Secretary, Fenner Brockway, as well as those Quakers, such as Stephen Hobhouse and Hubert Peet, whose passionate rejection of the spirit of force made it impossible for them to accept the sort of compromise advocated by their fellow Quaker, T. E. Harvey. No complete analysis of the absolutists was made, but the analyses of groups of absolutists published by the Friends Service Committee and by

[1] See p. 167, above.

Mrs. Hobhouse[1] clearly indicate that the majority were members of the I.L.P. or of the Society of Friends (or, of course, of both). There is some evidence, too, that the strains of absolutism were more easily borne by men of mature age: the nine prominent absolutists described by Mrs. Hobhouse have an average age of thirty-three.

In prison with the absolutists, and indistinguishable from them in the eyes of the law, were the 313 men whom the Central Tribunal had rejected as not genuine, as well as the shifting population of men returned to prison for disobeying the rules of the Brace Committee. This juxtaposition of the absolutists with the failures and the militants presented the prison authorities with a particularly difficult problem. The absolutists refused to obey some prison rules on the grounds of conscience; the failures and the militants often set out to undermine the system by calculated disobedience and contempt for authority. Yet the prison commissioners and individual prison governors could not easily differentiate between the two groups:

> On the one hand, genuine, well-conducted Absolutists, with high moral standards of their own, though differing from the rest of the community in the *application* of their sense of duty, and, on the other hand, men not in any sense genuinely conscientious and some of them guilty of grave misconduct. The administration of a common code to such different classes of prisoners was an almost impossible task: and it was still more impossible to distinguish the different classes and to treat them separately.[2]

For the prison authorities there was the additional problem of dealing with a large number of conscientious objectors[3] alongside the normal prison population. Experience with the suffragettes before the war suggested that concessions to a special group would cause 'dissatisfaction among ordinary prisoners';[4] and yet the Home Office found it increasingly difficult to justify the application of normal prison rules to men 'of good character and not of

[1] The Friends Service Committee, *The Absolutists' Objection to Conscription: a statement and an appeal to the conscience of the nation*, London, 1917, and Mrs. Henry (Margaret) Hobhouse, *I Appeal unto Caesar*, London, 1917.

[2] Conscientious Objectors in Prison, p. 7.

[3] Once the bulk of conscientious objectors had passed to the Home Office Scheme, the daily average in prison was about 1,200. See Prison Report, 1919 (Cmd.374), p. 22.

[4] See Prison Report, 1912 (Cd.6406), p. 11.

a class for whom prison arrangements were planned', particularly when these men were serving a third or fourth sentence for the same offence. Faced with this dilemma, the prison commissioners made repeated requests to be relieved of the responsibility for these military prisoners; as in the case of the Home Office Scheme, however, General Childs had no wish to alter an arrangement whereby the War Office retained its hold on the men concerned while leaving all the headaches of their everyday treatment to a civilian department.

At the outset Herbert Samuel (possibly prompted by Childs) had decided that prison discipline should not be relaxed for conscientious objectors, on the ground that such a concession 'would tend to encourage the evasion of military service on the plea of conscientious objection'.[1] In particular, Samuel rejected suggestions that conscientious objectors should be allowed certain privileges under Rule 243A, a rule introduced by Winston Churchill in 1910 to ameliorate the rigours of imprisonment for the suffragettes.[2] Conscientious objectors, in common with ordinary criminals, would be subject to the rules of the Third Division.[3] These rules, like those for Military Detention Barracks, had been designed to deter the brute elements in society, and their application to conscientious objectors gave rise to the familiar allegations of ill-treatment. But there was no victimization: conscientious objectors were treated as ordinary prisoners, until the autumn of 1917 when the letter of the law was relaxed in their favour. This did not mean that their sentence was light. The majority were sentenced to imprisonment 'with hard labour', and although the Dickensian phrase had legal rather than physical significance, the sentence still demanded that the prisoner should be kept in strict separation for the first twenty-eight days. After this period, he was allowed to work in association, and after two months, to communicate with and receive visits from relatives and 'respectable

[1] Conscientious Objectors in Prison, p. 1.

[2] For the introduction of the Rule see Prison Report 1912, p. 10; for its effect, E. Sylvia Pankhurst, *The Suffragette Movement*, London, 1931, p. 376.

[3] The First and Second Divisions were generally reserved for civil as distinct from criminal offenders. A prisoner in the First Division suffered little more than the loss of freedom; he lived in a special cell (cleaned by a prisoner in a lower division), enjoyed his own food, furniture, and books, was not required to work, and was relieved of any 'unaccustomed tasks or offices'. The Rules for the Second Division were a modified version of those for the First. Only prisoners in the Third Division were treated under the General Rules.

friends'. From six to ten hours each day the conscientious objectors were employed on making mailbags, a task that had the negative virtue of being in no way associated with the conduct of the war, though Clifford Allen with dogged logic wondered whether by making mailbags he was releasing other prisoners for war work.

The raw conditions and routine restrictions of Third Division were hard to accept for men who came from social groups outside the normal catchment area of the prisons. Conscientious objectors were repelled by the degradation of the individual and by the suppression of all decent and altruistic instincts, and particularly by the Rule of Silence that forbad all communication between prisoners and warders. Those who like Stephen Hobhouse announced their intention of disobeying this Rule were placed in solitary confinement. It was to be expected that the more intelligent and sensitive conscientious objectors would become ardent advocates of prison reform. 'What a generation of prison reformers we should make and must make,' wrote Hubert Peet between sentences, and he was not disappointed: the experiences of the conscientious objectors made a major contribution to the reforms of the post-war era.[1]

If the conscientious objectors found prison life distasteful, the prison officials found the conscientious objectors exasperating. The prison staff, from warder to governor, were experienced in dealing with ordinary criminals who 'worked the system' and thereby accepted it, but were nonplussed when a prisoner formally declared that as a matter of conscience he proposed to disobey the rules. Governors and Visiting Committees could and did punish conscientious objectors with restriction of diet,[2] periods of close confinement, loss of mattress and of other privileges, but, as the Prison Commission admitted, 'the question of dealing out just and adequate punishment in such cases is often beset with great difficulty'.[3] Before the Armistice, few conscientious objectors took

[1] See L. W. Fox, *The English Prison and Borstal Systems*, London, 1952, p. 61. One direct result of the conscientious objectors' experience was the Prison System Enquiry Committee established in January 1919 by the Executive of the Labour Research Department, whose report, edited by Stephen Hobhouse and Fenner Brockway, two absolutists, was published in 1922 as *English Prisons To-Day*.

[2] Punishment diet was similar to that prescribed for Military Detention Barracks: 1 lb. of bread plus water each day for three days, alternating with three days of normal diet, for a maximum of fifteen days.

[3] Prison Report, 1917, p. 11.

their protest against imprisonment to the lengths of a hunger strike; those who did were forcibly fed by a tube inserted in the nostril, an unpleasant procedure that placed a strain not only on the striker but also on the prison medical staff. When the striker's health deteriorated he was released for a time under the Prisoners (Temporary Discharge for Ill-health) Act of 1913,[1] the celebrated 'Cat and Mouse Act' that had been used to outmanoeuvre suffragettes who had been intent on victory or martyrdom.

The imprisonment of the absolutists did not at first provoke concern outside the circle of their friends. Though Asquith's Coalition Government had been anxious to avoid the prolonged imprisonment of conscientious objectors, it now considered that the procedure instituted by General Childs and Herbert Samuel provided a fair and adequate machinery for obtaining release, and that those who declined to avail themselves of it remained in prison of their own choice. This continued to be the official (and the popular) view while the absolutists were serving their initial sentence. Characteristically, no one appears to have looked beyond the point at which this sentence ended and the men were returned to their units. Perhaps Asquith imagined that after a spell behind bars the absolutists would settle for the Home Office Scheme, or even that the War Office would relent and discharge the men unconditionally. If so, he underestimated the inflexible will of the protagonists: in their own ways, General Childs and Clifford Allen were equally uncompromising. Official thinking on this issue was also confused by the facile assumption that the Central Tribunal's review of court-martial proceedings would inevitably result in the release of the genuine conscientious objectors, leaving the humbugs to suffer imprisonment. In this context, refusal to plead before the Central Tribunal was at first identified with insincerity, a conclusion that could hardly have been further from the truth. The fact that the absolutists were turning their backs on an offer that many politicians regarded as unwisely generous served to intensify the anger provoked by their tactics. The Government's hostility to the absolutists was vigorously—if somewhat incoherently—expressed by Lloyd George, who was Secretary of State for War in July 1916:

With that kind of men (*sic*) I personally have absolutely no sympathy whatsoever, and I do not think they ought to be encouraged. . . . I do

[1] 3 GEO 5, Ch. 4, 25 April 1913.

not think they deserve the slightest consideration. With regard to those who object to shedding blood it is the traditional policy of this country to respect that view, and we do not propose to part from it; but in the other case I shall only consider the best means of making the path of that class a very hard one.[1]

As a declaration of policy, this statement was soon forgotten; Lloyd George did nothing to make the absolutists' path a very hard one, on the contrary, as Prime Minister, he agreed to administrative changes that effectively eased their lot. The tone of his remarks proved to be a hostage to fortune, nevertheless,[2] and dismayed his admirers at the time. Seebohm Rowntree, the Quaker industrialist, urged him to reconsider his attitude:

Dear Lloyd George,

May I refer briefly to our conversation at luncheon about conscientious objectors? I feel that you are not doing justice either to yourself or to the extreme section of the C.O.s in the attitude you take up with regard to them.

I know some of the men who feel they cannot accept alternative service at the dictation of a tribunal. I do not share their view, but some of those who hold it are the salt of the earth—men whose lives are spent in useful and unselfish service of their fellows; and these men are to have their 'path made very hard'. . . .

I care so much for you, both as a friend and as an upholder of liberty, that I cannot contemplate without deep concern the way that you intend to deal with the sincere but extreme conscientious objectors. It would be a great relief to many of your truest friends if you would give further consideration to the matter. . . .[3]

In December 1916 Lloyd George became Prime Minister, and the immediate responsibility for the absolutists passed to the new Secretary of State for War, Lord Derby. It is Derby's misfortune that in appearance, as well as in reputation, he is the archetypal 'buffer' whose claims to political power rested not on ability but on inherited wealth and position. Haig dismissed him as a 'very weak-minded fellow', and certainly Childs seems to have found him easy to handle, though Derby's unsympathetic attitude to conscientious objectors was unlikely to provoke disagreement

[1] 5 HC 84, col. 1758–9.

[2] See e.g. Taylor, op. cit., pp. 54–5. According to Taylor, Lloyd George's attitude to the absolutists as revealed in this statement drove the first nail in the coffin of his radical reputation.

[3] Seebohm Rowntree to Lloyd George, 29 August 1916, Lloyd George Papers.

with his permanent officials. Derby readily endorsed the policy of no concessions to the absolutists, for there was no indication in December 1916 that it would lead him into a protracted conflict with the most powerful of his colleagues. But within six months of taking office he found that the repeated sentencing of conscientious objectors had become a subject of controversy in Government circles. In June 1917 thenumber of conscientious objectors serving a second or subsequent sentence had risen to six hundred,[1] and a formidable political lobby was urging the War Office to exercise clemency in the 'genuine' cases. For the majority of politicians and public men involved, concern had been prompted by the continued imprisonment of one man—Stephen Hobhouse. The story of their attempts to secure the release of this man, and of the others whom they considered genuine, has never been told.

In 1917 Stephen Hobhouse was thirty-six.[2] In August 1916 the Hoxton Local Tribunal had granted him exemption conditional on his joining the Friends Ambulance Unit. He had refused to accept or to appeal against this decision, and in October 1916 had been handed over to the military. After court martial and sentence for disobeying an order to put on uniform, he had refused to accept the conditions of the Central Tribunal's review of cases and had thus joined the body of absolutists. Though an Army Medical Board might well have recommended an unconditional discharge, he had declined to undergo an examination.

The presence of Stephen Hobhouse among the absolutists in prison was an embarrassment to the Government. It was not only that he was unfit to face a sentence in the Third Division; other absolutists, including Clifford Allen, suffered more permanent damage to their health in prison. But Hobhouse was alone among conscientious objectors in being both well-connected and widely recognized as a man of the highest integrity. Those who had scant sympathy with the pacifist position were prepared to believe that if the genuine conscientious objector existed at all, he existed in the person of Stephen Hobhouse.

Stephen was the eldest son of the Rt. Hon. Henry Hobhouse, a country gentleman of more than adequate means and modest

[1] Conscientious Objectors in Prison, p. 2.

[2] For the details of Stephen Hobhouse's life see Mrs. Henry Hobhouse, op. cit., pp. 20–22; Stephen Hobhouse, *Margaret Hobhouse and her Family*, privately printed, 1934, *passim*; and the same author's *Forty Years and an Epilogue: an autobiography, 1881–1951*, London, 1951, *passim*.

distinction, who had represented East Somerset as a Liberal and Liberal Unionist in the Commons for twenty years from 1886 to 1906. The family's fortunes had been established by profitable investment in the slave trade, a fact deplored by subsequent generations who nevertheless enjoyed the tangible benefits of Hapsden House with its 1,700 acres of fields and woodlands. In the family tradition, Stephen was sent to Eton and Balliol. With a First in Moderations and a Second in Greats, he entered the Board of Education and seemed set on a Civil Service career. Yet, before he was thirty, he had exchanged the Board of Education for a life of poverty and social work in London's East End, renounced his inheritance, and joined the Society of Friends. To those who knew of his life and work, his imprisonment under the Military Service Act was a scandal. With his second court martial in April 1917 the demands for his release became more insistent, and for eight months, until December, increasing pressure was put on the War Office to release administratively those conscientious objectors whose sincerity was regarded as self-evident. Lord Derby and General Childs could have withstood this pressure if it had been exerted by the predictable but ineffectual well-wishers of a liberal cause, but Stephen's mother was able to enlist the support of men who, after the Prime Minister, were among the most powerful in the Government.

Margaret Hobhouse possessed two great advantages in her struggle against the inflexibility of the War Office: the circle of her family's friends gave her ready access to political influence, and her own enterprise and stamina enabled her to outlast and outmanoeuvre even so skilful an opponent as General Childs. The championship of unpopular causes was in her blood: one of her ancestors had been attacked by hooligan patriots for refusing to celebrate British victories in the American War for Independence, and both her maternal and paternal grandfathers had been Radical M.P.s.[1] With an intense conviction in the justice of her cause she did not hesitate to approach every friend and relative whose name commanded attention. She was seldom rebuffed. Though her younger sister, Beatrice Webb, showed little interest in conscientious objectors except as a lever for prison reform, two older

[1] Richard Potter, M.P. for Wigan, and Lawrence Heyworth, M.P. for Derby. Richard Potter was a friend of the leading Radical, Sir John Cam Hobhouse, a relative of Stephen's grandfather.

sisters (Margaret was the seventh of nine daughters) had married respected and influential public men in Lord Courtney, an ageing but vigorously independent parliamentarian with pacifist convictions, and Lord Parmoor, a brilliant lawyer and former Conservative M.P. whose dislike of the war laid the foundations for his conversion to socialism.[1] Margaret's own husband, Henry Hobhouse, though he had been out of politics for a decade, retained many of the friendships he had built during his twenty years in the Commons. The Hobhouse family also counted among its allies such diverse figures as Charles Gore, Bishop of Oxford, George Bernard Shaw, and Lord Milner. It was Milner who made the first significant move to secure Stephen Hobhouse's release.

Initially, Milner tried to avoid raising Hobhouse's case in the War Cabinet, but Derby and Childs easily rode his unofficial approaches, and so on 9 May 1917 he wrote a long memorandum for his Cabinet colleagues condemning the present policy as too lenient to those whose sincerity was in doubt and too rigid where convictions were 'patently genuine'.[2] The previous day he had confided his intentions to Lord Selborne, his successor as High Commissioner in South Africa, and one of Margaret Hobhouse's earliest recruits:

My dear Selborne,

About the conscientious objectors, your view is precisely mine. I think the only way out of it is to deal with individual cases on their merits—just the thing you can never get a department to do. Unfortunately Derby, on whom it all depends, is, in matters of this kind, in the hands of his permanent officials, who of course have no flexibility. I have tried over and over again to make him exercise his commonsense in the matter, but in vain.

The only recourse, therefore, is to the Cabinet. I expect I shall be driven to it, although you can imagine how undesirable and unnecessary it is to have to take up the time of the Cabinet with a matter of this kind at the present juncture.[3]

In Liberal eyes, Milner's record in South Africa and his subsequent association with the far right in British politics, hardly fitted him

[1] He was a member of the Labour Cabinet of 1924, as was another of Margaret Hobhouse's brothers-in-law, Lord Passfield (Sidney Webb). Parmoor's son, Stafford Cripps, was a member of Attlee's post-war Labour Cabinet.

[2] CAB 24/12/677.

[3] Milner to Lord Selborne, 8 May 1917, Milner Papers 6.

for the role of champion in the absolutists' cause. The very week that Milner circulated his Memorandum to the War Cabinet, the Liberal *Daily News* attacked him as 'the Prussian ideal' and 'the negation of democracy'.[1] To his colleagues, Milner made no secret of the fact that his concern had been prompted by the imprisonment of Stephen Hobhouse:

> I will frankly admit that my attention was first drawn to this question by a necessity which lay upon me to enquire into the case of an individual who has been well known to me for many years.[2]

At Balliol, Milner had been a friend and contemporary of Henry Hobhouse, and at Stephen's christening had acted as proxy godfather. Later, Stephen's work in the East End had brought him into contact with Toynbee Hall, the social settlement of whose Council Milner was Chairman. But it would be wrong to interpret Milner's concern solely in terms of Stephen Hobhouse; he argued for the release of all genuine absolutists, and Hobhouse was not the only individual he cited as evidence for the War Cabinet.[3] Milner, the supreme administrator and advocate of compulsion, had little patience with a War Office policy that seemed to him to endorse the errors and inconsistencies of the first months of conscription; and as one who did not conceal his dislike of the democratic process,[4] he failed to understand why his colleagues were reluctant to discharge men who had been enlisted by Act of Parliament. 'All that appears to be required', he told them, 'is a greater elasticity of administration.'

It was the practice of Lloyd George's War Cabinet to summon men with specialist knowledge to the discussion of a particular topic; when Milner's Memorandum was considered on 22 May, General Childs (rather than Lord Derby), Walter Long, and Sir George Cave attended the meeting.[5] Childs put the War Office case: an administrative release was not possible without overriding the statutory tribunals and the law; and even if these consequences were accepted, there was no satisfactory way of differentiating

[1] *Daily News*, 12 May 1917. [2] CAB 24/12/677.

[3] In a memorandum dated 24 August 1917 (CAB 24/24/1833) Milner cited the case of Malcolm Sparkes, a Quaker who had done valuable work in the field of industrial relations.

[4] See especially Milner's attitude to the Irish Crisis 1912–14 as described in Gollin, op. cit., Chs. 8 and 9.

[5] CAB 23/4/257(3).

between the genuine absolutist and the political agitator. As for a discharge on medical grounds, this was not feasible while the standard of physical fitness required for military service was so low; Childs dismissed fears that the Government was in danger of creating martyrs, adding a little unwisely that 'in the present admirable conditions of prison life, there was no reason to apprehend such a fatality'.

On this occasion Childs's view prevailed, the War Cabinet deciding that the case for a further enquiry had not been established. Neither Milner nor Margaret Hobhouse was prepared to let the matter rest there. Margaret Hobhouse turned her attention to the Home Office. At the Cabinet meeting, Sir George Cave had supported Childs, but he does not appear to have resisted Mrs. Hobhouse for very long. Of the summer of 1917, the official report reads:

> The Army Council was particularly obdurate in refusing to release Stephen Hobhouse, a Conscientious Objector of the most genuine type, whose health was suffering, though his release was strongly urged by the Home Office and several Ministers.[1]

Meanwhile Milner's lead was attracting allies. The news that he was to raise the question of the absolutists in the Cabinet had already drawn support from Randall Davidson, the Archbishop of Canterbury:

> Stephen Hobhouse is of course the most conspicuous instance of a really fine fellow who is, or has been, suffering in mind and body on account of 'crankiness' which is in no sense mischievous in itself. . . . I do honestly think that the matter is one for the exercise of a rather arbitrary discretion in favour of men whose supposed 'persecution' is doing far more mischief than would be done by the relaxation of logical and technically defensible sternness, and the granting of release on condition that it is not used for promoting anti-war policy.[2]

Unlike some of those who privately gave encouragement to Margaret Hobhouse, Davidson was not afraid to advocate this policy in public. When the Lords debated the position of the absolutists, he urged the release of those of 'high character and unimpeachable motives', though disclaiming any sympathy for

[1] Conscientious Objectors in Prison, p. 2.

[2] Davidson to Milner, 21 May 1917, quoted in G. K. A. Bell, *Randall Davidson, Archbishop of Canterbury*, 2, London, 1935, pp. 821–2.

men who were 'certainly suffering from an overweening sense of personal infallibility and Pharisaic self-righteousness'.[1]

Davidson's interest turned out to be short-lived, but Milner found a more persistent ally in the President of the Board of Education, Herbert Fisher. Fisher does not appear to have been approached by Margaret Hobhouse, but as a Liberal and intellectual he deplored a policy that smacked of persecution, and his friendship with Gilbert Murray provided a link with the Hobhouse family. On 30 May, Fisher wrote to Milner:

My dear Milner,

I heartily approve your memo on Conscientious Objectors and am concerned to find that you did not succeed in carrying your point with the War Cabinet. I am persuaded that there is a very definite and *easily cognisable* class of cases in which unjust hardship is now being inflicted and that the Government will greatly suffer in the esteem of right-thinking persons, if no action whatever is taken in the direction which you indicate. . . . It is absurd to suppose that Stephen Hobhouse for instance is not a conscientious objector, seeing that he has been ready to undergo a long term of imprisonment rather than submit to Military discipline. And in such cases as these, it is surely wisest to admit an error has been committed and to release the man.[2]

Milner wasted no time in sending this letter on to Lloyd George with the comment, 'You might like to see the opinion of one whose judgement I am sure you will agree is worth considering on a matter of this kind.'[3]

Lloyd George had neither the time nor the inclination to become entangled in the complexities of this issue, yet it must now have been apparent to him that the War Cabinet's rejection of Milner's proposals had not been the last word. He therefore instructed his private secretary, Philip Kerr, to look into the whole question of the treatment of the absolutists and to make recommendations on future policy. It was a wise move. Within a few days, the Prime Minister received further evidence that the issue was still very much alive in a sharp note from Lord Henry Bentinck:

It is clear that a state of things exists which is a distinct failure of statesmanship, and a disgrace to our humanity, and I do not think I need give you any further proof for the need of the termination of what

[1] Davidson's speech, 5 HL 25, col. 330–33, 24 May 1917.
[2] Herbert Fisher to Milner, 30 May 1917, a copy in the Lloyd George Papers.
[3] Milner to Lloyd George, 1 June 1917, Lloyd George Papers.

can only tend to bring discredit on the Government and consequently a weakness in the cause of the Allies.[1]

And on the same day the Hobhouse lobby acquired a new and influential member. Lord Parmoor noted in his diary:

I have had an opportunity of speaking to General Smuts on the treatment of conscientious objectors; he expressed an opinion that the scandal of the present conditions should be altered, as it constituted an offence to the feelings of so many good men.[2]

Jan Christian Smuts had arrived in London in March as the South African member of the Imperial War Cabinet. The latter (the British War Cabinet sitting with Indian and Dominion representatives) met on selected days each week, so that Smuts was in a position to add his voice to that of Lord Milner, his former enemy. Smuts's qualities as a soldier did not prevent him choosing friends in England from among Quaker and Liberal families, some of whose members were already well-known to him.[3] It was indeed bad luck for General Childs that the Imperial War Cabinet should have brought to Downing Street the friend and admirer of Emily Hobhouse, Stephen's second cousin, whose exposure of the treatment of Boer women and children in British 'concentration camps' had scandalized patriotic opinion and endeared her to the people of South Africa.[4]

Yet another threat to the War Office policy appeared in the conclusions reached by Philip Kerr. Though Kerr may have researched the problem thoroughly, as a former disciple of Milner and member of the proconsul's 'kindergarten' in South Africa, he did not approach the problem from an entirely neutral standpoint. Before passing his conclusions on to the Prime Minister, Kerr asked Childs to read them. To Childs's consternation, they recommended the release of the absolutists on the ground that the tribunals had erred. 'I totally disagree with your

[1] Lord Henry Bentinck to Lloyd George, 15 June 1917, Lothian Papers 139/5. Bentinck was Conservative M.P. for Nottingham South.

[2] Lord Parmoor, *A Retrospect: looking back over a life of more than eighty years*, London, 1936, p. 119.

[3] For this period in Smuts's life see W. K. Hancock, *Smuts: the sanguine years 1870–1919*, Cambridge, 1962, pp. 425–8.

[4] Some 20,000 Boer women and children died in the camps, but the number would have been much higher if Emily Hobhouse had not exposed the conditions in the world's press.

proposals. . . .', Childs replied forcefully, 'the release of the first absolutist would be the beginning of the end.'[1] This reaction may have persuaded Kerr to modify the proposals he made to the Prime Minister; certainly Lloyd George made no move to initiate further discussion in the Cabinet. Childs, however, wished to secure his policy against future attack. Whereas the private lobbying had urged the release of men such as Stephen Hobhouse, public criticism of the War Office had concentrated on the injustice of the repeated sentences;[2] Childs therefore persuaded Derby that the practice of commuting longer sentences to 112 days should be abandoned so that the incidence of second and third courts martial would be reduced. He was confident that this measure would effectively put an end to the agitation on behalf of the absolutists. He wrote to Derby:

> I am bold enough to be emphatic in my suggestion that if you approve of my proposals we shall defeat the absolutist movement fully and finally.[3]

Childs's confidence proved to have been misplaced. The advocates of release had no intention of relaxing their efforts, and for once the climate of opinion was not entirely on the side of the War Office. In July and August the publicity given to the ill-treatment of Privates Gray and Brightmore revived earlier suspicions of the army's methods; and as the third anniversary of the outbreak of war passed, and the Battle of Passchendaele wound its bloody course through the wet summer and autumn, weariness and doubt were almost as common as rampant jingoism. In this context the suffering of the absolutists aroused more sympathy than would have been possible earlier in the year, or in the following spring when the last German offensive rekindled hostility to all conscientious objectors. The more favourable climate also owed something to Margaret Hobhouse's own success as a publicist. Frustrated in her private attempts to secure the release of her son, she tried to reach a wider audience by writing a brief account of the absolutists in which fact and polemic were skilfully

[1] Kerr's proposals dated 16 June 1917, and Childs's reply dated 18 June 1917, are in WO 32/2051/3302.

[2] See for example the debate in the Lords, 5 HL 25, col. 324–40, 24 May 1917.

[3] WO 32/2051/3302.

interwoven. With an evocative title, an eloquent introduction by Gilbert Murray, and prefatory notes of approval by members of the Hobhouse lobby, *I Appeal Unto Caesar* was published at the end of July.[1] Though it was ignored by the majority of newspapers and journals, the book was sympathetically reviewed in *The Times* and in *The Observer* (by John Galsworthy[2]), and sold 14,000 copies by October.

This publicity for the absolutists' cause does not appear to have worried Childs unduly but he was quick to spot the danger when Milner presented a copy to George V. He hastened to assure Wigram, the Assistant Private Secretary, that the book was 'part of a definite and dangerous propaganda':

> It is very desirable that the King should be aware of all the facts surrounding this venture of Mrs. Hobhouse as she is attempting to gain considerable backing from people like Parmoor, Courtney etc., who merely know one side of the question. Briefly Mrs. Hobhouse has attempted to convey the impression that the absolutists in prison are a body of intensely religious Christians. This is far from being the case. She is attempting to get absolute exemption for men who refuse to do anything whatever for their country and the day that *absolute* exemption is granted to anybody whether his objection be based on religious or on other grounds we are beaten.[3]

Childs's concern that the War Office should retain the confidence of the King was increased by his knowledge that a second—a more determined—attempt was currently being made by Milner to force a change of policy through the War Cabinet. Ironically, Milner's new offensive was facilitated by Childs himself.

Among the first politicians to whom Margaret Hobhouse had turned for help had been the Liberal members of Asquith's Coalition Cabinet: McKenna, Runciman, Samuel, Simon, and Asquith himself. With the exception of Simon, all had shared a collective responsibility for provisions which, however ambiguous, had implied that the out-and-out objector would receive an

[1] London, 1917. The 'notes' were written by Selborne, Parmoor, Bentinck, and Lord Hugh Cecil, the Conservative M.P. for Oxford University, who though not strictly a member of the Hobhouse lobby was nevertheless sympathetic to the cause of release.

[2] In 1916 Galsworthy had supported Gilbert Murray's efforts to secure better treatment for conscientious objectors. See H. V. Marrot, *The Life and Letters of John Galsworthy*, London, 1935, p. 755.

[3] Childs to Wigram, 17 September 1917, RA GV5910/2.

absolute exemption and were susceptible therefore to Mrs. Hobhouse's plea. Yet as the Liberal old guard they had little wish to ask favours of the men who had so rudely supplanted them, and it says much for Asquith's integrity that he was prepared to swallow his pride and request a meeting with Lord Derby. The meeting took place on 2 August in Asquith's room at the House of Commons, with McKenna and Childs supporting their respective chiefs.[1] But Asquith had nothing new to add to the familiar arguments for releasing those absolutists of whose good faith there was prima facie evidence. As with all the other advocates of release, Asquith seems to have believed that it was quite obvious which absolutists were genuine, that there was, in Herbert Fisher's words, 'a very definite and *easily cognisable* class of cases', and that there would be no difficulty in arranging for their release. As long as this remained the proposed alternative to War Office policy, Derby and Childs had little difficulty in seeing it off, and their task was made easier not harder by the presence of Stephen Hobhouse because the advocates of release were encouraged to argue individual cases. Even Derby recognized the flaw in this approach. 'The whole question of the release of conscientious objectors', he told Margaret Hobhouse, 'cannot depend upon one man; it must be treated and be dealt with as a general principle.'[2] When Derby passed on to the War Cabinet the précis of his discussion with Asquith, he wrote of Stephen Hobhouse:

> I do not think there is the least doubt in his case that he is a genuine Conscientious Objector—one of the very few who exist—and personally I should be glad to liberate him, but there is no method by which this can be done.

Although Childs admitted to Asquith that 'there were many hundreds of men who were forced into the Army through the ineptitude of the tribunals', Derby insisted that the Secretary of State could not be expected to select individual cases for fresh consideration. 'This', he complained, 'is asking me to pull chestnuts out of the fire to redeem Mr. Asquith's pledges and I have no wish to undertake a particularly disagreeable task.'

Childs's attack on the 'ineptitude of the tribunals' was unfor-

[1] Derby circulated a précis of the discussion (agreed with Asquith) with his own introductory remarks, on 21 August 1917. See CAB 24/23/1799.

[2] Derby to Margaret Hobhouse, 3 December 1917, WO 32/2051/3319.

tunate. It provoked the President of the Local Government Board, who blamed the War Office's Representative for many of the bad tribunal decisions. But while Hayes Fisher had clearly been stung by Childs's criticism, his Memorandum heartily endorsed War Office policy: 'For myself I am convinced that any concession of the kind suggested to the absolutist view would be disastrous.'[1] Much more serious from Childs's point of view was the fact that his remarks were also seized upon by Milner as fresh evidence that the whole question of the absolutists should be re-examined.[2] To the Prime Minister it was no doubt exasperating that this minor problem should continue to occupy the time and attention of his senior colleagues, yet Lord Milner was the one member of the War Cabinet on whose support he placed increasing importance during 1917,[3] and whose views, therefore, could not be ignored. The need to avoid alienating Milner would have been a more pressing argument with Lloyd George than the personal appeal he received from Margaret Hobhouse,[4] as would the desire to see this dispute, that had flared intermittently throughout the summer, now in public, now in the privacy of correspondence and Cabinet meetings, settled once and for all. On 8 October the War Cabinet at last yielded to Milner's pressure and agreed to set up a committee to consider the treatment of conscientious objectors and any possible legislation.[5]

The composition of the committee gave little hope to the advocates of release: the attitude of the Chairman, Sir George Cave, was at best ambiguous, and of the other members only Herbert Fisher was known to favour release. The chances of the committee recommending such a fundamental change in policy were further diminished by the Cabinet's insistence that General Childs should attend all the discussions. Childs himself contemplated this new development with equanimity. 'The position of the absolutist is

[1] CAB 24/25/1974.

[2] Milner circulated his second Memorandum urging release on 24 August: CAB 24/24/1833.

[3] See especially Gollin, op. cit., Chs. 15 and 16.

[4] Margaret Hobhouse to Lloyd George, 26 September 1917, Curzon Papers 10. The fact that this letter is in the Curzon Papers suggests that Curzon may have been taking an interest in the release of the absolutists some two months before his active intervention on their behalf.

[5] CAB 23/4/246(I). The committee members were: Sir George Cave (Chairman), George Barnes, Salisbury, Herbert Fisher, Hayes Fisher, and Ian Macpherson.

once more engaging the attention of the Cabinet,' he told Wigram, 'but I do not fear that our attitude towards them will be disturbed.'[1] Childs placed his confidence in the letter of the law. All the other arguments against the release of selected absolutists—that this would encourage men on the Home Office Scheme to adopt the absolutist position, that public opinion would be outraged, that the men were in prison of their own choice anyway—were secondary; the law had made provision for conscientious objectors, and whatever the failings of the statutory tribunals, their decisions could not arbitrarily be set aside without abandoning the whole basis of the Military Service Acts.

The force of the legal argument clearly impressed the Cabinet committee whose report expressed the view that to grant release to absolutists would 'in fact be a surrender to anarchy and the recognition of the right of an individual to disobey a statute if he disagrees with it'.[2] The committee's conclusion, which if not foregone was hardly unexpected, was that 'the proper course is to uphold the law'. But the committee did recommend that conscientious objectors who had been in prison for a substantial period and who had conducted themselves well should be allowed the privileges under Rule 243A. This concession did little to placate Fisher, who dissented from the committee's principal conclusion, and Milner, who had been thwarted once again. Both men counter-attacked vigorously, Milner in a further Memorandum to the War Cabinet,[3] Fisher in two personal letters—dated 18 and 20 October—to Lloyd George.[4] But, apart from the claim that public opinion was turning against the Government on this issue, a claim hotly disputed by other leading politicians, neither Milner nor Fisher had any new arguments to present; and when the War Cabinet came to consider the committee's report on 25 October it decided to endorse the conclusions.[5]

Though Milner in his Memorandum had warned that 'we have not heard the last of this question', the Prime Minister had every right to assume that the matter was now closed. In contrast to his earlier threat to make 'the path of that class a very hard one',

[1] Childs to Wigram, 11 October 1917, RA GV5910/5.
[2] The committee's report is CAB 24/29/2321, 16 October 1917.
[3] Milner's third Memorandum is dated 20 October 1917: CAB 24/29/2354.
[4] Both letters are in the Lloyd George Papers.
[5] CAB 23/4/257(3).

Lloyd George had taken steps to ensure that the case for release received a proper hearing. The War Office, too, could reasonably expect that its policy was secure for the remainder of the war. Yet, within a month, the politicians and the military had agreed upon a formula that resulted in the unconditional discharge of some three hundred absolutists including Stephen Hobhouse. The explanation of this dramatic reversal lies in the determination and resourcefulness of those who argued for the release of the genuine cases. Lord Milner and Margaret Hobhouse were in some ways an ill-assorted team but as campaigners they were complementary, the one tenacious, reserved, intellectually tough, the other unashamedly emotional, even self-indulgent in the promotion of her cause. Each reacted to the latest disappointment in characteristic fashion, Milner manoeuvring behind the scenes while Margaret Hobhouse recruited influential names for a memorial on the subject of the absolutists and a petition to the Home Secretary.

The Memorandum that Milner circulated for the War Cabinet meeting on 25 October does not appear to have been his only, or his principal, response to the Cabinet committee's report. On the morning of the meeting, *The Times* carried a remarkable leading article that urged the release of all absolutists and added a significant rider:

> One point is clear however. Men who, for whatever reason, persistently decline to do their duty as citizens place themselves permanently outside the community and have no title either to its protection or to the enjoyment of civil rights.[1]

The removal of civil rights, particularly of the franchise, had been discussed before both in the press and in Parliament, but never as a quid pro quo for the release of the absolutists. There are good reasons for thinking that this formula of release coupled with disfranchisement came from Lord Milner. In October 1917 Lord Northcliffe was in the U.S.A. and the Editor of *The Times*, Geoffrey Dawson, had a free hand to take a line on conscientious objectors that might not have commended itself to his chief;[2] and

[1] *The Times*, 25 October 1917.

[2] Northcliffe did not see the paper between 2 June and 11 November; see Reginald Pound and Geoffrey Harmsworth, *Northcliffe*, London, 1959, p. 590. During this period Dawson 'could conduct *The Times* on his own lines'; see J. E. Wrench, *Geoffrey Dawson and Our Times*, London, 1955, p. 150.

Dawson was one of Milner's most loyal disciples, a former member of the Kindergarten, and a man to whom Milner had often turned in the past when he had wished to give public expression to his opinions.[1] That a leading article echoing many of the arguments Milner had used in his memoranda should have appeared on the morning of the decisive War Cabinet meeting cannot be accepted as a mere coincidence. The article was almost certainly a move in Milner's campaign, and if it failed to influence the War Cabinet on this occasion, the new formula of release and disfranchisement had not been rejected as such.

Three weeks later, on 14 November, the House of Lords, effectively prevented by the Prime Minister from discussing questions of high policy, found time to turn its attention once again to the subject of conscientious objectors. At one point in the debate Lord Curzon intervened to say that while he did not think that there was a case for releasing the absolutists, he was prepared to consult the Home Secretary about 'greater elasticity' in their treatment.[2] As a member of the War Cabinet Curzon would have known about the proposed relaxation of prison discipline under Rule 243A and it may have been this to which he referred. Or he may have been ready to press for something more. Herbert Fisher suspected the latter and wrote at once. To the well-worn arguments for the release of the 'genuine' absolutists, Fisher added a fresh twist:

> These men are *ex hypothesi* cranks. They are morbid, obstinately tenacious of opinion, intractable, in many cases vain to the verge of lunacy. All these defects are enormously magnified by prison treatment, than which nothing can be considered more injurious to the preservation of mental balance and sanity.[3]

And he concluded on a note that was calculated to touch Curzon at a sensitive point:

> Please pardon this long epistle—but I am concerned lest the Muse of History should attach a reproach to the otherwise good name of our Government.

Curzon's reputation is above all that of an ambitious man, acutely conscious of the judgement of posterity but prepared to abandon

[1] Gollin, op. cit., p. 268. [2] 5 HL 26, col. 1011, 14 November 1917.

[3] Herbert Fisher to Curzon, 15 November 1917, Curzon Papers 72.

policies and accept humiliations rather than risk a setback to his career. But if Curzon was the 'political jumping-jack' of Beaverbrook's contemptuous phrase, he was not the man to court Lloyd George's disfavour by reopening a question that the Prime Minister now regarded as closed. Yet this is precisely what Curzon did on receiving Fisher's letter. His motives were no doubt mixed. He had not been approached by Margaret Hobhouse and with Lord Milner his relations were cool: the two former proconsuls had little in common, though they met daily in the War Cabinet, and had shared a romantic attachment to the actress Elinor Glyn, whose boudoir was carpeted with the tiger-skins they had shot in their respective outposts.[1] But, like Milner, Curzon was an administrator rather than a politician despite his pretensions to the premiership, and the sheer muddle of the policy for conscientious objectors must have provoked him. Then again there would be the satisfaction of coming to the aid of Stephen Hobhouse, a fellow alumnus of Eton and Balliol, and of putting one across Lord Derby, an old antagonist.[2] Or Curzon may simply have decided that the moment was propitious to cut through the deadlock on the absolutists and earn the gratitude of the swelling number of influential men who were sufficiently disturbed by the present policy to put their names to Margaret Hobhouse's memorial.

In the late afternoon of 19 November Curzon met Derby, Childs, and Cave at the War Office.[3] It must have been a difficult meeting, with Derby and Childs reluctant to discuss the question of release, Curzon anxious not to go away empty-handed, and Cave torn between his respect for the law and his desire to see the Home Office relieved of the responsibility for men whose presence was a continuous threat to the standards of the prison service. After the meeting Curzon scrawled a brief note to Herbert Fisher:

> Many thanks for your letter re C.O.s. I fought a good fight for them this afternoon at the W.O. and think that I got something substantial.[4]

[1] Milner's love for Elinor Glyn was not returned, but neither was Elinor Glyn's for Curzon. Curzon was aware that Milner was a rival but not vice versa. As for the tiger-skins, which gave rise to a celebrated jingle, they long outlasted the proconsuls in Elinor Glyn's private life. These affairs are described in Anthony Glyn, *Elinor Glyn: a biography*, London, 1955, pp. 126–9.

[2] For the hostility between Curzon and Derby, see Randolph S. Churchill, *Lord Derby, King of Lancashire*, London, 1959, p. 259.

[3] A Memorandum of the meeting is in WO 32/2051/3319.

[4] Curzon to Herbert Fisher, 19 November 1917, H. A. L. Fisher Papers I.

Curzon was not exaggerating. Derby and Childs had agreed that the War Office should authorize the release of any absolutists reported to be medically unfit by the prison doctor. Although Cave had mentioned that Stephen Hobhouse's health was not such as to warrant discharge from prison on medical grounds, Curzon had evidently decided that this was a detail on which the War Office would gladly display elasticity. Sure enough, the following morning Derby wrote to suggest that the medical discharge should be granted when the prison doctor decided that the man was never likely to become a soldier and that it was injurious for him to stay in prison, a formula that might have been tailored to fit Stephen Hobhouse's condition.[1]

It could be argued—and no doubt was by Curzon—that release on medical grounds met all the War Office objections: it did not undermine the law, it would not encourage an extension of absolutism, and it obviated the need to make an arbitrary distinction between the genuine absolutists and the others. Yet it could not be disguised that the position General Childs had defended so stubbornly since the spring had been breached if not overrun. It seems improbable that the War Office professionals, Macready and Childs, would have allowed this to happen without extracting a comparable concession from their opponents, such as the loss of civil rights proposed by Milner in *The Times*, but there is no mention of this in the report of the meeting on 19 November.

On 20 November the House of Commons was debating the Representation of the People Bill, and the order paper included an amendment in the name of Sir George Younger that was designed to disfranchise conscientious objectors who had been court-martialled or exempted from all military service.[2] When a similar amendment had been proposed in June, the Government's opposition had been stated unequivocally by Cave:

> So far as I have the power, so far as the Government has the power, to influence the vote of this House, we think the House will be best consulting its own dignity and the interests of justice by declining to accept this amendment.[3]

[1] Derby to Curzon, 20 November 1917, WO 32/2051/3319.

[2] The debate on Younger's amendment is 5 HC 99, col. 1135–1274, 20 and 21 November 1917.

[3] Cave's speech against the amendment is 5 HC 95, col. 331–6, 26 June 1917.

Among those who followed the Home Secretary's lead and voted against the amendment were the other members of the Administration present, Bonar Law, Walter Long, Hayes Fisher, and Stanley Baldwin. Now, five months later, Government opposition to the disfranchisement of conscientious objectors was withdrawn. Bonar Law announced that the issue would be left to a free vote of the House and declared his own intention of voting for an amendment which he regarded as a 'direct deterrent' to the growth of the absolutist movement. Sir George Cave, to his credit, said that he could not vote for the amendment and abstained, but his colleagues did not share his compunction: Walter Long, Hayes Fisher, and Stanley Baldwin joined Bonar Law in voting for disfranchisement. With this implicit Government backing, the amendment was carried by 209 votes to 171.

It is possible that the Government's volte-face on the disfranchisement of conscientious objectors (a volte-face that Bonar Law denied had ever occurred) had been agreed some weeks beforehand, in which case Curzon would have been able to present it to Derby and Childs as a new and powerful deterrent that would cover the release of those absolutists who were medically unfit. On the other hand the Government may not have come to a firm decision to withdraw its opposition to disfranchisement before 19 November, so that this may have been the quid pro quo that Derby and Childs required for the concession they made to Curzon. To a greater or lesser extent, therefore, the release of Stephen Hobhouse appears to have been dependent upon the disfranchisement of the conscientious objectors for five years after the end of the war.[1]

There was no immediate announcement of the arrangements for release on medical grounds, and those most closely concerned were not informed. On 27 November Herbert Fisher passed on to Gilbert Murray the contents of Curzon's hurried note, but clearly did not know the nature of the concession that Curzon had obtained.[2] Two days later, the Memorial calling for an end to repeated sentences and the Petition for the release of Stephen Hobhouse, both of which were the fruits of Margaret Hobhouse's

[1] See p. 235, below.

[2] Herbert Fisher to Gilbert Murray, 27 November 1917, H. A. L. Fisher Papers 7.

crusading zeal, were presented. The signatories to the Memorial[1] were predominantly churchmen, and included eighteen diocesan bishops, eight bishops suffragan, seven deans, and two hundred other clergy. There were laymen and clerics, such as George Lansbury and William Temple, who had already spoken out against the repeated sentencing of conscientious objectors, and many others such as Dick Sheppard, the founder of the Peace Pledge Union in 1934, who were now prepared to add their names to the protest. The Petition in the name of Mr. and Mrs. Henry Hobhouse was sent to the Home Secretary, with a copy for Lord Derby.[2] Though modestly signed, it was accompanied by useful references. One of these came from General Smuts, whose ignorance of the fact that Stephen Hobhouse was shortly to be released adds to the conspiratorial air that surrounds the origin of the War Office concession.

My dear Lord Derby,

Mr. and Mrs. Hobhouse have petitioned the Home Secretary for the release of their son *Stephen Hobhouse*. I pray you to give your support to the petition as the case of Stephen Hobhouse is causing profound misgiving to thousands of good people who are by no means in favour of C.Os. It is so exceptional and outstanding that I hope the Army Council may see its way to discharge him from the Army.

Yours sincerely,
J. C. Smuts.[3]

Derby replied to Margaret Hobhouse on 3 December. The announcement was now so close that he could afford to raise her hopes:

The whole matter is under consideration and if a decision is arrived at which will give freedom to your son to carry on his work amongst the poor, I personally shall rejoice with you in his release as an individual.[4]

The following day Curzon told the House of Lords that the Army Council would authorize the release and transfer to the Reserve of those absolutists reported by the Home Office to be in a poor state of health.[5] Though as members of the Reserve they were still liable for service, the War Office had no intention of recalling

[1] See WO 32/2051/3319. [2] Ibid.
[3] J. C. Smuts to Derby, 1 December 1917, WO 32/2051/3319.
[4] Derby to Mrs. Hobhouse, 3 December 1917, WO 32/2051/3319.
[5] 5 HL 27, col. 53–6, 4 December 1917.

them to the colours, so that their release was in effect unconditional. Four days later Stephen Hobhouse was discharged from Exeter Prison and directed to the lodgings his wife had taken in the city; as a final gesture of courtesy to their distinguished but embarrassing prisoner, the authorities had given his wife a confidential warning that he was about to be released.

The reaction to the release of Stephen Hobhouse was mixed. 'That pernicious woman Margaret Hobhouse', as Childs had called her in one of his less charitable moments,[1] was not unnaturally delighted at the success of her campaign, but she did not propose to slacken her efforts to obtain the release of all the absolutists. Emily Hobhouse wrote gushingly and inaccurately to Smuts, 'Dear Angel that Openeth Prison Doors',[2] but Curzon appears to have received neither thanks nor recognition. Although Clifford Allen was released shortly after Stephen Hobhouse, the suspicion remained that the War Office concession was primarily a response to influential pressure. In the Commons, the Government's motives were challenged by Joseph King, a Liberal and member of the U.D.C.:

Why has he been let out? Because you dare not keep him in. He comes of a very distinguished family; he had an uncle in the House of Lords; he is a very distinguished man himself. You dared not keep him in. You will keep many men in even when you are warned that if you keep them in they will die. They do in fact die. But you dared not keep Stephen Hobhouse in to die in prison. There is but one chance for many of these men—either release by death or release by favouritism.[3]

The evidence that is now available does little to discredit Mr. King's analysis.

Stephen Hobhouse and Clifford Allen were among the first of 333 absolutists released under the War Office concession during the next eighteen months.[4] As is not infrequently the case when concessions are granted under pressure, the release on medical grounds and the privileges allowed under Rule 243A provoked probably as much criticism as they prevented. The Home Office

[1] In a letter to Wigram, 11 October 1917, RA GV5910/5.
[2] Quoted in Hancock, op. cit., p. 461.
[3] 5 HC 103, col. 1597–8, 28 February 1918.
[4] This is the figure given in *The Tribunal*, 8 January 1920. The Home Office did not publish a figure.

was attacked from both sides. Visiting Committees protested that the concessions were undermining discipline in the prisons and advised governors to deny all privileges to conscientious objectors who were difficult to control.[1] On the other hand there were allegations (hardly surprising in view of the Visiting Committees' advice) that Rule 243A was not being fairly applied; more seriously, the Home Office was accused of failing to recommend the release of absolutists whose health was deteriorating. To counter this charge explicit instructions were given to governors and medical officers to report any case in which physical *or* mental health was being impaired by imprisonment.[2] While there may have been prisons where these instructions were narrowly interpreted, it was also true that some conscientious objectors deliberately courted ill-health by discarding overcoats in bitterly cold weather and by refusing to see the prison doctor, forms of non-cooperation that must have seemed logical to the individuals concerned but which the Home Office could be forgiven for regarding as perversity. For the dedicated but humourless Chairman of the N.C.F., Clifford Allen, even the onset of tuberculosis could be turned to good account. Before his release, he had written to a Fellowship official:

> I suggest best way to rouse opinion re the Absolutists (out of my case) is to wait until I have had about 30 to 40 days BW, no mattress, no exercise and punishment cell and 60 or 90 days solitary confinement etc. Then all this following upon the Doctor's original fear of serious consequences might provide material for 'Scandal propaganda', adjournment debate etc. on the Absolutists' persecution. . . .[3]

Nine conscientious objectors died in prison.[4] Though their deaths were from natural causes they were remembered as martyrs. For the absolutists, the claim to this title was not altogether presumptuous as they alone had refused to make any significant compromise with the Military Service Acts, yet even here death, though no less tragic, was an incidental not a direct result of Government policy. Statistics do not invalidate the facts in a particular case but it is worth observing that nine deaths among a

[1] Conscientious Objectors in Prison, p. 3. [2] Ibid.

[3] Clifford Allen to Catherine Marshall, July 1917, quoted in Martin Gilbert, *Plough My Own Furrow: the story of Lord Allen of Hurtwood as told through his writing and correspondence*, London, 1965, p. 86.

[4] This is the official figure given in 5 HL 34, col. 161, 3 April 1919. The N.C.F. claimed ten men died.

prison population of some 1,200 conscientious objectors over a period of three years was a lower death rate than for prisoners as a whole;[1] and this was despite the fact that the conscientious objectors were ill-equipped in physique and experience to face the rigours of the Third Division and sometimes adopted tactics—such as hunger striking—that undermined their own health.[2]

However neatly the deaths of conscientious objectors could be contained within the official statistics, a technique at which Cave was particularly adept when answering awkward questions in the House, the severe effect of long imprisonment was an important factor in keeping the fate of the absolutists before the public. In 1918 the calls for release tended to come from outside the Government, and from groups rather than individuals; of those who had worked so hard for the release of Stephen Hobhouse, only his mother, Lord Parmoor, and Herbert Fisher continued the campaign on behalf of all the absolutists. Milner appears to have taken no further interest in the matter. In April 1918 he left the War Cabinet to succeed Lord Derby as Secretary of State for War, thus assuming the responsibility for the conscientious objectors in prison that he had accused Derby of exercising so rigidly. Milner's arrival at the War Office was not marked by any particular 'elasticity of administration' as far as the conscientious objectors were concerned. When he received an appeal for the release of Barratt Brown, a Quaker whose credentials were as impeccable as those of Stephen Hobhouse, he was 'unable to help'.[3]

[1] Deaths from natural causes per 1,000 prisoners were 6·1 in local prisons and 9·3 in convict prisons in the year March 1917 to March 1918; the figures for 1918–19 were 7·2 and 16·5, an increase caused by the influenza epidemic. The deaths among conscientious objectors during this period were equivalent to about 3·8 per 1,000 prisoners. See Prison Reports, 1918, p. 22, and 1919, p. 24.

[2] There is some evidence that a significant number of conscientious objectors suffered from poor health before they were conscripted. The Pelham Committee found that of 3,964 conscientious objectors 874 had defective health and that the health of a further 860 could only be described as 'fair'. The Brace Committee reported that 'many of the men were feeble in physique', and the Prison Report for 1917, the year when the largest number of conscientious objectors was received into prison, stated that the general standard of physique was much inferior compared with previous years and that the daily average in prison hospitals was the highest on record.

[3] The appeal was made by Sir Oliver Lodge, Principal of Birmingham University, and Professor J. H. Muirhead, the University's Professor of Philosophy. At the time of his arrest Barratt Brown was lecturer in philosophy at the Friends' educational centre, Woodbrooke, near Birmingham. The correspondence is in WO 32/2052/3390.

Milner, unlike Derby, had to deal with few personal approaches on the behalf of absolutists, and he was probably shrewd enough to recognize the ambivalence that lay behind some of the public protestations. In January 1918 the Annual Conference of the Labour Party passed a resolution calling for the release of all conscientious objectors in prison, and a similar resolution was unanimously accepted by the I.L.P. Conference in April.[1] But the Labour movement had one eye on the future. In the spring of 1918 Clifford Allen noted in his diary:

> How very sad it is to see how everyone has lost heart in the usefulness of the C.O. stand.[2]

Labour's concern for the conscientious objectors in prison, many of whom were fellow socialists, was tinged with an anxiety not to be too closely identified with men who were not likely to be an asset in an election campaign. Their resolutions were also rendered partly ineffective by the military crisis of April and May which precluded for the time being any further consideration of release.

When the crisis had passed and the way opened to ultimate victory, the Home Office made one final attempt to resolve the problem of the absolutists short of actual release. Cave and his permanent officials were encouraged (so they later claimed) by 'influential persons sympathizing with the absolutists' to believe that if the absolutists were transferred to a special establishment and granted the maximum freedom consistent with their status as prisoners, they would work well and cause no trouble.[3] That such advice could have been given and accepted indicates an astonishing failure to grasp the essentials of the absolutists' position. For the Home Office, however, the scheme's obvious futility may well have been overlooked in the eagerness to separate the absolutists from the militants and so provide an opportunity to restore some semblance of discipline in the prisons.

The scheme was launched in August: absolutists who had served the equivalent of a two-year sentence were transferred to Wakefield Prison (evacuated as a work centre after the Whitsun fracas),

[1] Report of the Annual Conference of the Labour Party, 1918, p. 136; Report of the Annual Conference of I.L.P., 1918, p. 72.

[2] Gilbert, op. cit., p. 109.

[3] Conscientious Objectors in Prison, p. 4. The 'influential persons' probably included Parmoor.

where they were to be treated much like men undergoing preventive detention; they would be allowed to wear their own clothes, mix and smoke freely after working hours, and enjoy generous privileges with regard to letters and visits. But the whole experiment was based on a false hypothesis: the absolutists would not cooperate in any way that would compromise their total rejection of the Military Service Acts.[1] They elected their own committee, organized 'a perfectly voluntary service for food and sanitation', and declared that they would undertake no other work. Home Office officials, apparently taken unawares by this attitude, tried to enforce a nine-hour work-day but got nowhere; even more disillusioning for the department that had always argued that the absolutists at least were 'well-conducted' was the collapse of discipline at Wakefield. By the end of September the Home Office had had enough; the Wakefield experiment, as well-intentioned and badly conceived as ever, was abandoned, and the men returned to normal prison life. In a lame attempt to save face the Home Office claimed that 'the experiment, though it failed, had the advantage of diminishing for a time the flood of criticism based on the alleged persecution of Conscientious Objector prisoners'.[2] If this was true, the respite was brief. The signature of the Armistice in November created a new situation: recruiting under the Military Service Acts was suspended, local and appeal tribunals held final, self-congratulatory meetings, and the nation prepared for a general election. Demobilization emerged as a prominent and controversial issue. The new situation was not altogether favourable to the conscientious objectors in prison. Though the end of the war strengthened the argument for release, the priorities for demobilization were sufficiently unpopular without adding the premature discharge of soldiers who had refused to serve. Appeals for the release of all conscientious objectors in prison, however influentially signed, stood little chance of succeeding until the demobilization of serving soldiers was well advanced.[3]

[1] For the men's views see *The Friend*, 20 September 1918.

[2] Conscientious Objectors in Prison, p. 4.

[3] There were numerous appeals, some more influential than others. In November 1918 eighty-three M.P.s urged the Prime Minister to sanction release. In December a major petition for release was sponsored by Parmoor, Gilbert Murray, Colonel John Buchan, and the Master of the Temple. In April 1919 a more modest petition was presented by the residents of Portishead. The last two petitions are in the Lloyd George Papers.

This delay inspired a wave of hunger strikes. In the first three months of 1919, 130 conscientious objectors had to be temporarily released under the 'Cat and Mouse Act' after periods of forcible feeding, and at the end of March the Home Office issued confidential instructions that forcible feeding should be abandoned with the result that the hunger strikers earned their temporary release very quickly.[1] The delay also gave the militants an opportunity to promote unrest and to disrupt the routine of the prisons. Their direct action against authority was most effective and, from the point of view of the conscientious objectors as a whole, most damaging at Wandsworth.

Wandsworth Prison was divided into a civil and a military wing, the former containing civilian criminals and military personnel who had been sentenced to imprisonment, the latter containing soldiers who had been sentenced to detention. Among the 220 military prisoners in the civil wing were 108 conscientious objectors, many of whom were not absolutists but the extreme anti-authoritarians who had been turned down by the Central Tribunal or sent back to prison from the Home Office Scheme.[2] The difficulties of controlling a prison holding these different groups were exacerbated by the privileges that the conscientious objectors enjoyed under Rule 243A, privileges that were understandably resented by the other prisoners and that gave the militants the freedom to organize. The subversion of authority which had begun on a limited scale in 1918 with meetings at which 'The Red Flag' was sung and 'extreme socialist views promulgated', became more ambitious when the Governor took no effective disciplinary action. Attempts were made to goad the soldiers in the detention barracks into resisting authority, though fortunately for the soldiers a mutiny was averted. On the civil side, no direct incitement was necessary; the other military prisoners, inspired by the success of the militants, attacked the warders. This incident persuaded the Prison Commission that the Governor should, in the official euphemism, be sent on leave, and an Acting Governor appointed to restore order.

When the Acting Governor, Major George Blake, made his

[1] Conscientious Objectors in Prison, p. 6.

[2] For the events at Wandsworth see Wandsworth Prison (Allegations against Acting Governor) (Cmd.131, 1919). The inquiry was conducted by Mr. Albion Richardson, M.P.

initial inspection with the Chief Warder, he soon discovered how successful the militant conscientious objectors had been in reducing the prison to a state of near-anarchy:[1]

When we came inside the prison there was in that hall you have just seen, C.2 they call it, a gang of men, I did not know who they were, drawn up, and they were singing and making an awful noise absolutely unheard of in any prison I had been in. I said, 'Silence'. One man shouted out, 'Get your hair cut', another made a disgusting and offensive noise with his mouth, some other men made some other remarks, and somebody shouted out from the back, 'Who is this bloody swine?' or 'Hark at the bloody swine'.

Blake and the Chief Warder then entered one of the workshops:

In the workshop there were some decently behaved people sitting down and working quietly, and the officer in charge reported, 'All correct, Sir.' Then from the other door marched in, singing 'The Red Flag', a gang of these Conscientious Objectors. They were noisy, and I saw the other men were getting restive at once. Nearly all the prisoners were soldiers, you know. There was a restive look about them. I said, 'March these men out'. I rather think I said, 'March these noisy devils out of here. I won't have them disturbing the decently behaved and respectable prisoners.' I had a purpose in saying that. As they went out they started shouting and yelling, and so for the benefit of everyone concerned I shouted to these men, 'You damned mutinous swine, I have come down here to restore order, and if you do not behave yourselves I will give you hell.' I did not know what to do with these fellows. The prison was in an appalling state; I simply cracked a whip at them; I lashed out at them with my tongue. I called them 'Damned mutinous swine', most disgusting words to use but I am not apologising for it. It was the only thing to do.

The methods Blake used to discipline the militant conscientious objectors were the subject of an official inquiry which concluded that the Acting Governor had shown a 'want of discretion' in his selection of epithets but that otherwise his conduct had been free from reproach. Though some of the absolutists at Wandsworth had tried to restrain the extremists, they had soon discovered that in an open conflict with authority the anarchists were contemptuous of the convictions that motivated the majority of conscientious objectors, a home truth that the pacifist movement was slow to absorb.

[1] Both quotations are from Major Blake's evidence to the inquiry.

In January 1919 the responsibility for the conscientious objectors in prison had passed to a new Secretary of State for War, Winston Churchill, and a new Home Secretary, Edward Shortt.[1] Inheriting a responsibility that was likely to bring discredit whichever way it was handled, Churchill must have been relieved to learn that his military advisers now favoured release. The logic of the War Office position was clear: now that the Military Service Acts had been suspended, there was no law to undermine and no recruiting to prejudice. Churchill wasted no time in proposing to the Cabinet that the conscientious objectors who had served two years should be released at once, but the balance of opinion at the Cabinet meeting was still against release until demobilization was further advanced.[2] The activities of the militants helped to confirm this view: members of the Cabinet who opposed Churchill argued that many of the conscientious objectors in prison were 'revolutionaries', 'blackguards', and 'Bolsheviks' whose discharge at this time would be bitterly resented.

This decision did not satisfy the War Office which displayed as much determination to get the conscientious objectors out of its system as it had previously shown in thwarting the advocates of release. Churchill prosecuted the military case with characteristic force. When the matter was again raised in the Cabinet on 17 March, he 'strongly pressed for the release of these prisoners. . . . He wished vigorously to protest, both against the invidious position in which he was at present placed, and also against the severity of these men's present treatment, to the continuance of which his military advisers were strongly opposed.'[3] But the Cabinet stalled once again and Churchill, obviously under considerable pressure from the military, had to renew the attack a fortnight later. The military members of the Army Council, he claimed on this occasion, were unanimous that the rank and file of the army would accept the release of the conscientious objectors without protest. Appropriately it was Curzon, sensing once again perhaps that the moment was right, who threw his weight behind the War Office

[1] Although Lloyd George appointed a full Cabinet it did not meet as such until October; meanwhile the War Cabinet continued to function and to summon Ministers and experts to its meetings.

[2] Churchill's proposals are in his memorandum, CAB 24/75/6873, and the meeting to discuss them was on 26 February 1919, CAB 23/9/537(5).

[3] CAB 23/9/545(I).

and swung the Cabinet in favour of release along the lines that Churchill had proposed.[1]

This decision of 3 April was applied to all conscientious objectors who had served twenty months (the minimum of a two-year sentence), time spent in military custody or on the Home Office Scheme being allowed to count towards the total. This enabled the Home Office to release the majority of conscientious objectors from prison by the end of May, and the remainder—some 213 men—by the beginning of August.[2] At Childs's suggestion, all were discharged from the army with ignominy for committing a disgraceful offence, a formula that somewhat unnecessarily ensured that they would be court-martialled if they attempted to re-enlist.

[1] CAB 23/10/553(I), 3 April 1919.
[2] For these dates see Conscientious Objectors in Prison, p. 6.

CHAPTER ELEVEN

AFTERMATH

There was little justice in the order in which the different groups of conscientious objectors were released. Men who had suffered the least disruption of their civilian lives were the first to be freed from their obligations under the Military Service Acts: by February 1919 all those doing work of national importance under the tribunals or the Pelham Committee had been allowed to go home. In April the Home Office closed its work centres, formally discharged the men on exceptional employment, and began the systematic release of the conscientious objectors in prison. But the demobilization of the Non-Combatant Corps, whose members had been willing to fulfil the role originally proposed for all conscientious objectors, was not completed until January 1920.

Release did not automatically remove the penalties associated with being a conscientious objector. In some walks of life the stigma of having been a conchie was a bar to promotion, even to employment itself, and all conscientious objectors were open to discrimination if their war record (or rather lack of one) became known. For those who were insulated against the world by their membership of an apocalyptic sect, neither official nor unofficial penalties mattered much. Disfranchisement was irrelevant to men who regarded themselves as travellers in a foreign country and uninterested in the nature of the government. Even for the non-sectarian, the loss of the vote was hardly the severe penalty that Lloyd George's Cabinet had claimed. The reason was that in many areas disfranchisement was enforced half-heartedly or not at all. Under the Representation of the People Act, 1918,[1] conscientious objectors who had been exempt from all military service or who had been court-martialled (that is to say all conscientious

[1] 7 and 8 GEO 5, Ch. 64, 6 February 1918. Section 9 (2) covers the disfranchisement of conscientious objectors.

objectors except those who had enlisted in the Non-Combatant Corps) were disqualified from voting in a national or local election for five years after the end of the war. As the state of war was not legally concluded until 31 August 1921, the disqualification lasted until 30 August 1926.[1] The Act provided that where conscientious objectors could satisfy the Central Tribunal that they had done work of national importance the disqualification would be lifted, but of some five thousand men who could have applied for the removal of this penalty, only 404 did so.[2] The other-worldly commitments of the sectarians could not account for a lack of interest on this scale and the Central Tribunal was obliged to recognize that in many cases conscientious objectors had been included in the voting register because the registration officer had been ignorant of the facts. 'There seems no other conclusion possible', the Central Tribunal reported in 1922, 'but that the section has failed of its intended effect.'[3] This failure does not appear to have worried the government of the day, which was perhaps reluctant to draw attention to an act of discrimination that was best forgotten.

Restriction on the promotion and employment of conscientious objectors in the civil service was a more effective penalty, though the number of men involved was small. During the war the obsession with equal sacrifice had insisted that where conscientious objectors were allowed to remain in the service on the grounds that it was work of national importance, this period of their careers should neither earn increments nor count towards pension.[4] After the war the Government was at first unwilling to re-employ conscientious objectors on a permanent basis unless they had served in the Non-Combatant Corps, a policy that Randall Davidson criticized as 'an act of real unfairness'.[5] Subsequently, in 1920, the Treasury agreed to distinguish between conscientious objectors with a record of cooperation and good conduct who were restored to full establishment privileges, and the absolutists and

[1] SR&O 1921, No. 1276. See also G. P. Warner Terry, *The Representation of the People Acts 1918 to 1928*, London, 1928, p. 44.

[2] Supplementary Report of the Central Tribunal, 1922. In 318 cases the disqualification was removed.

[3] Supplementary Report of the Central Tribunal, 1922.

[4] CAB 23/4/298(18), 14 December 1917.

[5] In a letter to Austen Chamberlain, 19 November 1919, quoted in Bell, op. cit., 2, p. 953.

militants who were discharged from the civil service. As a result of this decision 230 conscientious objectors were reinstated and joined the 50 non-combatants who, since 1917, had been recognized as still on the establishment. Approximately 70 conscientious objectors were now discharged, though for some the discharge was a formality as they had already resigned. The Treasury also decided that conscientious objectors should not be promoted over the heads of ex-soldiers and that any application to join the civil service from a conscientious objector should be rejected.[1] These restrictions remained in force until 1929, when, despite the protests of the British Legion, conscientious objectors became eligible for promotion and for employment in all departments except defence.[2]

Conscientious objectors were also refused reinstatement in the Metropolitan Police. Nevil Macready, who had been appointed Commissioner in September 1918, argued that conscientious objectors would be a liability in a tight corner,[3] an argument he may have remembered twenty-five years later when a former conscientious objector, Herbert Morrison, assumed ministerial responsibility both for the police and for internal security.[4]

It was rare to find a conscientious objector who had been a policeman but a commonplace to find one who had been a teacher. Despite the defeat of Lord Charnwood's proposal in 1917, some Education Committees were accused of refusing to re-employ conscientious objectors.[5] While discrimination against conscientious objectors who wished to teach may have been more widespread than these few recorded cases, it was by no means universal: the headmaster of one independent public school with a Nonconformist tradition, Bishop's Stortford College, engaged no fewer than three conscientious objectors as masters in the immediate post-war years.[6]

[1] See Report from the Select Committee on the Civil Service (Employment of Conscientious Objectors), H.M.S.O., 10 April 1922.

[2] See Treasury Circular E.1206/4, 'Civil Service and Conscientious Objectors', 10 September 1929. The British Legion protest was made through Resolution No. 143 of their Annual Conference in 1930.

[3] Macready, op. cit., 2, pp. 388–9.

[4] Morrison was Secretary for Home Affairs and Home Security from 1940 to 1945.

[5] See *The Tribunal*, 12 June 1919.

[6] The headmaster, F. S. Young, also refused to continue military training for the boys in peacetime despite representations from the War Office.

With the exception of the ex-servicemen's organizations, which watched keenly for any indulgence towards those who had refused to fight, society soon lost interest in the conscientious objector. The conscientious objectors themselves showed little inclination to live in the past. When the N.C.F. held its first post-war convention in November 1919, its members rejected a proposal that the Fellowship should continue its work. Instead, the young activists turned their attention to the promotion of a world-wide renunciation of war, an idealistic concept that was soon to become a popular obsession in progressive circles. Former absolutists founded the No More War Movement in 1921[1] and played the leading role in the War Resisters International which established its headquarters in London in 1923.[2] Wherever the pacifist backlash against the war was expressed in organizational terms, ex-conscientious objectors were involved: they helped to found pacifist groups within the major Protestant Churches[3] and were prominent among the sponsors of that archetypal renunciation of war, the Peace Pledge of 1934.[4]

Although pacifism between the wars owed much to former conscientious objectors, of the three absolutists whose example and leadership had made them the most celebrated opponents of conscription, only Fenner Brockway continued to play an active role. He was Chairman of the No More War Movement and of the War Resisters International. In 1938 he attempted to revive the spirit of the N.C.F. by founding a No Conscription League, but there was little support for a cause that had once inspired such dogged loyalty. The possibility of the reintroduction of conscription in 1938 also moved Clifford Allen to dream of a new campaign against the old enemy, but by this time he was much too ill to offer effective opposition. Allen's health never recovered from the

[1] For the early years of this movement see W. J. Chamberlain, *Fighting for Peace*, London, 1929, pp. 118–29. Chamberlain had been an absolutist.

[2] For the origins of this movement see *War Resisters of the World* (an account of the movement in twenty countries and a report of the International Conference held at Hoddesdon, England, July 1925), published by the W.R.I., 1925. This organization is still active.

[3] Groups were started as follows: the Congregational Peace Crusade (1926); the Baptist Pacifist Fellowship (1932); the Methodist Peace Fellowship (1933); the Anglican Pacifist Fellowship (1937). PAX, organized by Roman Catholics but open to Christian pacifists of all denominations, was started in 1936.

[4] Among the initial sponsors of the Pledge were two former absolutists, James Hudson and Wilfred Wellock.

effects of his imprisonment. Though he was Chairman of the I.L.P. in 1923 he was forced to resign two years later, and while Brockway was able to fight elections and, eventually, to become a well-established Labour M.P., Allen's intense interest in politics had to be satisfied with the activities of ginger groups and the correspondence columns of *The Times*. In 1931 Allen was offered a peerage by Ramsay MacDonald for the not very flattering reason that the Prime Minister needed socialist allies in the Lords. Allen accepted, just as Fenner Brockway accepted a life peerage when he was defeated in the General Election of 1964. The Chairman and Secretary of the N.C.F., a militantly progressive organization pledged to subvert the law, thus ended their public careers as Baron Brockway and Lord Allen of Hurtwood.[1] Both men also came to reject an absolute pacifist position, Brockway because he recognized that it was inconsistent with his support of the Republicans in Spain, Allen because absolute pacifism could not be reconciled with his advocacy of a strong and effective League of Nations. Clifford Allen died of tuberculosis in Switzerland in 1939; for a further thirty years Fenner Brockway continued to promote those progressive causes such as Colonial Freedom and Peace in Vietnam, that in spirit if not in substance were the natural offspring of the No Conscription Fellowship.

Stephen Hobhouse spent the first years after his release from prison preparing the evidence for the Labour Research Department's enquiry into the prison system. This period of intensive work following closely upon his own imprisonment caused a breakdown in health from which he never fully recovered. In 1921 he passed the responsibility for the prison enquiry on to Fenner Brockway and the published report entitled *English Prisons To-Day* appeared over both their names. For the rest of his life Stephen Hobhouse was a semi-invalid, a role for which his years of indifferent health had prepared him but in which he was obliged to live on the family's investments, a dependence upon unearned income that he had always sought to avoid. But there were com-

[1] Two other conscientious objectors—Herbert Morrison and F. W. Pethick-Lawrence—also ended their public careers in the House of Lords. Pethick-Lawrence was called up in 1918 at the age of 46 and was one of the few 'political' objectors to be granted exemption. An Etonian, he must surely have been the only Captain of the Oppidans ever to become a conscientious objector. See F. W. Pethick-Lawrence, *Fate Has Been Kind*, London, 1943, p. 118.

pensations. He was able to devote time to the writings of the mystical philosophers and to strengthen his pacifist convictions by a study of the teaching of Mahatma Gandhi. His books on mysticism sold few copies, but the pacifist pamphlets he wrote during the Second World War were widely read by a new generation of conscientious objectors. *Christ and Our Enemies*, a pamphlet urging reconciliation and forgiveness, was also officially issued to all army and air force chaplains in 1945. Stephen Hobhouse died on Easter Morning 1961 at the age of seventy-nine.

Margaret Hobhouse did not long survive her son's release from prison. The battle with inflexible officials, the constant lobbying, and protracted correspondence had all taken their toll. In March 1918 her spirit sustained a cruel blow when her youngest son, Paul, was reported 'missing presumed killed' during the German offensive. For eight months she continued to write to him 'in occupied territory' on the slender hope that he was a prisoner, but at the Armistice it was the letters that came back marked 'Undeliverable. Return to sender'. In her grief she sought consolation in spiritualism but lost none of her contempt for stupidity in the administration of this world. In 1919 she renewed her struggle with the War Office, whose officials were refusing to allow feeding bottles to be sent to orphaned babies in Germany; and shortly before her death in the spring of 1921, she was eagerly recruiting subscribers to the cost of Stephen's prison enquiry.

Margaret Hobhouse's former antagonists at the War Office, Generals Macready and Childs, found no shortage of peacetime opportunities to exercise their particular skills. As Commissioner of the Metropolitan Police Nevil Macready successfully disposed of a Police Strike, outmanoeuvred the handful of militant constables, and carried through much needed reforms. In March 1920 Lloyd George asked him to take command of the forces in Ireland, a task that perhaps no other soldier could have carried through successfully. Macready, the expert in the use of troops in aid of the civil power, steered the authorities through the final confused and murderous years of British engagement in Ireland. When the last troops withdrew in December 1922, Macready sailed with them. A few days later he left the army and entered on nearly a quarter of a century of uneventful retirement. His friend and disciple, Wyndham Childs, had left the army in the previous year. At the age of forty-four, Childs had achieved the rank of Major-

General and the unusual distinction of a double knighthood.[1] Following Macready's example, he joined the police as Head of the Special Branch at Scotland Yard, a role that admirably suited his talent for combining toughness with finesse. Macready, whose father had been born during the French Revolution and whose uncle had fought at Waterloo, lived to witness the defeat of Nazi Germany and the first Atomic Bomb.[2] He died in January 1946. Faithful to the last, General Childs followed his beloved chief to the grave a few months later.

Of the members of Lloyd George's Government who had been concerned with the treatment of conscientious objectors, only a few were in a position to apply their experience when conscription was reintroduced in 1939. Milner, Curzon, Walter Long, and Sir George Cave had all died in the 1920s, but Winston Churchill, as Prime Minister in 1940, roundly condemned a revival of the sort of public hostility to conscientious objectors that had characterized the home front in 1918,[3] and Herbert Fisher, as Chairman of the Appellate Tribunal for conscientious objectors in 1939 and 1940, played an important role in executing the provisions for conscience in the Military Training Act.[4] Lloyd George himself was a member of the House that debated these provisions, as were a number of men who had had direct experience of the problem in the First World War. That these provisions were so generous and comprehensive was a reflection partly of the existence of this experience and partly of the fundamental changes in the organization of recruiting that had been initiated as early as 1917.

In August 1917 the Ministry of National Service, which had been established in March and was now reconstituted, was given control over both civilian and military manpower. As Macready and other senior officers had been urging since the decision to

[1] He received one knighthood at the end of the war and another when he left the War Office in March 1921.

[2] His father, William Charles Macready, the actor, had been seventy when Nevil was born in 1862. Father and son thus spanned one hundred and fifty-four years.

[3] When conscientious objectors were dismissed by some employers Churchill told the Commons: 'Anything in the nature of persecution, victimisation, or man-hunting is odious to the British people.' 5 HC 370, col. 284, 20 March 1941.

[4] Fisher had left the Board of Education in 1922 and had been elected Warden of New College in 1925. He commuted from Oxford to attend tribunal meetings. On his way to one meeting he was knocked down by a motor-cycle and died of his injuries on 18 April 1940.

introduce conscription, the War Office was relieved of all responsibility for the recruiting procedure. The Military Representative at the tribunals became the National Service Representative, who as the agent of the supreme manpower authority was no longer obsessed with obtaining recruits for the army; and the Army Medical Boards, whose standards and scruples had been widely questioned, were replaced by National Service Medical Boards which examined conscripts before enlistment and which had no motive for turning a blind eye to chronic illness or incapacity.[1] In the following year the reform of the recruiting organization was taken a stage further when the power to appoint members of local tribunals was transferred from the local registration authorities to the Local Government Board.[2] None of these changes had a significant effect on the treatment of conscientious objectors in the First World War, but they established the principle of civilian control over the recruiting procedure, and it was this that made possible the sophisticated and flexible arrangements for conscientious objectors in the Second World War.

Between 1919 and 1939 plans for mobilization in the event of a future war retained a statutory exemption from service on the ground of conscience.[3] When the decision was taken in April 1939 to reintroduce a limited measure of conscription, this exemption was automatically included in the draft Bill which was prepared by the Ministry of Labour.[4] As in the Military Service Act of 1916, the claim to exemption would be subject to the discretion of a tribunal, but whereas the Local Government Board had conceived the tribunal system as an extension of local government, the Ministry of Labour drew on its experience of specialist tribunals such as the Courts of Referees under the Unemployment Insurance Acts.[5] The result was that the tribunals in the Second World War were semi-professional bodies appointed by the Minister and

[1] For these changes see *The Recruiting Code*, published by the Ministry of National Service, January 1918, pp. 63 and 96.

[2] SR&O 1918, No. 495, Pt. I, 1.

[3] See H. M. D. Parker, *Manpower: a study of wartime policy and administration*, London, 1957, pp. 41–4.

[4] The draft Bill is in Public Bills Volume IV, Session 8 November 1938 to 23 November 1939, Bill 115. Section 3 deals with conscientious objection. Under SR&O 1939, No. 1118, the Ministry became 'of Labour and National Service'.

[5] For the law relating to the Courts of Referees see the Unemployment Insurance Act 1935 (25 GEO 5, Ch. 8, 26 February 1935), secs. 40–46.

dealing exclusively with applications from conscientious objectors. As had been the practice with Courts of Referees, the chairmen of local tribunals were to be men with legal training. In constitution and performance the local tribunals bore little resemblance to their counterparts in the First World War, but this improvement was the result of changes in the organization of recruiting and not of a conscious attempt to avoid the pattern of 1916.

While the tribunals themselves were the product of experience in other fields, the law they administered enshrined all the important lessons that had been learnt from the treatment of conscientious objectors in the First World War. In 1916 many conscientious objectors had refused to accept the decision of the tribunal because the only form of exemption offered had been from combatant duties; the law had seemed to imply that this was the correct, even the sole exemption for applicants on conscientious grounds. The widespread arrest and court martial of conscientious objectors had followed, a process that Asquith's Government had proved powerless to prevent. In 1939 this was avoided by the Government's recognition that there were different categories of conscientious objection, all of which had to be comprehended by the law. The Prime Minister, Neville Chamberlain, who as Chairman of the Birmingham Local Tribunal in 1916 had heard one applicant after another reject his offer of exemption from combatant duties only,[1] explained these categories to the Commons:

> There is the most extreme case where a man feels it is his duty to do nothing to aid or comfort those who are engaged in military operations. . . . We learned something about this in the Great War and I think we found that it was both a useless and exasperating waste of time and effort to attempt to force such people to act in a manner which was contrary to their principles.
>
> Then there is another category, who take a less extreme view. . . . They will therefore be glad, provided that their scruples are not infringed, to undertake work which could be represented as work of national importance, although not connected directly or indirectly with military service. Then, again, there is another category still less extreme. Their view is that they are not prepared to put themselves in a position where they might be called upon to take life, but they have no objection, on the contrary they are eager and anxious, to do their share in saving

[1] See for example the report of the hearing in the *Birmingham Gazette*, 9 March 1916.

life. . . . they do not even want to be left out of the military forces, provided their work in the military forces can be confined to non-combatant duties.[1]

The draft of the Military Training Bill also provided for forms of exemption that were consistent with the range of conscientious objections recognized. The chances of a conscientious objector establishing the ground of his application only to be offered a form of exemption that he could not accept were small, and this was in striking contrast to the experience of conscientious objectors in 1916.

When the provisions for conscientious objectors were debated in the Commons they were warmly welcomed by those members who were able to make an informed comparison with the provisions of the Military Service Act. The Quaker, T. E. Harvey, who had been a member of the Pelham Committee and had concerned himself with the treatment of conscientious objectors throughout the First World War, was probably better qualified than any other member of the House to make such a comparison:

I want to pay the warmest tribute to the effort that has been made by the Government to deal fairly with the conscientious objector. I believe the proposals contained in the Bill in this respect are immeasurably better than the proposals in the 1916 Act.[2]

Memories of the 1916 Act (though not always accurate or even relevant) also prompted some amendments. The Commons was not short of members who thought they could remember exactly what had gone wrong last time. Apart from those members, such as Lloyd George, Winston Churchill, and Neville Chamberlain, who had experienced the problem of the conscientious objector from the point of view of the authorities, there were six M.P.s—George Benson, Arthur Creech Jones, James Maxton, Herbert Morrison, F. W. Pethick-Lawrence, and Sidney Silverman—who had applied to the tribunals for exemption on conscientious grounds in the First World War. There was also an M.P., Brigadier Page Croft, who had been noted by General Childs as a parliamentary opponent of the conscientious objector in the previous war, but who now supported the provisions for conscience in the Military Training Bill.

[1] 5 HC 346, col. 2097–8, 4 May 1939.
[2] 5 HC 346, col. 2179, 4 May 1939.

In these circumstances attempts to improve the already generous provisions met with little opposition. In some cases amendments gave legal expression to fears that had their origin in the First World War: thus Ernest Brown, the Minister of Labour, agreed that the Bill should specify that work of national importance should be 'of a civil character and under civilian control' and that in appointing tribunals he should 'have regard to the necessity of selecting impartial persons'.[1] Members were sometimes so anxious to prevent a repetition of the mistakes of 1916 that they failed to appreciate the fundamental changes already embodied in the Bill. Lloyd George, whose Government had severed the military connection with recruiting in 1917, still wanted to be sure that the Minister would exclude 'pukka soldiers' from the tribunals.[2] There was a tendency to melodramatize the maladministration of the First World War and, in the absence of official statistics, to exaggerate the number of conscientious objectors who had been refused exemption. On one point, however, there was no call for melodrama or exaggeration: it was sufficient that M.P.s remembered that the repeated sentences imposed on the absolutists had been the one aspect of official policy that had been widely condemned at the time. To prevent this happening again, the Government accepted the need for legal machinery to discharge from the army a soldier who had committed an offence for conscientious reasons. It was fitting that this amendment should be urged on the Government by Arthur Creech Jones, who as an absolutist had suffered four courts martial in the First World War.[3]

With these amendments, the Military Training Act became law on 26 May 1939: a few months later the change from peacetime training to wartime national service did not alter the principle of civilian recruiting or restrict the legal provisions that had been made for conscientious objectors. In concept and execution these provisions enabled those affected by the Act to exercise freedom of

[1] These assurances were honoured in the Military Training Act (2 and 3 GEO 6, Ch. 25), 1939, 3 (8) and Schedule Part II.

[2] 5 HC 347, col. 1301–2, 16 May 1939.

[3] 5 HC 347, col. 1689–90, 18 May 1939. In Attlee's post-war Labour Government Creech Jones became Secretary of State for the Colonies. This Government contained two other former C.O.s: Herbert Morrison as Lord President and Lord Pethick-Lawrence as Secretary of State for India and Burma.

conscience to a degree unequalled in any other country. It was an achievement of which the nation had a right to be proud and to which the lessons of experience made an important contribution. The long drawn out conflict between conscience and government in the First World War had not been in vain.

APPENDIXES

A. Membership of five local tribunals, 1916.
B. Central Tribunal: Members, 1915–1919.
C. Pelham Committee: Nature of objections of men referred to the Committee.
D. Central Tribunal: Questionnaire.
E. Central Tribunal: Classification of cases reviewed by the Tribunal I.
F. Certificates of exemption granted on conscientious grounds and in force in England and Wales, 28 April 1917.
G. Central Tribunal: Classification of cases reviewed by the Tribunal II.
H. Pelham Committee: Occupations to which men were assigned.
I. Pelham Committee: Occupations in which men were allowed to remain.

APPENDIX A ANALYSIS OF THE MEMBERSHIP OF FIVE LOCAL TRIBUNALS IN 1916

Chelsea

The Rt. Hon. Lord William Pickford	
Cllr. Major-General E. H. Sartorius, V.C.	Retired soldier
Cllr. the Hon. W. Sidney, J.P.	Barrister
Cllr. W. J. Mulvey, J.P.	Veterinary Surgeon
Cllr. R. Salisbury	Builder and Decorator
Cllr. F. M. Snagge, J.P.	Barrister
Cllr. T. D. Blanch	Carriage Builder
Cllr. T. J. Welch, J.P.	Schoolmaster
Mr. A. Fiddes	Local Sec. of the Amalgamated Union of Shop Assistants, Warehousemen and Clerks
Mr. J. W. Turner	Pres. of local branch of National Amalgamated Society of Operative House and Ship Painters and Decorators

Neath

Ald. H. P. Charles	Solicitor
Ald. H. Morgan	Woollen Merchant
Ald. D. Davies	Tinplate Worker
Cllr. Harry	Tinplate Worker
Cllr. Jones	Railway Signalman
Cllr. John Rees	Builder
Cllr. W. B. Trick	Auctioneer

Lanark County

Colonel King Stewart	Landed Proprietor
Sir Simon Lockhart	Landed Proprietor
Mr. George Fraser	Estate Factor
Mr. Robert Lambie	Portioner
Mr. J. Anderson	Coalmaster
Mr. Owen Coyle	Trade Union Secretary

Mr. J. Sullivan	Miner's Agent
Mr. Gavin Hamilton	Farmer and Banker
Mr. W. Love	Provision Merchant
Mr. J. Raeside Auld	Commercial Traveller
Mr. Hay Shennan	Sheriff Substitute

Norwich

Ald. E. E. Blyth	Solicitor
Ald. G. H. Morse	Brewery Director
Ald. J. A. Porter	Timber Merchant
Cllr. R. W. Bishop	Jeweller
Cllr. F. H. Bassingthwaite	Baker and Grocer
Mr. J. G. Gordon-Munn	Doctor of Medicine
Mr. E. Reeve	Solicitor
Cllr. J. Crotch	Company Director
Mr. A. Walker	Pres. local branch of Typographical Association
Mr. J. Mason	Sec. the Sick Benefit Branch of Norwich Boot and Shoe Operatives Union

Wigan

Cllr. A. E. Baucher	Solicitor
Cllr. J. I. Anson Cartwright	Postal Official
Ald. A. S. Hilton	Estate Agent
Ald. J. T. Grimshaw	Master Baker
Mr. T. Holland	Tailor
Ald. J. N. Cheetham	Colliery Checkweightman
Ald. T. Ashton	Wholesale Fish Merchant
Cllr. T. J. Arkwright	Master Tailor
Mr. J. M. Ainscough, J.P.	Managing Director, Furniture and Drapery Store
Mr. W. Johnson, J.P.	Master Builder
Mr. R. Prestt	Engineering Trade Union Official

APPENDIX B MEMBERS OF THE CENTRAL TRIBUNAL, 1915–1919

Source: Report of the Central Tribunal, pp. 4–5

1. The Rt. Hon. Lord Sydenham of Coombe, Secretary of Committee of Imperial Defence, 1904–7, Governor of Bombay, 1907–13; Chairman of Tribunal from October 1915 to June 1916.
2. Sir George Younger, Bt., Unionist M.P. (Ayr Burghs).
3. Sir Francis Charles Gore, Barrister.
4. Sir Cyril Jackson, Barrister, Chairman of the L.C.C., 1915, ex-Chief Inspector, Board of Education.
5. G. J. Talbot, Esq., K.C., Fellow of All Souls.
6. The Marquess of Salisbury; Chairman of the Tribunal, June 1916–September 1917.
7. The Rt. Hon. George Barnes, Labour M.P. (Glasgow Blackfriars), General Secretary of Amalgamated Society of Engineers.
8. Sir A. L. Firth, Bt., President of the Association of Chambers of Commerce of Great Britain.
9. Sir A. O. Williams, Chairman of Quarter Sessions.
10. Sir R. W. Carlyle, Indian Civil Service, 1878–1915.

These ten members constituted the Central Tribunal as gazetted in March 1916. The following members were appointed after March 1916 to fill vacancies created by the resignation of some of the original members:

11. The Rt. Hon. Lord Richard Cavendish, Liberal Unionist M.P. (Lonsdale), 1895–1906, served in war 1914–15, wounded.
12. J. F. L. Brunner, Esq., Liberal M.P. (Northwich).
13. James O'Grady, Esq., Labour M.P. (East Leeds), Secretary of the National Federation General Workers.
14. The Rt. Hon. the Viscount Hambledon, Conservative M.P. (Strand), 1891–1910, served in war 1915–16, Gallipoli; Chairman of the Tribunal, September 1917–December 1918.
15. Robert Tootill, Esq., Labour M.P. (Bolton), Secretary of the Bolton Trades Council.
16. Captain the Hon. Evan Charteris, K.C., served in war 1916–18.

APPENDIX C PELHAM COMMITTEE'S ANALYSIS OF THE NATURE OF THE OBJECTIONS OF MEN REFERRED TO THE COMMITTEE

Source: Report of the Pelham Committee, Schedule 4

Christadelphian	1,716
Plymouth Brethren	145
Society of Friends	140
Methodist	112
Baptist	73
Jehovah's Witnesses	66
Congregational	65
Anglican	51
Adult School	17
Unitarian	14
7th Day Adventist	10
Community of the Son of God	9
Roman Catholic	9
Jewish	8
Peculiar People	8
Presbyterian	7
Salvation Army	7
Christian Scientist	5
Pentecostal	4
Apostolic Faith	3
Christian Israelite	3
Church of Christ	3
Jewish Christian Church	3
Spiritualist	3
Theosophist	3
Tolstoyan	3
Nazarite	2
Brotherhood Church	1
Buddhist	1
Church Army	1
Church of God	1
Church of Scotland	1
Dependent Cokler	1
Dowie's Church	1

Faithist	1
Lutheran	1
New and Latter House of Israel	1
New Thought School	1
Second Adventist	1
Swedenborgian	1
Theistic	1
Denomination not stated	240
Moral	199
Political	42
Nature of objection not stated	1,050
	3,964

APPENDIX D CENTRAL TRIBUNAL QUESTIONNAIRE

Source: Report of the Central Tribunal, p. 34

Application on the Grounds of Conscientious Objection

1. State precisely on what grounds you base your objection to combatant service.
2. If you object also to non-combatant service, state precisely your reasons.
3. Do you object to participating in the use of arms in any dispute, whatever the circumstances and however just, in your opinion, the cause?
4. Would you be willing to join some branch of military service engaged not in the destruction but in the saving of life? If not state precisely your reasons.
5. (a) How long have you held the conscientious objections expressed above?
   (b) What evidence can you produce in support of your statement? Please forward written evidence (from persons of standing if possible) which should be quite definite as to the nature and sincerity of your conscientious objections.
6. (a) Are you a member of a religious body, and if so, what body?
   (b) Is it one of the tenets of this body that no member must engage in any military service whatsoever?
   (c) Does the body penalise in any way a member who does engage in military service; if so, in what way?
   (d) When did you become a member of that body?
7. (a) Are you a member of any other body one of whose principles is objection to all forms of military service and if so what body?
   (b) When did you become a member?
8. Can you state any sacrifice which you have made at any time because of the conscientious objections which you now put forward?
9. (a) Assuming that your conscientious objections were established, would you be willing to undertake some form of national service (other than your present work) at this time of national need?
   (b) What particular kinds of national service would you be willing to undertake (state all different kinds)?
   (c) Have you since the war broke out been engaged in any form of philanthropic or other work for the good of the community? If so give particulars.

(d) What sacrifice are you prepared to make to show your willingness without violating your conscience to help your country at the present time?

10. (a) If you are not willing to undertake any kind of work of national importance as a condition of being exempted from military service state precisely your reasons; and also

(b) How you reconcile your enjoying the privileges of British citizenship with this refusal?

APPENDIX E

Source: Report of the Central Tribunal, p. 25

'Classification of men who, having alleged conscientious objection as the reason of the breach of discipline for which they had been sentenced by court martial, have had their cases investigated by the Central Tribunal (up to and including December 31st, 1918), distinguishing for each category those who were in possession of exemption of some kind after their cases had been finally disposed of by the Tribunals.'

Category[1]	After disposal of case by Tribunals men who were in possession of:				Total	Men who had not applied to any Tribunal for exemption *on the ground of conscientious objection*	Grand total
	Exemption from combatant service only	Other forms of exemption which have expired by lapse of time or for some other reason	No exemption				
			Cases in which Tribunals refused exemption	Cases in which Tribunals originally gave some form of exemption but later withdrew it			
A	1,639	42	1,808	74	3,563	815	4,378
B	21	—	100	—	121	75	196
C	4	—	20	1	25	21	46
D	12	—	92	2	106	161	267
E	260	47	266	5	578	114	692
Other recommendations	33	3	57	—	93	48	141
Total.. ..	1,969	92	2,343	82	4,486	1,234	5,720

[1] For the classification into these categories see pp. 164–5.

APPENDIX F

Source: Lothian Papers, Box 139/5

'Certificates of exemption granted on conscientious grounds in force in England and Wales on 28 April 1917. (The figures are estimates based on returns from nearly 90 per cent of the Tribunals.)'

Tribunals	Absolute	Conditional	Other certificates (excluding non-combatant)	Total	From combatant service only	Grand Total
Central	0	121	4	125	97	222
58 Appeal	50	1,620	180	1,850	1,580	3,430
1157 Urban	190	1,630	380	2,200	3,440	5,640
650 Rural	30	180	60	270	500	770
	270	3,551	624	4,445	5,617	10,062

The analysis drawn up for Lloyd George by Philip Kerr in June 1917.

APPENDIX G

Source: Report of the Central Tribunal, p. 24

'Number of conscientious objectors interviewed by the Tribunal in years 1916, 1917 and 1918: the number and proportion assigned to the various classes.'

		Number of men interviewed by the Tribunal	Classification					Other recommendations
			A	B	C	D	E	
1916	Number	2,288	1,953	85	29	40	165	16
	Proportion per cent.	100	85·4	3·7	1·3	1·7	7·2	0·7
1917	Number	2,267	1,591	40	12	104	443	77
	Proportion per cent.	100	70·2	1·8	0·5	4·6	19·5	3·4
1918	Number	1,165	834	71	5	123	84	48
	Proportion per cent.	100	71·6	6·1	0·4	10·6	7·2	4·1
Total	Number	5,720	4,378	196	46	267	692	141
	Proportion per cent.	100	76·5	3·4	0·8	4·7	12·1	2·5

APPENDIX H PELHAM COMMITTEE: OCCUPATIONS ASSIGNED TO MEN

Source: Report of the Pelham Committee, Schedule 15

Agriculture	1,064
Forestry, saw milling, timber work	30
Controlled Establishments	851
Government contractors	70
Textiles	37
Railways, Docks, Shipping	40
Mercantile Marine	3
Mines	25
Flour mills	49
Food manufacture and distribution	65
Chemists and drug manufacturing	8
Bakers	16
Boot and shoe operatives, tanners, etc.	15
Tailors	3
Hospitals, asylums, etc.	80
Welfare Work, Y.M.C.A., F.A.U.	116
Municipal and public utility	30
Civil Service	20
Education	7
Veterinary surgeons and research chemists	4
Printing	4
Banking	2
Dental mechanic	1
Wheelwright	1
Undertaker	1
	2,542

APPENDIX I PELHAM COMMITTEE: OCCUPATIONS IN WHICH MEN WERE ALLOWED TO REMAIN

Source: Report of the Pelham Committee, Schedule 13

Controlled Establishments	301
Government contractors	60
Textiles	56
Railways, Docks, Shipping	70
Mercantile Marine	2
Mines	111
Agriculture	14
Food manufacture and distribution	33
Flour mills	5
Bakers	24
Master grocers, dairymen, builders, farmers, and saw millers	35
Boot and shoe operatives, tanners, etc.	40
Tailors	12
General Post Office	74
Civil Service	16
Municipal and public utility	42
Education	28
Doctors, dentists, chemists, opticians, accountants, etc.	22
Dispensers and dental mechanics	5
Hospitals, asylums, etc.	1
Welfare Work	7
Secretaries, cashiers, and clerks	43
Managers, merchants, commercial travellers	27
Printing	11
Steeplejack	1
Trade union official	1
Tobacco drier	1
Deputy consul	1
Waiter	1
Chauffeurs	2
	1,046

Note: 124 cases were withdrawn before work was assigned. In 252 cases no recommendation was made; these included men rejected or discharged, or who refused to take up work.

NOTE ON SOURCES

Much of this book is based on the unpublished material in the records of government departments and the private papers of individuals. All departmental records are now accessible, but in the case of the tribunal records the condition of inspection is that the names of individual conscientious objectors are not given. Few tribunal records have in fact survived, though the number might well have been smaller. In 1919 the responsibility for these records passed from the doomed Local Government Board to the nascent Ministry of Health. Two years later the Ministry decided that all personal papers relating to exemption on the ground of conscientious objection and all tribunal minute books with the exception of those of the Central Tribunal, should be destroyed.[1] Fortunately, this decision was somewhat less sweeping in execution; the papers of two appeal tribunals, the Middlesex in England and the Lothian and Peebles in Scotland, were also preserved as part of the official records. In addition the Scottish Home and Health Department preserved a few files dealing with the constitution and operation of tribunals in Scotland. Three local authorities, the London County Council and the Borough Councils of St. Marylebone and Camberwell, did not destroy the minute books in their possession; there may have been others who showed an understandable disinclination to destroy local war records and I am conscious that I have not explored this possibility as thoroughly as I might have done. It is also a matter of chance that the Report and Minutes of the Pelham Committee have survived. The Board of Trade has no records of the Committee, but one of the Committee members, T. E. Harvey, retained a copy of the Report and of the Minutes among his private papers. Other collections of private papers have also been rich sources of information, though some that might have proved valuable, such as those of Walter Long and Nevil Macready, have been destroyed.

[1] 'Schedule containing lists of particulars of certain classes of documents relating to Tribunals under the Military Service Acts 1916–1918 which are not considered of sufficient public value to justify preservation by the Public Record Office, 8 November 1921.' MH 47/3.

SOURCES

A. MANUSCRIPT SOURCES

Battersea Central Library
Letter Books of the Battersea Local Tribunal 1915–1917

Beaverbrook Foundations
Selected letters from the Lloyd George Papers

Bodleian Library, Oxford
Asquith Papers
H. A. L. Fisher Papers
Gilbert Murray Papers

British Library of Political and Economic Science
Independent Labour Party Papers
Beatrice Webb Diaries
Passfield Papers

Camberwell Town Hall
Minutes of Camberwell Local Tribunal 1915–1918

County Hall, London
Minutes of the County of London Appeal Tribunal 1915–1918

County Records Office, Bedford
Correspondence of Bedfordshire Appeal Tribunal 1916

Friends' House, London
T. E. Harvey Papers (including Pelham Committee Papers)
Arnold Rowntree Papers
Minutes of the Meeting for Sufferings 1915

Home Office
The Home Office and Conscientious Objectors: A Report prepared for the Committee of Imperial Defence 1919:
Part I. The Brace Committee
Part II. Conscientious Objectors in Prison

House of Lords Record Office
Herbert Samuel Papers

Kedleston Hall, Derby
Curzon Papers Section E 1915–1919

New College, Oxford
Milner Papers

Public Record Office
Cabinet Papers
Home Office Papers Class 45
Kitchener Papers
Ministry of Health Papers Classes 10 and 47
War Office Papers Class 32

St. Marylebone Town Hall
Minutes of St. Marylebone Local Tribunal 1915–1918
Minutes of St. Marylebone Local Recruiting Committee 1915

Scottish Record Office
Lothian Papers
Lothian and Peebles Appeal Tribunal Papers
Scottish Home and Health Department Papers Class 25478S

University of South Carolina
Clifford Allen Papers

Windsor Castle
Royal Archives

Miscellaneous Letters
Arthur Creech Jones to Dr. Salter (undated copy)
E. M. Forster to the author, 13 February 1963
David Garnett to the author, 6 March 1965
James Strachey to the author, 16 March 1965

B. OFFICIAL PUBLICATIONS

Command Papers

1912

Cd.5978 40th Annual Report of the Local Government Board, 1910–1911

Cd.6406 Report of the Commissioners of Prisons and Directors of Convict Prisons, 1912

1916

Cd.8149 Report on Recruiting by the Earl of Derby, K.G., Director-General of Recruiting

Cd.8331 45th Annual Report of the Local Government Board, 1915–1916

1917
Cd.8550 Committee on Employment of Conscientious Objectors: Rules
Cd.8627 Committee on Employment of Conscientious Objectors: Rules
Cd.8697 46th Annual Report of the Local Government Board, 1916–1917
Cd.8764 Report of the Commissioners of Prisons and Directors of Convict Prisons, 1917
Cd.8884 Committee on Employment of Conscientious Objectors: Additional Rules

1918
Cd.9005 War Cabinet Report, 1917
Cd.9157 47th Annual Report of the Local Government Board, 1917–1918
Cd.9174 Report of the Commissioners of Prisons and Directors of Convict Prisons, 1918

1919
Cmd.131 Inquiry held into the Allegations made against the Acting Governor of Wandsworth Prison
Cmd.374 Report of the Commissioners of Prisons and Directors of Convict Prisons, 1919

1921
Cmd.1193 General Annual Reports of the British Army for the period from 1st October, 1913 to 30th September, 1919

1947
Cmd.7225 Ministry of Labour and National Service Report for the years 1939–1946

Local Government Board:
Circulars, 1914–1919, Vols. 79–84, Ministry of Health, Class 10, Public Record Office
War Office:
Army Orders, 112/1916, 179/1916, 203/1916
Army Council Instructions, 431/1916, 551/1916, 1300/1916
Group and Class Systems: Notes on their Administration under the Military Service Act, by Lord Derby, February 1916
Manual of Military Law, the War Office, 1914
Parliamentary Debates

Recruiting Code, Ministry of National Service, January 1918
Registration and Recruiting, the War Office, August, 1916
Report of the Central Tribunal, February 1919
Report from the Select Committee on the Civil Service (Employment of Conscientious Objectors), April 1922
Rules for Military Detention Barracks and Military Prisons 1912
Statistics of the Military Effort of the British Empire in the Great War 1914–1920, the War Office 1922
Statutory Rules and Orders
Treasury Circular E. 1206/4, 10 September 1929

C. SELECT BIBLIOGRAPHY

Addison, Christopher, *Politics from Within, 1911–1918: I*, London, 1924
Amery, L. S., *My Political Life: 3, 1929–1940*, London, 1955
Armitage, F. P., *Leicester 1914–1918: the war-time story of a Midland town*, Leicester, 1933
Arthur, Sir George, *Life of Lord Kitchener: 3*, London, 1920
Asquith, Earl of Oxford and, *Memories and Reflections: 3*, London, 1928
Aulard, F. V. A., *Actes du Comité de Salut Public: 6*, Paris, 1893
Bainton, R. H., *Christian Attitudes towards Peace and War*, London, 1961
Barnes, George N., *From Workshop to War Cabinet*, London, 1924
Beaverbrook, Lord, *Politicians and War, 1914–1916*, London, 1959 ed.
Men and Power, 1917–1918, London, 1956 ed.
Bell, G. K. A., *Randall Davidson, Archbishop of Canterbury*, 2, London, 1935
Bell, Julian, ed., *We Did Not Fight, 1914–1918: experiences of war-resisters*, London, 1935
Blake, Robert, *The Unknown Prime Minister: the life and times of Andrew Bonar Law, 1858–1923*, London, 1955
Boulton, David, *Objection Overruled*, London, 1967
Braithwaite, Constance, *Legal Problems of Conscientious Objection to Various Compulsions under British Law*, Friends' Historical Society, 1968
Brittain, Vera, *The Rebel Passion: a short history of some pioneer peace-makers*, London, 1964
Brock, Hugh, *The Century of Total War*, Peace News Pamphlet, London, 1961
Brockway, Fenner, *Inside the Left*, London, 1942
Outside the Right, London, 1963
See also Hobhouse, Stephen
Butler, J. R. M., *Lord Lothian*, London, 1960

Catchpool, Corder, *On Two Fronts: letter of a Conscientious Objector*, London, 1919

Chamberlain, W. J., *Fighting for Peace*, London, 1929

Childs, Maj.-Gen. Sir Wyndham, *Episodes and Reflections*, London, 1930

Churches of God, *Report of the Conferences of Representative Overseers of the Churches of God in the British Isles and Overseas, 1935–1940*

Churchill, Randolph S., *Lord Derby, 'King of Lancashire'*, London, 1959

Churchill, Winston S., *The World Crisis, 1916–1918: I*, London, 1927

The Second World War, I, London, 1948

Cohen, Percy, *Unemployment Insurance and Assistance in Britain*, London, 1938

Cole, Clara Gilbert, *The Objectors to Conscription and War*, Manchester, 1936

Cole, G. D. H., *British Working Class Politics, 1832–1914*, London, 1946

A History of the Labour Party from 1914, London, 1948

Cole, Marley, *Jehovah's Witnesses: the new world society*, London, 1956

Courtney, Kate, *Extracts from a Diary during the War*, printed for private circulation, 1927

Crosby, G. R., *Disarmament and Peace in British Politics, 1914–1919*, Cambridge, Mass., 1957

Cross, F. L., ed., *The Oxford Dictionary of the Christian Church*, London, 1957

Dearle, N. B., *Dictionary of Official War-Time Organisations*, London, 1928

Donington, Robert and Barbara, *The Citizen Faces War*, London, 1936

Durbin, E. F. M., and Catlin, George, eds., *War and Democracy: essays on the causes and prevention of war*, London, 1938

Edwards, M., *Methodism and England: a study of Methodism in its social and political aspects during the period 1850–1932*, London, 1943

Edmunds, Brigadier-General Sir James E., *Official History of the Great War: Military Operations, France and Belgium 1916*, London, 1932

Elton, Lord, *The Life of James Ramsay MacDonald, 1866–1919*, London, 1939

Ensor, R. C. K., *England, 1870–1914*, London, 1936

Falls, Cyril, *War Books: a critical guide*, London, 1930

Fay, Sir Sam, *The War Office at War*, London, 1937

Feiling, Keith, *The Life of Neville Chamberlain*, London, 1946

Field, G. C., *Pacifism and Conscientious Objection*, Cambridge, 1945

Fisher, H. A. L., *An Unfinished Autobiography*, London, 1940

Flugel, J. C., *Man, Morals and Society: a psycho-analytical study*, London, 1945

Fox, L. W., *English Prisons and Borstal Systems*, London, 1952

Freud, Sigmund, 'Warum Krieg?', *Psychological Works* (Standard Edition), Vol. XXII, London, 1964

Friends Service Committee, *The Absolutists' Objection to Conscription: a statement and an appeal to the conscience of the nation, May, 1917*

Fry, A. Ruth, *A Quaker Adventure*, London, 1926

Garnett, David, *The Flowers of the Forest*, London, 1955

Gilbert, Martin, *Plough My Own Furrow: the story of Lord Allen of Hurtwood as told through his writing and correspondence*, London, 1965

Glover, Edward, *War, Sadism and Pacifism*, London, 1933

Glyn, Anthony, *Elinor Glyn: a biography*, London, 1955

Gollin, A. M., *Proconsul in Politics: a study of Lord Milner in opposition and in power*, London, 1964

Gooch, G. P., *Life of Lord Courtney*, London, 1920

Graham-Harrison, Sir William, 'An examination of the main criticisms of the Statute Book', *Journal of the Society of the Public Teachers of Law*, 1935

Graham, John W., *Conscription and Conscience: a history 1916–1919*, London, 1922

Graves, Robert, *Goodbye to All That*, London, 1929

Grunhut, Max, *Penal Reform*, Oxford, 1948

Hall, Hubert, *British Archives and the Sources for the History of the World War*, London, 1925

Hamilton, Mary Agnes, *Arthur Henderson: a biography*, London, 1938

Hanak, H., 'The Union of Democratic Control during the First World War', *Bulletin of the Institute of Historical Research*, XXXVI, 94, November, 1963

Hancock, W. H., *Smuts: the sanguine years, 1870–1919*, Cambridge, 1962

Hankey, Lord, *The Supreme Command, 1914–1918*, London, 1961

Harrod, R. F., *The Life of John Maynard Keynes*, London, 1951

Hastings, James, ed., *Encyclopaedia of Religion and Ethics*, Edinburgh, Vol. IV, 1911, Vol. VI, 1913, Vol. VIII, 1915, Vol. XI, 1920

Hayes, Denis, *Conscription Conflict*, London, 1949

Challenge of Conscience: the story of the Conscientious Objectors of 1939–1949, London, 1949

Hirst, Margaret E., *The Quakers in Peace and War*, London, 1923

Hobhouse, Mrs. Henry (Margaret), *I Appeal Unto Caesar*, London, 1917

Hobhouse, Rosa Waugh (Mrs. Stephen Hobhouse), 'An Interplay of Life and Art: an autobiography' (unpublished manuscript in the London Library), 1958

Hobhouse, Stephen, 'An English Prison from Within', *Quarterly Review*, July, 1918

Margaret Hobhouse and Her Family, privately printed, 1934

Forty Years and An Epilogue: an autobiography, 1881–1951, London, 1951

Hobhouse, Stephen, and Brockway, Fenner, *English Prisons To-Day*, London, 1922

Hunter, E. E., *The Home Office Compounds*, N.C.F., 1917

Huxley, Aldous, ed., *Letters of D. H. Lawrence*, London, 1932

Independent Labour Party, *Report of the Annual Conference of the Independent Labour Party 1918*

Iremonger, F. L., *William Temple, Archbishop of Canterbury: his life and letters*, London, 1948

James, Stanley B., *The Men Who Dared*, London, 1917

Jannaway, F. G., *Without the Camp: being the story of why and how the Christadelphians were exempted from military service*, privately published, London, 1917

Jauncey, L. C., *The Story of Conscription in Australia*, London, 1935

Jenkins, Roy, *Asquith*, London, 1964

Johnstone, J. K., *The Bloomsbury Group*, New York, 1963

Kellogg, Walter, *The Conscientious Objector*, New York, 1919

Labour Party, *Report of the Annual Conference of the Labour Party 1918*

Legge, J. C., 'Australia and the Universal Training Law', *Army Review*, January, 1913

Liddell Hart, B. H., *The Real War 1914–1918*, London, 1930

Lloyd, E. M. H., *Experiments in State Control at the War Office and the Ministry of Food*, Oxford, 1924

Lloyd, Roger, *The Church of England in the Twentieth Century*, London, 1946

Lloyd George, David, *War Memoirs: 2*, London, 1933

Long, Walter (Viscount), *Memories*, London, 1923

Maccoby, S. M., *English Radicalism 1886–1914*, London, 1953

English Radicalism: the end?, London, 1961

McKenna, Stephen, *Reginald McKenna, 1863–1943*, London, 1948

McKenzie, R. T., *British Political Parties*, London, 1955

McNair, John, *James Maxton: the beloved rebel*, London, 1955

Macready, Sir Nevil, *Annals of an Active Life*, 2 vols., London, 1924

Magnus, Philip, *Kitchener*, London, 1958

Mallet, Sir Charles, *Lord Cave: a memoir*, London, 1931

Marrot, H. V., *The Life and Letters of John Galsworthy*, London, 1935

Marsh, David C., *The Changing Social Structure of England and Wales, 1871–1951*, London, 1958

Martin, D. A., *Pacifism: an historical and sociological study*, London, 1965

Marwick, Arthur, *Clifford Allen: the open conspirator*, London, 1964
The Deluge: British society and the First World War, London, 1965
Mennonite Publishing House, *The Mennonite Encyclopedia: 3*, Scottdale, 1957
Middleton, T. H., *Food Production in War*, Oxford, 1923
Morrison, Lord, of Lambeth, *Herbert Morrison: an autobiography*, London, 1960
Morrison, Sybil, *I Renounce War: the story of the Peace Pledge Union*, London, 1962
Murray, Gilbert, *An Unfinished Autobiography with contributions by his friends*, edited by Jean Smith and Arnold Toynbee, London, 1960
National Peace Council, *Peace Year Book*, London, 1939
No Conscription Fellowship, *The No Conscription Fellowship: a souvenir of its work during the years 1914–1919*, London, 1919
Oakley, W. H., *Guildford in the Great War*, Guildford, 1934
Ogg, David, *H. A. L. Fisher, 1865–1940: a short biography*, London, 1947
Owen, Frank, *Tempestuous Journey: Lloyd George his life and times*, London, 1954
Pankhurst, E. Sylvia, *The Suffragette Movement*, London, 1931
Parmoor, Lord, *A Retrospect: looking back over a life of more than eighty years*, London, 1936
Parker, H. M. D., *Manpower: a study in war-time administration*, London, 1957
Peel, Mrs. C. S., *How We Lived Then, 1914–1918*, London, 1929
Peet, Hubert W., 'Some Fruits of Silence', *Friends Quarterly Examiner*, April, 1920
'112 Days Hard Labour', *The Ploughshare*, April, 1917
Pelling, Henry, *The British Communist Party: a historical profile*, London, 1958
Pethick-Lawrence, F. W., *Fate Has Been Kind*, London, 1943
Petrie, Charles, *Walter Long and His Times*, London, 1936
Playne, Caroline, *Society at War 1914–1916*, London, 1931
Britain Holds On 1917–1918, London, 1933
Plowman, Max, *Bridge Into the Future*, Letters edited by D. L. P., London, 1944
Pollard, Robert S. W., 'Conscientious Objectors in Great Britain and the Dominions', *Journal of Comparative Legislation*, 28 (1946), Pts. 3 and 4
'Tribunals for Conscientious Objectors', in R. S. W. Pollard (ed.), *Administrative Tribunals at Work: a symposium*, London, 1950
Pound, Reginald, and Harmsworth, Geoffrey, *Northcliffe*, London, 1959
Prestige, G. L., *The Life of Charles Gore: a great Englishman*, London, 1935

Rae, J. M., 'The Development of official treatment of conscientious objectors to military service, 1916–1945', unpublished Ph.D. Thesis, University of London, 1965

Ram, Sir Granville, 'The Improvement of the Statute Book', *Journal of the Society of the Public Teachers of Law*, 1951

Roberts, R. Ellis, *H. R. L. Sheppard: life and letters*, London, 1942

Rogers, P. G., *The Sixth Trumpeter: the story of Jezreel and his tower*, London, 1963

Ronaldshay, Earl of, *The Life of Lord Curzon: 3*, London, 1928

Rose, Gordon, *The Struggle for Penal Reform*, London, 1961

Samuel, Viscount, *Memoirs*, London, 1945

Sassoon, Siegfried, *Memoirs of an Infantry Officer*, London, 1930

Scott Duckers, J., *Handed Over*, London, 1917

Simon, Viscount, *Retrospect*, London, 1952

Snowden, Philip (Viscount), *British Prussianism: the scandal of the tribunals*, Manchester, 1916

An Autobiography, 1864–1919, London, 1934

Society of Friends, *Peace Among the Nations: being the testimony of the Society of Friends on war*, London, 1915

Spender, J. A., and Asquith, Cyril, *Life of Herbert Henry Asquith: 2*, London, 1932

Spinks, G. Stephens, *Religion in Britain since 1900*, London, 1952

Stone, G. F., and Wells, Charles, *Bristol and the Great War 1914–1918*, Bristol, 1920

Sweet, William Warren, *The Story of Religion in America*, New York, 1950 ed.

Sydenham, Lord, of Combe, *My Working Life*, London, 1927

Tatham, M., and Miles, J. E., *The Friends Ambulance Unit 1914–1919: a record*, London, 1919

Taylor, A. J. P., 'Politics in the First World War', *Proceedings of the British Academy*, XLV, London, 1959

English History, 1914–1945, London, 1965

Terry, G. P. W., *The Representation of the People Acts, 1918–1928*, London, 1928

Thomis, Malcolm Ian, 'The Labour Movement in Great Britain and Compulsory Military Service, 1914–1916', unpublished M.A. Thesis, University of London, 1959

Tudur Jones, R., *Congregationalism in England, 1662–1962*, London, 1962

Underwood, A. C., *A History of the English Baptists*, London, 1947

University Group on Defence Policy, *Who was for Munich?: the role of the peace movements in the 1930s*, London, 1959

War Resisters of the World: an account of the movement in twenty countries and a report of the international conference held at Hoddesdon, Herts., England, July 1925

Watch Tower and Bible Tract, *Jehovah's Witnesses in the Divine Purpose*, New York, 1959

Wilcox, F. McL., *Seventh Day Adventists in Time of War*, Washington, D.C., 1936

Wilson, B. R., *Sects and Society: a sociological study of three religious groups in Britain*, London, 1961

Wolfe, Humbert, *Labour Supply and Regulation*, Oxford, 1923

Woodcock, George, *Anarchism: a history of libertarian ideas and movements*, London, 1963

Woolf, Leonard, *Beginning Again: an autobiography of the years 1911–1918*, London, 1964

Wrench, John Evelyn, *Geoffrey Dawson and Our Times*, London, 1955

Alfred, Lord Milner: the man of no illusions, 1854–1925, London, 1958

Wright, Edward Needles, *Conscientious Objectors in the Civil War*, Philadelphia, 1931

Young, G. M., *Stanley Baldwin*, London, 1952

D. NEWSPAPERS AND PERIODICALS

(i) *National*

Daily Mail
Manchester Guardian
The Nation
The Times
Westminster Gazette

(ii) *Provincial*

Birmingham Gazette
Cardiff Times
Cornwall County News
Eastern Daily Press
Glasgow Herald
Harrow Observer
Hereford Journal
Leeds Mercury
Wakefield Express

(iii) *Specialist*

C.B.C.O. Bulletin
The Christadelphian
C.O.s' Hansard
The Friend
The Justice of the Peace
Labour Leader
Law Journal
Local Government Chronicle
Mennonite Quarterly Review, Indiana
Ministry of Labour Gazette
National Message
Socialist Standard
The Tribunal
The Venturer

INDEX

(Conscientious objector *abbreviated to* CO *throughout*)

Absolute exemption, in Military Service Bill, 31, 46–8; N.C.F.'s policy on, 92–3; tribunals' policy on, 113, 118–23; number awarded to COs, 130

Absolutists, the, 89–90; number of, 166–7; treatment of, **201–33**; disfranchisement of, 234–5; discharged from Civil Service, 235–6

Advisory Committees, appointed by War Office, 17–18; influence on tribunals, 62, 96

Aggression, a characteristic of some COs, 86

Agriculture, Board of, 169

Allen, Clifford, Chairman of N.C.F., 12, 84, 167; opinion of General Childs, 138; attacks Home Office Scheme, 173; an absolutist, 201, 207, 225–6; diary quoted, 228; subsequent career and death, 237–8

Alternativists, the, 88–9

Amery, L. C. M. S., supporter of Lord Milner, 8; drafts compulsory service scheme, 20

Anarchists, as COs, 85–6; on Home Office Scheme, 176, 185–6; in prison, 202, 230–31

Army Council, letter on treatment of COs, 143; and commutation of sentences, 148; and death penalty, 150; and Home Office Scheme, 162, 165, 167, 181, 189; and COs in prison, 211, 224, 232

Army Medical Boards, 52, 241

Army Order X, 159, 164

Army Reserve W, 161

Asquith, H. H., Liberal Prime Minister, 1, 3; and voluntary recruiting, 2–5, 9, 14–16, 19–21; and drafting of Military Service Bill, 22–32; introduces Bill to Commons, 33–6; and Labour opposition, 38–9; and compulsory vaccination, 43–4; meetings with Gilbert Murray, 128, 152–4; and transfer of COs to civil power, 158–61; death of eldest son, 180; end of premiership, 181; urges release of absolutists, 215–16

Asquith, Raymond, killed in action, 180

Australia and compulsory military training, 7, 28

Australian Defence Act, 1910, model for British bill, 28–32, 35

Australian Freedom League, 19

Baldwin, Stanley, and disfranchisement of COs, 223

Balfour, A. J., 10

Balfour, Lady Betty, 10

Balliol College, Oxford, 208, 210, 221

Baptist Church, 76

Barlinnie Prison, 164

Barnes, George, 217 n.5

Barratt Brown, A., 227

Barrhead Local Tribunal, 103

Battersea Local Tribunal, 98, 100

Beaverbrook, Lord, 221

Bedford Appeal Tribunal, 59

Bell, Clive, 82

Benedict XV, Pope, 80

Benson, George, 243

Bentinck, Lord Henry, letter to Lloyd George on absolutists, 212–13

Bevin, Ernest, 85, 129 n.5, 198 n.2

Birmingham Local Tribunal, 55, 78, 242

Bishop's Stortford College, 236

Blake, Major, Acting Governor of Wandsworth Prison, 230–31
'Bloomsbury Group', 30, 81–2
Bonar Law, A., Conservative Leader, 5; on Military Service Bill, 28, 42
Boulogne, COs sent to, 154–5
Brace Committee, established, 161; responsible for Home Office Scheme, **162–190**; reconstituted, 186; and Pelham Committee, 197; men rejected by, in prison, 202
Brace, William, Under Sec. of State, Home Office, 38 n.3, 182; as Chairman of Committee on Employment of COs, 161, 167, 169, 178, 184, 186
Bradford Local Tribunal, 106
Brightmore, Private James, ill-treatment of, 144–7, 187, 214
Briscoe, Major E. W., appointed to Brace Committee, 186
British Legion, protests against employment of COs, 198 n.3, 236
British Prussianism: the Scandal of the Tribunals, 108
British Socialist Party, 84
Brockway, Fenner, Editor of *Labour Leader*, 11; and the origins of N.C.F., 11–12; on the death of Walter Roberts, 179; an absolutist, 201; subsequent career, 237–8
Brooke, Lt.Col. Reginald, ill-treatment of COs by, 149–50
Brown, Ernest, Minister of Labour in 1939, 60–61, 244
Burns, John, resignation, 3; criticizes magistrates, 57

Camberwell Local Tribunal, 57, 62, 63, 121
Campbell-Bannerman, Sir H., 3
Canadian Military Service Act, 1917, 49–51
Casement, Sir Roger, 182
Cave, Sir George, Home Secretary, 182; reconstitutes Brace Committee, 186–7; and the absolutists, 210–11, 221–2, 227–8; and disfranchisement of COs, 222–3
Cecil, Lord David, and Home Office Scheme, 178
Cecil, Lord Hugh, supports Margaret Hobhouse, 215 n.1
Cecil, Lord William, Bishop of Exeter, on COs at Dartmoor, 185, 187
Central Tribunal, appointed under Derby Scheme, 17; given statutory authority, 32; membership of, 59–60, 249; and the exemption of COs, 69, 81, 82, 90, 97, 104, 114, 116–17, 120, 125, 130; as Advisory Body to Army Council, 127, 160–61, 162–8, 169, 173, 175, 181, 185, 188–90, 201–2; and Pelham Committee, 197; and disfranchisement, 235
Chamberlain, Neville, Chairman of Birmingham Local Tribunal, 55, 78; Prime Minister, 242–3
Chantilly, Inter-Allied Conference at, 20
Charnwood, Lord, proposes ban on CO teachers, 199–200, 236
Childs, Major-General Sir Wyndham, wants exemption for religious COs only, 29–30; Director of Personal Services, 64, 89; hostile to political objectors, 116; opposed to absolute exemption of COs, 123; early career and character, 136–8; and treatment of COs in the army, 138–50; views on death penalty, 151, 156–7; drafts Army Order X, 159–61; and the Central Tribunal's review of cases, 162–7; and Home Office Scheme, 169, 172, 175, 181; and the Non-Combatant Corps, 191, 194; and the absolutists, 203, 205, 206, 208; resists attempts to release Stephen Hobhouse, 209–18; concession to Lord Curzon, 221–3; opinion of Margaret Hobhouse, 225; subsequent career and death, 239–40
Christadelphians, petition to Parliament, 12; as COs, 71, 74, 88–9; special exemption for, 113–15, 129, 130; and Pelham Committee, 196–7
Christian Israelites, 77
Christian Scientists, 81
Church Army, 80 n.5
Church of Christ, 77
Church of England, 78–9
Church of Jesus Christ of Latter Day Saints, 80 n.5
Churches of God, 75
Churchill, Winston, not opposed to

conscription, 7; introduces Rule 243A, 203; advocates release of COs in prison, 232–3; condemns victimization, 240
Civil Service, and employment of COs, 235–6
Cleethorpes, South Sea Lane Camp, 144–5
Conditional exemption, provision for in Military Service Bill, 31; amendment to cover COs, 45–6; tribunals' policy on, 123–7; Asquith proposes extension of, 128; number of certificates issued, 130–32; work done by COs granted, 195–200
Congregational Union, 79
Conscription, Asquith's policy on, 1–2, 14–16; historical reasons for opposition to, 5–6; campaign in favour of, 7–9; opposition to in 1915, 9–13, 18–19; decision to introduce, 20–21
Conservatives, join Coalition, 5; favour conscription, 7; and .provisions for COs, 42–5, 160, 169
Courtney, Lord, 209, 215
Courts of Referees, model for tribunals in Second World War, 241–2
Craig, Capt, C., 34
Craik, Sir Henry, 110
Creech Jones, Arthur, as socialist CO, 84; as M.P., 243; moves amendment to Military Training Bill, 244
Crewe, Lord, member of Cabinet Committee on Military Service Bill, 22 n.1
Curzon, Lord, advocates conscription, 7, 10, 14, 20; member of Cabinet Committee on Military Service Bill, 22; obtains the release of absolutists, 220–25; supports Churchill on release of COs in prison, 232–3

Daily Mail, 8, 34, 36, 146, 186
Daily News, 14, 210
Dartmoor Prison, taken over by Brace Committee, 183–4. *See also* Princetown Work Centre
Davidson, Randall, Archbishop of Canterbury, 79; urges release of Stephen Hobhouse, 211–12; criticizes discrimination against COs, 235
Davies, David, letter to Gilbert Murray, 154, 159
Dawson, Geoffrey, Editor of *The Times*, 219–20
Death penalty, COs liable to, 150–57
Denbigh Local Tribunal, 122
Dependent Coklers, 76–7
Derby, Lord, Director-General of Recruiting, 15, 19–20, 33, 64, 101; and COs sent to France, 152–3; becomes Secretary of State for War, 181–2; supports Childs's policy, 206–8; and the release of Stephen Hobhouse, 209, 216, 221–4; leaves War Office, 227
Derby Scheme, 15–19; statistics for, 20; and the introduction of conscription, 22–5, 32, 39, 52–4, 58–63, 94–5
de Rothschild, Major L., a military representative, 102
Detention barracks, COs in, 148–50, 154, 160
de Vitoria, Francisco, on the Just War, 80
Dillon, James, 41
Director of Public Prosecutions, and anti-war literature, 18
Disfranchisement of COs, proposed by *The Times*, 170, 219–20; debates on, 222–3; ineffective in practice, 234–5
Dowie's Church, 77
Dyce, Home Office Camp at, 176; conditions at, 177–9; camp closed, 183

Easter Rising, 128, 153
Elliot, Brigadier-General, and the treatment of COs, 144–6
English Prisons To-day, 238
Ethical Church, 80 n.5
Eton College, 208, 221, 238 n.1
Exemption from combatant service only, in draft Military Service Bill, 30–31; Asquith emphasizes, 36; in United States and colonial Acts, 49–50; tribunals favour, 127–8; Asquith proposes abolition of, 128; number of certificates issued, 131–2. *See also* Absolute exemption; Conditional exemption

Exeter Prison, Stephen Hobhouse released from, 225

Field Punishment No. 1, 148–50
Findlay, Lord, on absolute exemption, 120
Firth, Henry, death at Princetown, 188
Fisher, H. A. L. (Herbert), President of Board of Education, 199; opposes ban on CO teachers, 199–200; advocates release of absolutists, 212, 217–18, 220–21, 223, 227; Chairman of Appellate Tribunal, 240
Fisher, W. Hayes, President of Local Government Board, 47; criticism of military representatives, 103; on absolute exemption, 121; opposes release of absolutists, 217
Foch, Marshal, 63
Forster, E. M., 'develops conscientious objection', 70
Free Churches, 79
Friends, Society of, 12, 37, 42, 58, 72–3, 76, 113, 124, 202, 208. *See also* Quakers
Friend, The, 109, 112, 119, 128, 141
Friends Ambulance Unit, 35–6, 69, 113, 124–5, 130, 197, 207
Friends, Young Men's Service Committee, 12
Fryer, Major, and Brightmore case, 145

Gallipoli, 2, 20
Galsworthy, John, 215
Garnett, David, 82
Geddes, Aukland, Director of Recruiting, 64–6
George V, King, Lord Derby a friend of, 15; Samuel reports to, 41, 46, 156; approves of scheme to employ COs, 184; and of Bishop of Exeter's proposals, 187; Childs warns against Mrs. Hobhouse, 215
Glasgow Local Tribunal, 98
Gloucester Appeal Tribunal, 97
Glyn, Elinor, 221
Gore, Charles, Bishop of Oxford, 79; calls for better treatment of COs, 108; friend of the Hobhouses, 209
Graham, John, on women tribunal members, 56; and death sentences, 152–3
Grant, Duncan, 82
Gray, Private John, ill-treatment of, 143–4
Grey, Sir Edward, Foreign Secretary, 5; and Cabinet crisis over conscription, 26
Gresson, Lt. Col., and Gray case, 143–4
Grimshaw, Major, and Brightmore case, 145–6
Group System, 16, 39, 95
Guild of the Pope's Peace, 80

Haig, Field Marshal Sir D. 63, 206
Haldane, Lord, 170
Hampstead Local Tribunal, 106–7
Hardie, Keir, 11
Harrogate Local Tribunal, 106
Harrow-on-the-Hill Local Tribunal, 56–7
Harvey, T. E., proposes amendment on conditional exemption, 45–6, 88; correspondence from tribunal applicants, 108; a member of the Pelham Committee, 125 n.4; and COs sent to France, 155; views on Non-Combatant Corps, 193; tribute to government on provisions for COs in Military Training Bill, 243
Health, Ministry of, policy on tribunal records, 259
Henderson, Arthur, joins Coalition Cabinet, 5; attempts to postpone conscription, 38; in War Cabinet, 181
Hereford Appeal Tribunal, 106
Hicks, E. L., Bishop of Lincoln, 79, 108
Hobhouse, Charles, supports conscription, 37
Hobhouse, Emily, and General Smuts, 213, 225
Hobhouse, Henry, 207, 209
Hobhouse, Margaret, starts campaign for release of son, 208–9; recruits influential support, 211; publishes book on absolutists, 214–15; Childs warns King against, 215; Asquith supports, 216; appeals to Lloyd George, 217; petitions Home Secre-

tary, 219, 223–4; efforts on behalf of other absolutists, 225; death, 239
Hobhouse, Paul, reported missing, 239
Hobhouse, Stephen, sincerity acknowledged, 73; an absolutist, 207–8; campaign for the release of, **208–225**; subsequent career and death, 238–9
Home Grown Timber Committee, and employment of COs, 171, 174, 183
Home Office, Herbert Samuel succeeds Simon at, 41; responsibility for COs in army transferred to, 67, 159–61, 163–4, 166; Sir George Cave succeeds Samuel at, 182; and treatment of COs in prison, 202–3; urges release of Stephen Hobhouse, 211; and release of absolutists in poor health, 224–6; and the Wakefield experiment, 228–9; abandons forcible feeding, 230; releases COs in prison, 233
Home Office Scheme, origins of, 159–61; organization of, 168–73; initial difficulties of, 174; types of CO on, 175–6; attitude of Parliament towards, 178–80; Rules for, 182, 187; public hostility to, 185–6; Exceptional Employment on, 188; disbanded, 190, 234
Hoxton Local Tribunal, grants exemption to Stephen Hobhouse, 207
Hull, Atwick Camp, 143
Hunt, Major, attacks COs, 170

I Appeal Unto Caesar, published, 215
Imperial War Cabinet, brings General Smuts to London, 213
Independent Labour Party, condemns war, 11; provides leadership of N.C.F., 12; M.P.s in, oppose conscription, 26, 37; as a source of political COs, 83–4, 116; members of, become absolutists, 202; Annual Conference calls for release of COs, 228; Clifford Allen Chairman of, 238
Inland Revenue, Board of, provides work for COs, 171
International Bible Students Association, *see* Jehovah's Witnesses
Ireland, conscription not applied to, 34; deserters seek refuge in, 65; proposal to extend conscription to, 156–7
Irish Members, support Asquith's Liberal Government, 3; and voting on Military Service Bill, 37

Jannaway, F. G., negotiates Christadelphian exemption, 114–15
Jehovah's Witnesses, as COs, 74, 75, 77; on Home Office Scheme, 176
Jewish Christian Church, 80 n.5
Joynson-Hicks, W., attempts to limit conscientious objection in law, 42
Just War, 80

Keeble, S., condemns war, 80
Kerr, Philip, researches CO problem for Lloyd George, 212; recommends release of absolutists, 213–14
Keynes, Maynard, testifies for James Strachey, 100
King, Joseph, on Stephen Hobhouse's release, 225
Kinloch-Cooke, Sir C., criticizes Home Office Scheme, 186
Kitchener, Lord, joins Asquith's Cabinet, 3–4, 5; reluctant to give lead on conscription, 7–8; hostility to political COs, 29, 140; responsible for call-up, 52; chooses Macready as Adjutant General, 63; defends 'horseplay' among soldiers, 139; condemns physical coercion of COs, 142; announces transfer of COs to civil power, 158; death, 155
Knutsford, COs attacked at, 189

Labour, Ministry of, prepares draft Military Training Bill, 241–2
Labour Leader, condemns war, 11; invites men of military age to join N.C.F., 11–12; exposes tribunal irregularities, 108
Labour Party, leader in Coalition Cabinet, 5; and conscription, 9, 37–9; differences on nuclear disarmament, 85; represented on Central Tribunal, 60, 249; Annual Conference calls for release of COs, 228
Labour representative, a statutory requirement on tribunals, 54, 56–8,

60; abused at Leeds Local Tribunal, 99
Labour Research Department, inquiry into prison system, 204 n.1, 238
Lanarkshire Appeal Tribunal, policy on socialist COs, 116-17
Lansbury, George, conflict with Ernest Bevin, 85; signs Memorial on repeated sentences, 224
Lawrence, D. H., dislikes compulsion, 85
League of Nations, Clifford Allen supports, 238
Leeds Local Tribunal, parties equally represented on, 56; rowdyism at, 99
Leicester Local Tribunal, 98
Liberal Party, and the conduct of the war, 3; retains key posts in Coalition, 5; opposed to conscription, 7-9; and Military Service Bill, 26–7, 30, 37; doubts about tribunal system, 43–5, 53
Llanelly R.D.C., provides work for COs, 171, 174
Lloyd George, David, no doctrinaire objection to conscription, 7; misleading statement on death penalty, 151; considers extension of conscription to Ireland, 156–7; becomes Prime Minister, 181; appoints H. A. L. Fisher to Board of Education, 199; statement on absolutists, 205–6; Seebohm Rowntree letter to, 206; asks Philip Kerr to research CO problem, 212; Milner, and Bentinck, letters to, 212–13; does not act on Kerr's proposals, 214; agrees to Cabinet Committee on COs, 217; H. A. L. Fisher's letters to, 218; and Military Training Bill, 240, 244
Local Government Board, responsible for National Register, 14; and for tribunals under Derby Scheme, 16–17; consultations on Military Service Bill, 22; responsible for tribunals under Bill, 32; Walter Long's association with, 39–40, 63; and appointment of tribunal members, 52–4; John Burns as President of, 57; not responsible for tribunal expenses, 63; and tribunal procedure, 67, 97, 117, 119; W. Hayes Fisher as President of, 103, 217; inquires into absolute exemption, 121–2; congratulates tribunal members, 133
Local Registration Authorities, 16, 52
London Appeal Tribunal, 98; Chairman's statement of aims, 109–10; decision on Christadelphian appeals 114–15; scheme for payment of COs, 198
Long, Walter, favours conscription, 7; President of Local Government Board, 14; instructs local authorities to appoint tribunals, 16; chairman of Cabinet Committee on Military Service Bill, 20, 22–3; career and character, 40; steers Military Service Bill through Commons, 39–47; on latitude allowed to COs, 49; partly to blame for Bill's limitations, 51; adapts tribunal system for conscription, 52–60, 63; announces arrangements for alternative service, 92, 125; guides tribunals on procedure, 95–6, 100, 105, 107–8, 112, 119; dismisses criticism of tribunals, 109; blames applicants, 110; views on absolute exemption, 123; misleading statement on death penalty, 151; elder son killed, 180; becomes Colonial Secretary, 182
Lothian and Peebles Appeal Tribunal, 68, 97
Lunacy Commissioners, 190
Lutheran Church, 80 n.5

Macbean, Captain, and Brightmore case, 145–6
Macdonald, J. Ramsay, pleads for more intelligent use of COs, 178
McKenna, Reginald, Chancellor of the Exchequer, 5; opposes conscription, 9; persuaded not to resign, 25–6; supports Asquith on release of absolutists, 215–16
Maclean, Sir Donald, Chairman of London Appeal Tribunal, 109–10
Macpherson, J. I., statement on Brightmore case, 145
Macready, Lt. General Sir Nevil, Adjutant General, wants exemption restricted to religious objectors,

29–30; responsibility for call-up, 52, 63–5; hostile to political objectors, 116; Memorandum on COs, 135, 147, 158; association with Wyndham Childs, 136–7; endorses Childs's policy for COs, 138–9; condemns physical coercion of COs, 142; and Brightmore case, 146; dismisses Lt. Col. Brooke, 149; and death penalty, 156–7; and Non-Combatant Corps, 192–4; subsequent career and death, 239–40

Manchester Guardian, publishes Private Brightmore's letter, 145

Marsh, Edward, testifies to courage of Francis Meynell, 100

Marxists, at Tonypandy, 137; on Home Office Scheme, 176

Maxton, James, at local tribunal, 103; as M.P., 243

Maxwell, Lt. General Sir J. G., and Brightmore case, 144–5, 147

Mellor, Judge, a tribunal chairman, 110; and conditional exemption, 126

Methodist Church, strong pacifist minority in, 79

Metropolitan Police, COs refused reinstatement in, 236

Meynell, Francis, Roman Catholic CO, 80, 100

Middlesex Appeal Tribunal, statistics of, 98; questions for COs, 106; follows Central Tribunal's decision on Christadelphians, 114; and absolute exemption of COs, 118–19, 122; and conditional exemption, 126; reluctance to allow appeals by COs, 129

Military representatives, under Derby Scheme, 17–18; under conscription, 62, 66–7, 96–7, 99, 101–4, 111, 113–14, 116, 126, 129; blamed for bad tribunal decisions, 103, 217

Military Service (No. 2) Act, 1916, drafted, 22–32; Asquith introduces to Commons, 33–6; vote on First Reading, 37; Committee Stage, 39–48; compared with United States and colonial Acts, 48–51; becomes law, 52; does not provide sufficient recruits, 66; no one department responsible for, 67; N.C.F. tries to force repeal of, 90, 91–2; High Court rulings on, 104, 120; no definition of conscientious objection in, 112; recruits deemed to have been enlisted by, 134; safeguard against death penalty in, 150; recruiting under, suspended, 229

Military Service Act, 1916 (Session 2), 48–9; specifies exemptions available to COs, 120, 126–7

Military Service (No. 2) Act, 1918, 48–9

Military Training Act, 1939, 60, 240–45

Militia Acts, 6, 27–8, 34–5

Milner, Lord, an advocate of conscription, 8–10; criticizes tribunals, 121; joins War Cabinet, 181; plays leading role in release of Stephen Hobhouse, 209–22; becomes Secretary of State for War, 227–8

Moore, G. E., 82

Morley, Lord, resignation, 3

Morrison, Herbert, works under Pelham Committee, 196; Home Secretary in Second World War, 236, 243

Muggletonians, 76–7

Murray, Gilbert, discusses exemption of COs with Asquith, 128; letter to Samuel quoted, 134; anxiety about COs sent to France, 152–4, 155; told of Cabinet decision on COs, 158–9; writes introduction to *I Appeal Unto Caesar*, 215; sponsors petition for release of COs, 229 n.3

Nairn Appeal Tribunal, 109

Nation, The, 14, 50

National Register, 1915, 13–14, 37

National Service, Ministry of, 63, 102–3, 240–41

National Service Act, 1939, 244

National Service Bill, 1909, 7

National Service League, 6–8, 15

New Zealand Military Service Act, 1916, 49–50

Nield, Herbert, Chairman of Middlesex Appeal Tribunal, urges Samuel to prosecute N.C.F., 111; note on tribunal's powers, 119; integrity of, 122

No Conscription Fellowship (N.C.F.), origins of, 11–12; activity during

Derby Scheme, 18–19; military hostility to, 29–30, 116; tactics of, 39, 90–93, 100, 118; and socialism, 82–5; anarchists in, 85; criticizes tribunals, 108, 109; accused of coaching COs, 110–11; wants political objection recognized, 113; Childs's ambivalent attitude towards, 140; and COs in the army, 141, 143–4, 152, 158; and Home Office Scheme, 165, 167, 173, 175; holds post-war convention, 237

No More War Movement, former absolutists in, 237

Non-Combatant Corps, 87; deserters from, arrested, 126–7; contains men resisting orders, 152; Army Order establishing, 191; duties undertaken by, 192–3; excluded from pay increase, 194; demobilization of, 234; and discrimination, 235–6

Non-combatant duties, available to attested men, 25; under Australian Act, 30; in draft Military Service Bill, 31; Asquith emphasizes, 35–6; specified in other conscription laws, 50; COs' attitude to, 87–8; tribunals favour, 127–8; Asquith suggests abolishing, 128; nature of, 192–3

Northcliffe, Lord, his newspapers demand conscription, 8–9; absence gives Editor of *The Times* a free hand, 219

Nottinghamshire Appeal Tribunal, 97

Observer, 215

Orthodox Church, 80

Outhwaite, R. L., proposes amendment to Military Service Bill, 44; compliments tribunals, 109

Page-Croft, Brigadier, 243

Parliamentary Counsel's Office, 23

Passchendaele, Battle of, 214

Peace Pledge Union, 224, 237

Peculiar People, 77

Peet, Hubert, 204

Pelham Committee, 115; appointed, 125–6, 128; policy of, 195–200; men working for, released, 234

Pentecostal Churches, 75–6

Pethick-Lawrence, F. W., CO who becomes M.P., 243

Pitt, William, cited by Asquith, 34

Playne, Caroline, recalls hostility to COs, 189

Plowman, Max, resigns commission, 70; letter on COs, 114

Plymouth, meeting on COs at, 186

Plymouth Brethren, 74–5, 77; on Home Office Scheme, 176

Post Office, and employment of COs, 169

Princetown Work Centre, adapted from Dartmoor Prison, 184; unrest among COs at, 185–6, 188–9

Prison Commission, offers Dartmoor Prison to Brace Committee, 184; asks to be relieved of responsibility for COs, 203; appoints Acting Governor at Wandsworth, 230

Prison Visiting Committees, and punishment of COs, 204; protest at relaxation of rules for COs, 226

Prisoners (Temporary Discharge for Ill-Health) Act, 1913, 205, 230

Protected industries, 13; men released to army from, claim to be COs, 68–9, 165

Psycho-analysts, and the motives for conscientious objection, 86–7

Quakers, 25, 26; excepted from Militia Acts, 27, 35; as tribunal members, 57; as COs, 72–3, 77; tribunals' attitude to, 113; and alternative service, 124–5; as absolutists, 201–2, 227. *See also* Society of Friends

Railway Executive Committee, and employment of COs, 159

R.A.M.C., 71

Rechabites, Independent Order of, 80

Reconciliation, Fellowship of, 12

Recruiting, statistics for, 4, 20; history of, 5–7; military role in, 16–18, 62–7; under civilian control, 63, 103, 240–41

Recruiting Officers, 16–17, 65–6

Recruiting Committees, 13, 62

Red Cross, the, 35, 70

'Red Flag,' the, sung at tribunal hearings, 99; provokes ban on propaganda, 180; sung by COs, 186, 231

Representation of the People Act, 1918, 70–71, 222, 234–5

Road Board, employs COs, 169, 171, 174, 177, 183
Roberts, Walter, death at Dyce, 179–80
Roman Catholic Church, and conscientious objection, 78, 80
Rowntree, Arnold, proposes amendment on conditional exemption, 45–6, 88
Rowntree, Seebohm, letter to Lloyd George on COs, 206
Rule 243A, and suffragettes, 203; application to COs, 218, 220, 225–6, 230
Runciman, Walter, opposes conscription, 9, 215

St. Marylebone Local Tribunal, 62, 96, 104
Salford Local Tribunal, 126
Salisbury, Lord, Prime Minister, 6
Salisbury, Lord, Chairman of Central Tribunal, 59; criticizes Brace Committee, 181
Salter, Dr. A., letter from Creech Jones to, 84
Salvation Army, 80
Samuel, Herbert, Home Secretary, 41, 46; states official policy on N.C.F., 111; and transfer of COs to civil power, 159–61, 167; rulings on employment of COs, 169, 171, 172–3; opinion of COs, 174–5; replaced by Sir George Cave, 181–2
Sandemanians, 77
Sandhurst, 136, 144
Sandhurst, Lord, 199–200
Sassoon, Siegfried, 70
Scotland Yard Special Branch, Childs appointed to, 240
Selborne, Lord, supports Milner on conscription, 8; letter from Milner to, 209
Seventh Day Adventists, 73–4, 75–6, 87–8, 193
Shaw, Bernard, friend of Hobhouses, 209
Sheppard, H. R. L., 224
Shortt, Edward, Home Secretary, 232
Silverman, Sidney, CO who becomes M.P., 243
Simon, Sir John, Home Secretary, 5; opposes conscription, 7; reluctant to prosecute N.C.F., 18–19; member of Cabinet Committee on Military Service Bill, 22; reminds colleagues that there will be COs, 25; resigns, 26–7; fails to rally opposition in Commons, 36–7
Sims, Mr., member of Camberwell Local Tribunal, 57
Sinn Fein, and conscription in Ireland, 156–7
Skeffington, Sheey, arbitrary execution of, 153
Smith, F. E., member of Cabinet Committee on Military Service Bill, 22 n.1
Smuts, General J. C., arrives in London, 213; urges release of Stephen Hobhouse, 224; letter from Emily Hobhouse to, 225
Snowden, Philip, wants women on tribunals, 56; speeches on tribunal hearings, 100, 108–9; and dismissal of Lt. Col. Brooke, 149 n.4
Socialists, and the outbreak of war, 11; and conscription, 84–5; tribunals hostile to, 115–17; blamed for trouble in Non-Combatant Corps, 192; among prisoners at Wandsworth, 230
Somme, Battle of, 142
South Africa, 8, 31, 35, 136–7
South Yorkshire Appeal Tribunal, 129
Spiritualism, 78
Stamfordham, Lord, Private Secretary to George V, 184
Stanton, C. B., hostile to COs, 179–80, 199
Stevenson, Capt., Deputy Governor of Wormwood Scrubs, 169; advises Brace Committee, 172; Inspector of Home Office Camps, 186–7
Stop the War Committee, 13
Strachey, James, a CO, 82, 100; on aggression in COs, 86–7
Strachey, Lytton, 82
Suffragettes, 203, 205
Supplementary Report of Central Tribunal, 1922, 70–71
Sutherland, George, 141
Swedenborg Society, 80 n.5
Sydenham, Lord, Chairman of Central Tribunal, 59

Temple, William, criticizes tribunals, 108
Tennant, H. J., Under Secretary of State for War, and Pelham Committee, 125; and 'horseplay' among soldiers, 139; announcements on death penalty, 155–6
Terrell, Major Henry, joins Brace Committee, 186; inquires into strike at Princetown, 188–9
Theosophists, 80 n.5
Thring, Sir Arthur, drafts Military Service Bill, 23
Times, The, 8, 33, 38, 108, 140, 170, 177, 194, 215, 219, 222, 237
Tolstoy, Leo, inspiration of pacifist anarchists, 85
Toynbee Hall, 210
Trade, Board of, and employment of COs, 67, 169; appoints Pelham Committee, 125
Trade unions, oppose conscription, 9–10, 38–9; representatives on tribunals, 60, 61; and Home Office Scheme, 171, 173
Treasury, the, limits finance for Home Office Scheme, 169, 171–2; and employment of COs in civil service, 235–6
Tribunal, The, 92, 102, 108, 141, 143, 179
Tribunals, under Derby Scheme, 16–18; in Military Service Bill, 31–2; debate on, 43–5; in Canadian Military Service Act, 51; appointment of, 52–61; links with military recruiting, 61–3; disposal of applications, **94–133**; accused of ineptitude, 216–17; in Second World War, 241–2. *See also* Central Tribunal

Unemployment Insurance Acts, 241
Union of Democratic Control, 13, 30, 225
Unitas Fratrum, excepted from Militia Acts, 27
United States Selective Service Act, 1917, 49-50
Universalists, 80 n.5

Vaccination Acts, 28–9, 43–4, 57, 94

Wakefield Express, provokes hostility to COs, 189
Wakefield Prison, used as work centre, 173, 180, 183, 189; absolutists sent to, 228–9
Wandsworth Military Detention Barracks, ill-treatment of COs in, 149–50
Wandsworth Prison, unrest among COs in, 230–31
War Agricultural Committees, 183
War Cabinet, 46, 67, 103, 109, 121, 130, 181, 194; and the release of absolutists, 209, 210–13, 217–21, 232–3
War Office, 3, 13; and Derby Scheme, 16–18; and drafting of Military Service Bill, 22–4, 25; hostility to non-religious COs, 29–30, 116; role in conscription, 52, 64–7; reluctant to refer soldiers to tribunals, 95–6; and military representatives, 96, 101–4; and N.C.F., 111, 140; exempts Christadelphians, 114–15; and exemption available to COs, 123–4, 126, 128; and treatment of COs in the army, 140, 142, 143–5, 149, 155–7; and transfer of COs to civil power, 161, 167; and Home Office Scheme, 181; and Non-Combatant Corps, 193; and absolutists, 203, 205, 208, 210, 213–15, 217, 219, 221–2, 224–5; advocates release of COs in prison, 232–3
War Resisters International, 237
Warwick Work Centre, 173, 180, 183
Webb, Beatrice, on conscription, 10; on COs, 85; on tribunals, 100–101; Margaret Hobhouse's sister, 208
Wedgewood, Commander, 170
Wesleyan Methodist Peace Fellowship, 79
Westminster Gazette, 36
Wigram, Lt. Col. Clive, Assistant Private Secretary to George V, 123, 215, 218, 225
Winnington-Ingram, A. F., Bishop of London, in favour of the war, 79
Work of national importance, *see* Pelham Committee

Younger, Sir George, proposes disfranchisement of COs, 222–3; member of Central Tribunal, 249